On the Write Track

Beginning Literacy
for Secondary Students

Deborah Becker Cotto
Prince George's County
Public Schools

Alta Book Center
Publishers

Deborah Becker Cotto teaches in the Prince George's County Public Schools, Maryland, U.S.A.

Acquisitions Editor: Aarón Berman
Content Editor: Sharron Bassano
Cover Art: Bruce Marion
Text Design: Detta Penna
Production: Penna Design and Production
Interior Art: Janet Childs and Michael Bulkley

ISBN 1-882483-38-3

This book is dedicated
to my husband, Dennis,
for providing the faith, support,
and infinite patience
without which I could not have
completed this book.

Also to my students,
for their enthusiasm, hard work,
and endurance;
they make the effort
well worth it!

Acknowledgments

Special thanks are given to my editor, Sharron Bassano, who has
provided generous encouragement and great ideas from the start
and who is a joy to work with.

Thank you, Dr. Jodi Crandall at the University of Maryland, Baltimore
County, for taking the time to contribute advice.

Thank you, Dr. John Nelson, for helping me "way back when" in
graduate school, and who suggested publishing this book.

Finally, I would like to acknowledge Aarón Berman and Simón
Almendares at Alta Book Center Publishers, not only for believing
in and supporting this book, but also for protecting the integrity
and quality of the educational materials they publish.

Table of Contents

Introduction

On the Write Track: Beginning Literacy for Secondary Students is a textbook for secondary students who have had limited or interrupted exposure to formal schooling and need to build basic literacy and English language skills for functioning in an academic setting. The text was designed specifically for teaching literacy in the ESOL classroom and is particularly useful for multilevel classrooms where student needs are diverse.

The objective of **On the Write Track** is to provide a text that addresses the specific needs of the beginning literacy learner and at the same time present age-appropriate material for secondary-level students. **On the Write Track** will enable students to:

- develop the literacy skills needed to begin reading and writing independently in English;
- acquire initial oral and aural English language skills needed to begin functioning in social and academic settings;
- build vocabulary and background knowledge in the content areas.

Integrating the objectives of teaching literacy, language, and exposure to the content areas allows teachers flexibility in adapting this text to the specific needs of each classroom and each student.

The Student Text

On the Write Track's student text is organized into ten chapters that introduce basic vocabulary and concepts through everyday themes that students can easily relate to: *Numbers, Letters, Who Are You?, Where Are You From?, In the Classroom, In School, The Calendar, The Weather, Families,* and *Communities.* Academic content and skills, such as mapping, graphing, and measurement, are taught in connection with the themes presented in each chapter. Each chapter also introduces math and problem-solving activities to build numeracy and critical thinking skills. Simple group and pair activities enable students to build cooperative learning skills. The student text also features a unique reference section that students can use to locate commonly used vocabulary and academic content.

The Teacher's Guide

On the Write Track's Teacher's Guide provides helpful background information and guidelines for teaching beginning literacy students, as well as step-by-step instructions for presenting each page of the student text. The Teacher's Guide also includes numerous extension activity ideas as well as reproducible blackline masters.

A
Get Ready

In this chapter, you will:

____ Trace left to right, top to bottom.

____ Find top, bottom, left, and right.

____ Match pictures and numbers.

____ Count from 1 to 10.

____ Read and write numbers from 1 to 10.

____ Dictate numbers.

____ Complete patterns.

____ Identify more and less.

____ Solve problems.

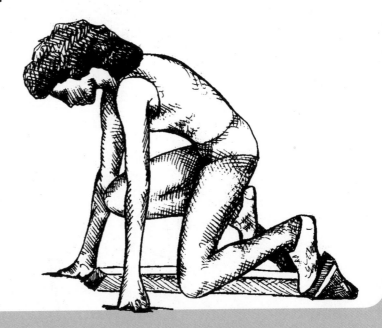

TRACING

A. Trace the lines from left to right.

1.

2.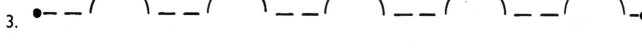

3.

4.

5.

B. Trace the road from start to finish.

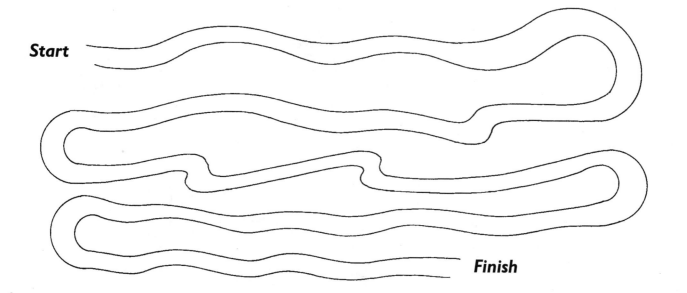

Start

Finish

TRACING

A. Trace the lines from top to bottom.

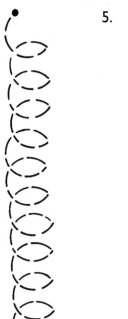

B. Find the path through the maze from start to finish.

Start

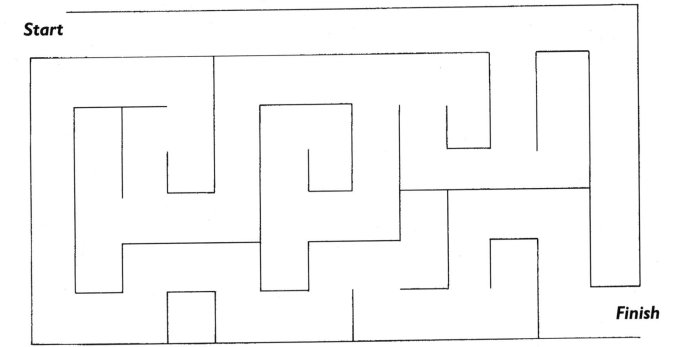

Finish

TOP AND BOTTOM

A.

- **Listen** to your teacher.
- **Color** the side your teacher says: *top* or *bottom*.

1.

top
bottom

2.

top
bottom

3.

top
bottom

4.

5.

6.

B.

- **Work** with a partner.
- **Tell** your partner *Color the top* or *Color the bottom*.
- **Take turns.**

1.

2.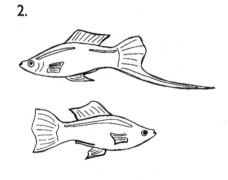

3.

LEFT AND RIGHT

A.

- **Listen** to your teacher.
- **Color** the side your teacher says: *left* or *right*.

1.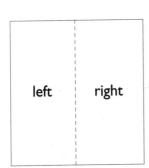

left | right

2.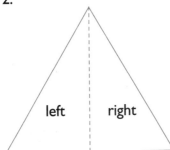

left | right

3.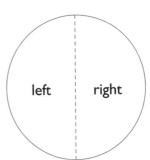

left | right

4.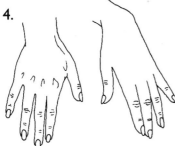

5.

6.

B.

- **Work** with a partner.
- **Tell** your partner *Color the left* or *Color the right*.
- **Take turns.**

1.

2.

3.

MATCHING

- **Match** the same pictures.

SAME NUMBERS

• **Circle** the numbers that are the same as the first number.

0	⓪	8	⓪	10	⓪
1	1	4	7	1	10
2	4	5	2	7	2
3	8	3	3	6	3
4	4	4	7	4	9
5	6	9	5	5	2
6	6	9	5	9	6
7	1	2	7	7	1
8	8	9	3	8	8
9	6	8	9	0	9
10	10	1	0	10	10

WRITING PRACTICE

• **Trace** and **copy**.

0 0̄ ̄ ̄ ̄ ̄   1 1̄ ̄ ̄ ̄ ̄   2 2̄ ̄ ̄ ̄ ̄
              ○   ○ ○

3 3̄ ̄ ̄ ̄ ̄   4 4̄ ̄ ̄ ̄ ̄   5 5̄ ̄ ̄ ̄ ̄
○ ○ ○   ○ ○   ○ ○ ○
              ○ ○   ○ ○

6 6̄ ̄ ̄ ̄ ̄   7 7̄ ̄ ̄ ̄ ̄   8 8̄ ̄ ̄ ̄ ̄
○ ○ ○   ○ ○ ○ ○   ○ ○ ○ ○
○ ○ ○   ○ ○ ○   ○ ○ ○ ○

9 9̄ ̄ ̄ ̄ ̄   10 1̄0̄ ̄ ̄ ̄
○ ○ ○   ○ ○ ○ ○ ○
○ ○ ○   ○ ○ ○ ○ ○
○ ○ ○

NUMBERS MATCH

- **Count** the objects.
- **Match** the objects to the correct amount.
- **Write** the number on the line.

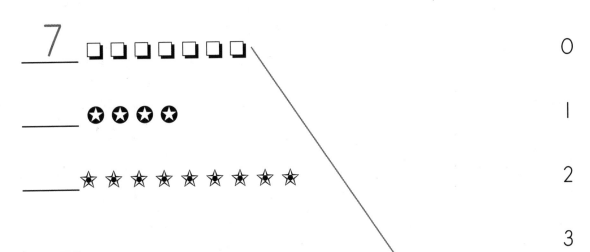

_7_ □ □ □ □ □ □   0

____ ✪ ✪ ✪ ✪   1

____ ★ ★ ★ ★ ★ ★ ★ ★   2

____   3

____ ✂ ✂   4

____ ☞ ☞ ☞ ☞ ☞ ☞ ☞ ☞ ☞   5

____ ➢   6

____ ● ● ● ● ●   7

____ ■ ■ ■ ■ ■ ■ ■   8

____ ✿ ✿ ✿ ✿ ✿ ✿   9

____ ❖ ❖ ❖   10

BAR GRAPH

• **Color** the correct number of squares in each column.

▓										
▓										
▓										
▓										

| 4 | 2 | 7 | 0 | 10 | 5 | 1 | 9 | 6 | 3 | 8 |

NUMBERS DICTATION

A. **Listen** and **circle** the numbers your teacher names.

1. | 0 | 1 | 2 |

4. | 5 | 6 | 7 |

2. | 3 | 4 | 5 |

5. | 8 | 9 | 10 |

3. | 3 | 1 | 5 |

6. | 7 | 10 | 5 |

B. *Partner A:* • **Circle** one number from each group.

• **Dictate** the numbers you circle to your partner.

Partner B: • **Listen** and **circle** the numbers your partner names.

1. | 0 | 2 | 4 |

4. | 4 | 9 | 1 |

2. | 1 | 3 | 5 |

5. | 5 | 0 | 10 |

3. | 4 | 6 | 8 |

6. | 9 | 6 | 7 |

C. *Partner A:* • **Listen** and **circle** the numbers your partner names.

Partner B: • **Circle** one number from each group.

• **Dictate** the numbers you circle to your partner.

1. | 3 | 2 | 1 |

4. | 6 | 8 | 10 |

2. | 4 | 0 | 2 |

5. | 9 | 6 | 8 |

3. | 5 | 6 | 7 |

6. | 9 | 5 | 4 |

MORE NUMBERS DICTATION

- **Write** the number you hear.
- **Show** how many.

Example: 3 ● ● ● ○ ○ ○ ○ ○ ○ ○

1. _____   ○ ○ ○ ○ ○ ○ ○ ○ ○ ○

2. _____   ○ ○ ○ ○ ○ ○ ○ ○ ○ ○

3. _____   ○ ○ ○ ○ ○ ○ ○ ○ ○ ○

4. _____   ○ ○ ○ ○ ○ ○ ○ ○ ○ ○

5. _____   ○ ○ ○ ○ ○ ○ ○ ○ ○ ○

6. _____   ○ ○ ○ ○ ○ ○ ○ ○ ○ ○

7. _____   ○ ○ ○ ○ ○ ○ ○ ○ ○ ○

8. _____   ○ ○ ○ ○ ○ ○ ○ ○ ○

9. _____   ○ ○ ○ ○ ○ ○ ○ ○ ○

10. _____   ○ ○ ○ ○ ○ ○ ○ ○ ○

Chapter A

PATTERNS

- **Complete** the pattern.

MORE OR LESS?

A. • **Write** > if the first number is more.

   • **Write** < if the first number is less.

   • **Write** = if the numbers are the same.

1.   5 _<u>></u>_ 3   6.   7 _____ 7

2.   2 _____ 9   7.   3 _____ 4

3.   10 _____ 10   8.   0 _____ 10

4.   8 _____ 6   9.   5 _____ 5

5.   0 _____ 1   10.   7 _____ 6

B. • **Write** your own problems.

   • Have a partner **solve** them.

1.   _<u>3 < 4</u>_   6.   _____

2.   _____   7.   _____

3.   _____   8.   _____

4.   _____   9.   _____

5.   _____   10.   _____

PROBLEM SOLVING

• **Complete** the pictures.

1.		
2.		
3.		
4.	XXXXXXX	XXX
5.		
6.	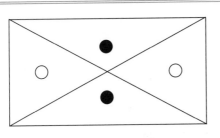	

B
Get Set

In this chapter, you will:

____ Identify same and different letters.

____ Read and write capital and lowercase letters.

____ Match capital to lowercase letters.

____ Dictate letters.

____ Spell words.

____ Count and write numbers from 11 to 20.

____ Solve problems.

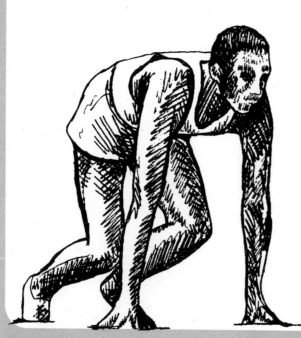

SAME LETTERS A–I

• **Circle** the letters that are the same as the first letter.

A	(A)	B	(A)	V	N
B	B	B	D	E	B
C	D	O	C	C	Q
D	P	D	D	O	D
E	E	E	F	E	B
F	F	E	P	T	F
G	O	C	G	G	Q
H	H	I	E	M	H
I	F	I	I	J	L

• **Point** to the letters your teacher names and **repeat.**

A B C D E F G H I

SAME LETTERS J–R

• **Circle** the letters that are the same as the first letter.

J	(J)	L	I	(J)	(J)
K	H	N	K	K	R
L	L	I	L	L	J
M	W	N	M	N	W
N	W	N	N	M	V
O	O	Q	C	O	D
P	R	P	F	A	P
Q	Q	O	Q	D	G
R	P	F	R	R	K

• **Point** to the letters your teacher names and **repeat.**

J K L M N O P Q R

SAME LETTERS S–Z

- **Circle** the letters that are the same as the first letter.

S	B	S	C	J	S
T	F	I	T	T	L
U	U	V	U	J	U
W	W	V	W	M	W
X	V	X	X	Y	W
Y	W	V	Y	A	Y
Z	Z	X	W	N	Z

- **Point** to the letters your teacher names and **repeat**.

S T U V W X Y Z

WRITING PRACTICE

- **Trace** and **copy**.

A  B C

D  E F

G   H   I   J

K   L   M   N

O   P   Q   R

S   T   U   V

W   X   Y   Z

LETTERS DICTATION

A.   **Listen** and **circle** the letter your teacher names.

1. | C | D | A | B |
|---|---|---|---|

4. | S | Q | R | T |
|---|---|---|---|

2. | H | E | G | F |
|---|---|---|---|

5. | U | V | W | X |
|---|---|---|---|

3. | K | L | J | I |
|---|---|---|---|

6. | Z | Y | U | X |
|---|---|---|---|

B.   *Partner A:*   • **Circle** one letter from each group.
                         • **Dictate** the letters you circle to your partner.

      Partner B: • **Listen** and **circle** the letters your partner names.

1. | O | C | Q | A |
|---|---|---|---|

4. | B | V | E | F |
|---|---|---|---|

2. | E | C | D | B |
|---|---|---|---|

5. | Q | K | U | A |
|---|---|---|---|

3. | N | W | M | V |
|---|---|---|---|

6. | P | T | C | E |
|---|---|---|---|

C.   *Partner A:*   • **Listen** and **circle** the letters your partner names.

      Partner B: • **Circle** one letter from each group.
                         • **Dictate** the letters you circle to your partner.

1. | C | Q | A | O |
|---|---|---|---|

4. | H | V | F | E |
|---|---|---|---|

2. | C | D | E | B |
|---|---|---|---|

5. | G | J | K | P |
|---|---|---|---|

3. | M | N | V | W |
|---|---|---|---|

6. | P | R | K | L |
|---|---|---|---|

DIFFERENT LETTERS a–i

• **Draw** an X over the letters that are different from the first letter.

a	a	b̶	a	⦸	q̶
b	b	b	d	p	b
c	d	o	c	c	q
d	p	d	d	b	d
e	e	g	o	e	c
f	f	f	r	t	f
g	q	p	g	g	q
h	h	l	b	y	h
i	f	i	i	j	l

• **Point** to the letters your teacher names and **repeat**.

a   b   c   d   e   f   g   h   i

DIFFERENT LETTERS j–r

- **Draw** an X over the letters that are different from the first letter.

j	j	l	i	j	j
k	h	r	k	x	k
l	l	i	l	l	t
m	w	m	m	n	w
n	n	w	n	m	u
o	q	o	c	a	o
p	r	p	b	p	q
q	q	p	q	d	b
r	t	f	r	r	r

- **Point** to the letters your teacher names and **repeat.**

j   k   l   m   n   o   p   q   r

DIFFERENT LETTERS s–z

• **Draw** an X over the letters that are different from the first letter.

s	s	j	c	z	s
t	f	l	t	t	l
u	u	u	v	n	u
w	w	v	w	m	w
x	v	x	x	y	z
y	w	y	y	y	v
z	z	s	w	s	z

• **Point** to the letters your teacher names and **repeat.**

s t u v w x y z

WRITING PRACTICE

• **Trace** and **copy.**

Aa Aa _____   Bb Bb _____

Cc Cc _____   Dd Dd _____

Ee Ee _____   Ff Ff _____

Gg Gg _____   Hh Hh _____

Ii Ii _____   Jj Jj _____

Kk Kk _____   Ll Ll _____

Mm Mm _____   Nn Nn _____

WRITING PRACTICE

- **Trace** and **copy**.

Oo Oo = = =   Pp Pp = = =

Qq Qq = = =   Rr Rr = = =

Ss Ss = = =   Tt Tt = = =

Uu Uu = = =   Vv Vv = = =

Ww Ww = = =   Xx Xx = = =

Yy Yy = = =   Zz Zz = = =

Chapter B

MATCHING LETTERS

A. **Match** the CAPITAL LETTERS to the lowercase letters.

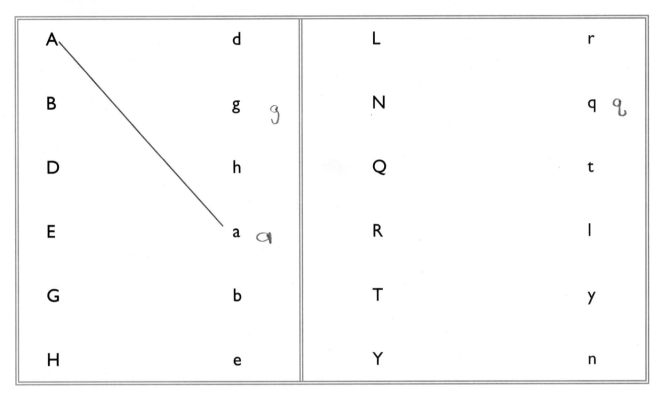

A	d	L	r
B	g	N	q
D	h	Q	t
E	a	R	l
G	b	T	y
H	e	Y	n

B. **Write** the missing CAPITAL letters.

A   B   <u>C</u>   D   _   F   _   H   I   J   _   _   M

_   O   P   _   R   S   T   _   _   _   X   Y   _

C. **Write** the missing lowercase letters.

___   b   c   d   ___   ___   g   h   ___   j   k   ___   ___

n   o   ___   q   ___   s   ___   u   v   ___   ___   ___   z

LETTERS DICTATION

A.   **Listen** and **circle** the letter your teacher names.

1.	e c f a	4.	t i j f
2.	r s t u	5.	c o d s
3.	b d p q	6.	g p q d

B.   *Partner A:*   • **Circle** one letter from each group.
                          • **Dictate** the letters you circle to your partner.

Partner B: • **Listen** and **circle** the letters your partner names.

1.	o c q a	4.	h y k b
2.	b d p q	5.	i j t l
3.	c o d s	6.	m n w u

C.   *Partner A:*   • **Listen** and **circle** the letters your partner names.

Partner B: • **Circle** one letter from each group.
                          • **Dictate** the letters you circle to your partner.

1.	o c q a	4.	h y k b
2.	b d p q	5.	i j t l
3.	c o d s	6.	m n w u

SPELLING DICTATION

Partner A: **Spell** each word to your partner.

1. write	2. read	3. say	4. copy
5. draw	6. color	7. name	8. number

- **Listen** and **write** the words your partner spells.
- **Check** your work.

1. _____   5. _____

2. _____   6. _____

3. _____   7. _____

4. _____   8. _____

Partner B: **Listen** and **write** the words your partner spells.

1. _____   5. _____

2. _____   6. _____

3. _____   7. _____

4. _____   8. _____

- **Spell** each word to your partner.
- **Check** your work.

1. listen	2. trace	3. check	4. write
5. draw	6. read	7. date	8. letter

CUT AND PASTE

• **Cut** and **paste** the letters you find in a magazine or a newspaper.

Aa
Ee
Gg
Mm
Rr
Tt

NUMBERS 11–20

A. • **Count** the letters.
• **Write** the numbers.

1. _____ AAAAAAAAAAA

2. _____ BBBBBBBBBBBBBBBBBB

3. _____ CCCCCCCCCCCCCCCC

4. _____ DDDDDDDDDDDD

5. _____ EEEEEEEEEEEEEEE

6. _____ FFFFFFFFFFFFFFFFF

7. _____ GGGGGGGGGGGGGGGGGGG

8. _____ HHHHHHHHHHHH

9. _____ IIIIIIIIIIIIII

10. _____ JJJJJJJJJJJJJJJJJJ

B. **Write** numbers 1–20 in order.

/
_____, _____, _____, _____, _____, _____, _____, _____, _____, _____,

_____, _____, _____, _____, _____, _____, _____, _____, _____, _____,

PROBLEM SOLVING

• **Complete** the letters.

1. b	l	2. f	ſ
3. d	c	4. g	c
5. q	ᴖ	6. e	–
7. k	ⱦ	8. m	n
9. R	\	10. T	–
11. E	L	12. X	/
13. W	V	14. N	\

Chapter B

1
Who Are You?

In this chapter, you will:

_____ Read and write ordinals 1st to 12th.

_____ Put words in ABC order.

_____ Complete a student I.D. Card.

_____ Address a letter.

_____ Answer questions about yourself.

_____ Write sentences about yourself.

_____ Ask questions about another person.

_____ Solve addition problems.

_____ Read and write numbers 1 to 100.

ORDINALS

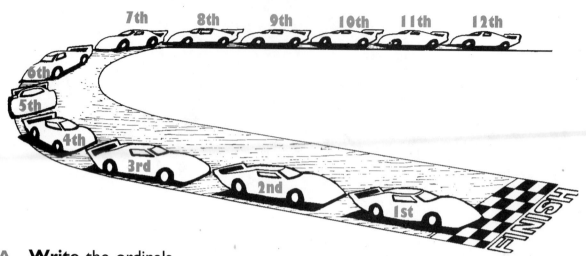

A. Write the ordinals.

1. A is the ___1st___ letter.

2. B is the _____ letter.

3. C is the _____ letter.

4. D is the _____ letter.

5. E is the _____ letter.

6. F is the _____ letter.

7. G is the _____ letter.

8. H is the _____ letter.

9. I is the _____ letter.

10. J is the _____ letter.

11. K is the _____ letter.

12. L is the _____ letter.

B. Order the pictures 1st to 6th.

SAME LETTERS

• **Circle** the letter groups that are the same as the first.

na	(na)	an	ma	no
me	ne	em	me	me
add	ada	add	add	dad
res	esr	ser	res	ers
tele	tele	tel	tell	tele
one	on	one	eno	noe
num	mun	num	nun	num
ber	ber	ber	ben	reb
age	ega	ade	age	age
gra	gra	agr	age	gra
ade	age	ade	ape	eda

MATCHING

• **Match** the words that are the same.

1. NAME		telephone
2. FIRST		last
3. LAST		grade
4. MIDDLE		first
5. ADDRESS		age
6. TELEPHONE		name
7. NUMBER		number
8. AGE		middle
9. GRADE		address

Chapter 1

VOCABULARY PRACTICE

A. • **Listen** to your teacher say the words.

    • **Circle** the beginning letter sound.

1. | l   m   n |

6. | f   t   p |

2. | s   v   f |

7. | n   m   h |

3. | l   r   w |

8. | g   u   a |

4. | d   n   m |

9. | d   b   g |

5. | a   e   o |

B. Put the words **in ABC order.**

name	1. _address_____
first	2. _____
last	3. _____
middle	4. _____
✔ address	5. _____
telephone	6. _____
number	7. _____
age	8. _____
grade	9. _____

VOCABULARY PRACTICE

A. **Count** the letters in the words from the Word File.

> **Word File**
>
> name   address   telephone
>
> number   age   grade

1. Write the word with 3 letters. _____

2. Write the word with 4 letters. _____

3. Write the word with 5 letters. _____

4. Write the word with 6 letters. _____

5. Write the word with 7 letters. _____

6. Write the word with 9 letters. _____

B. • **Match** the word to the same shape.

   • **Write** the word in the shape.

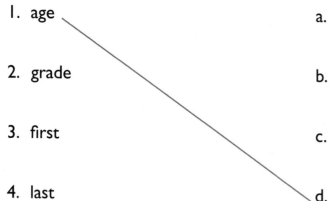

1. age

2. grade

3. first

4. last

5. address

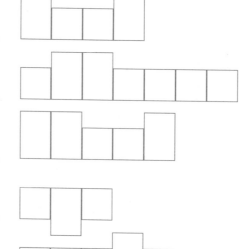

a.

b.

c.

d.

e.

SABA'S I.D. CARD

Saba   Miriam   Issac
First Name   Middle Name   Last Name

2335 Center Street, Apt. #7
Address

Baltimore   MD   21202
City   State   ZIP

(410) 555-5555   17   11
Telephone Number   Age   Grade

X   Saba M. Issac
Signature

STUDENT PHOTO

A. Answer the questions. Use Saba's I.D. card.

1. What is Saba's first name? _____

2. What is Saba's last name? _____

3. What is Saba's middle name? _____

4. What is Saba's address? _____

5. What is Saba's telephone number? _____

6. How old is Saba? _____

7. What grade is Saba in? _____

B. Practice your signature.

X _____   X _____

X _____   X _____

YOUR I.D. CARD

A. Complete your I.D. card.

_____

First Name   Middle Name   Last Name

_____

Address

_____

City   State   ZIP

_____

Telephone Number   Age   Grade

X _____

Signature

STUDENT PHOTO

B. Complete the sentences.

1. My first name is _____.

2. My middle name is _____.

3. My last name is _____.

4. My address is _____

_____.

5. My telephone number is _____.

6. I am _____ years old.

7. I am in the _____ grade.

ADDRESS A LETTER

A. **Match** the letter with the correct word.

1. ___B___ name

2. _____ street

3. _____ city

4. _____ state or province

5. _____ zip code

6. _____ return address

(A) Marc Durand
9 Pie-IX Boulevard
Montreal, QC H2N4B6
Canada

(B)→*Mr. Long D. Nguyen*

(C)→*90 Beach Street, Apt. #434*

Miami, FL 31090 U.S.

(D) **(E)** **(F)**

B. • **Address** the envelope to your school.

• **Write** your return address.

QUESTIONS

A. **Circle** the correct word to complete the questions.

1. What **(is)** / are your first name?

2. What **is** / are your last name?

3. What **is** / are your address?

4. What **is** / are your telephone number?

5. What grade **is** / are you in?

6. How old **is** / are you?

B. • **Complete** the questions.
   • **Use** words from the Word File.

Word File
What
How
is
are
telephone
middle
name

1. ____What____ is your first name?

2. What is your _____ name?

3. What is your last _____ ?

4. What _____ your address?

5. What is your _____ number?

6. _____ old are you?

7. What grade _____ you in?

PARTNER INTERVIEW

A. • **Ask** a partner the personal questions from page 42.
   • **Ask** your partner to spell the words.
   • **Write** the answers on the I.D. card.

First Name   Middle Name   Last Name
_____

Address
_____

City   State   ZIP

STUDENT PHOTO

_____
Telephone Number   Age   Grade

X _____
Signature

B. **Complete** the questions about your partner:
   • **Circle** the correct word.
   • **Write** the missing word.

1. **His / Her** first name is _____ .

2. **His / Her** middle name is _____ .

3. **His / Her** last name is _____ .

4. **His / Her** address is _____ .

5. **His / Her** telephone number is _____ .

6. **He / She** is _____ years old.

7. **He / She** is in the _____ grade.

WRITING SENTENCES

- **Answer** the questions in complete sentences.
- **Write** a . at the end of each sentence.

1. What is your first name?

   My first name is _____.

2. What is your last name?

   _____

3. What is your middle name?

   _____

4. What is your address?

   _____

   _____

5. What is your telephone number?

   _____

6. How old are you?

   _____

7. What grade are you in?

   _____

NUMBERS 1–100

- **Copy** the numbers.

1	2	3	4	5	6	7	8	9	10
1	*2*								
11	12	13	14	15	16	17	18	19	20
21	22	23	24	25	26	27	28	29	30
31	32	33	34	35	36	37	38	39	40
41	42	43	44	45	46	47	48	49	50
51	52	53	54	55	56	57	58	59	60
61	62	63	64	65	66	67	68	69	70
71	72	73	74	75	76	77	78	79	80
81	82	83	84	85	86	87	88	89	90
91	92	93	94	95	96	97	98	99	100

ADDITION

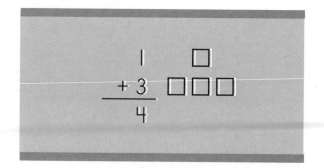

$$1 + 3 = 4$$

$$\begin{array}{r} 1 \\ + 3 \\ \hline 4 \end{array}$$

- **Solve** the problems.

1. ●● + ●●●●

   $2 + 4 = $ _____

2. ●●●● + ●●●●

   $4 + 4 = $ _____

3. ●●●●●● + ●●●

   _____ + _____ = _____

4. ●●●● + ●●●●

   ●●●●

   _____ + _____ = _____

5. $\begin{array}{r} 3 \\ + 5 \\ \hline \end{array}$

6. $\begin{array}{r} 9 \\ + 6 \\ \hline \end{array}$

7. _____

   + _____

   _____

8. _____

   + _____

   _____

PROBLEM SOLVING

- **Write** a math problem to show how much it is.
- **Solve** the problem.

1. How much is it?

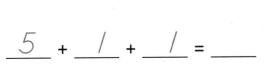  

5 + 1 + 1 = ____

2. How much is it?

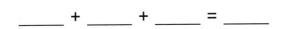  

____ + ____ + ____ = ____

3. How much is it?

 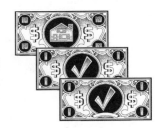

____ + ____ + ____ = ____

4. How much are they?

 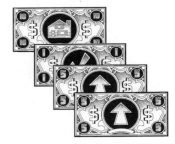

____ + ____ + ____ + ____ = ____

5. How much are they?

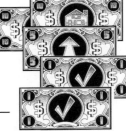 

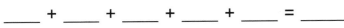

____ + ____ + ____ + ____ + ____ = ____

2
Where Are You From?

In this chapter, you will:

____ Describe where you and other people are from.

____ Make a bar graph.

____ Identify directions: up, down, left, and right.

____ Identify directions on a compass rose.

____ Identify continents and oceans on a world map and globe.

____ Read a globe.

____ Make a world map poster.

____ Solve subtraction problems.

____ Count money.

WHERE ARE YOU FROM?

- **Read** the sentences.

1. My name is Marc.
   I am from Canada.

2. Your name is Marie.
   You are from Haiti.

3. His name is Long.
   He is from Vietnam.

4. Her name is Saba.
   She is from Ethiopia.

5. Our names are Ana and Carlos.
   We are from Mexico.

6. Their names are Amar and Zinat.
   They are from Iraq.

7. I am from _____.

WHERE ARE WE FROM?

- **List** the names of some students in your class or group.

- **Write** a sentence about where each student is from.

For example: _____ Marc is from Canada. _____

1._____ is from _____.

2._____ is from _____.

3._____.

4._____.

5._____.

6._____.

7._____.

8._____.

9._____.

10._____.

BAR GRAPH

A. **Complete** the graph with information from page 49.

Where Are We From?

Number of Students

10
9
8
7
6
5
4
3
2
1
0

Country

B. **Complete** the sentences with data from the graph.

1. _____ students are from _____.

2. _____ students are from _____.

3. _____ students are from _____.

4. _____ students are from _____.

5. _____ students are from _____.

6. _____ students are from _____.

7. _____ students are from _____.

8. _____ students are from _____.

9. _____ students are from _____.

10. _____ students are from _____.

DIRECTIONS

up   **down**   **left**   **right**

• **Write** the direction.

1.   2.   3.   4.

left
_____   _____   _____   _____

5.   6.   7.   8.

_____   _____   _____   _____

9. 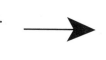   10.   11.    12.

_____   _____   _____   _____

13.   14.   15.   16.

_____   _____   _____   _____

THE COMPASS ROSE

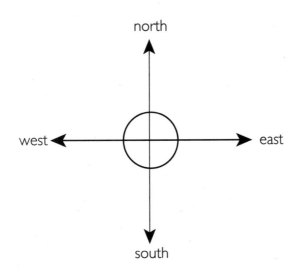

A. Read.

The compass rose has four **directions.**

The four directions are **north, south, east,** and **west.**

North is at the top. North points up.

South is at the bottom. South points down.

East is at the right. East points right.

West is at the left. West points left.

B. Complete the sentences.

1. The compass rose has ____four____ directions.

2. The four directions are _____, _____, _____, and

_____.

3. North points _____.   **Draw** an arrow pointing north: _____↑_____

4. South points _____.   **Draw** an arrow pointing south: _____

5. East points _____.   **Draw** an arrow pointing east: _____

6. West points _____.   **Draw** an arrow pointing west _____

THE WORLD MAP

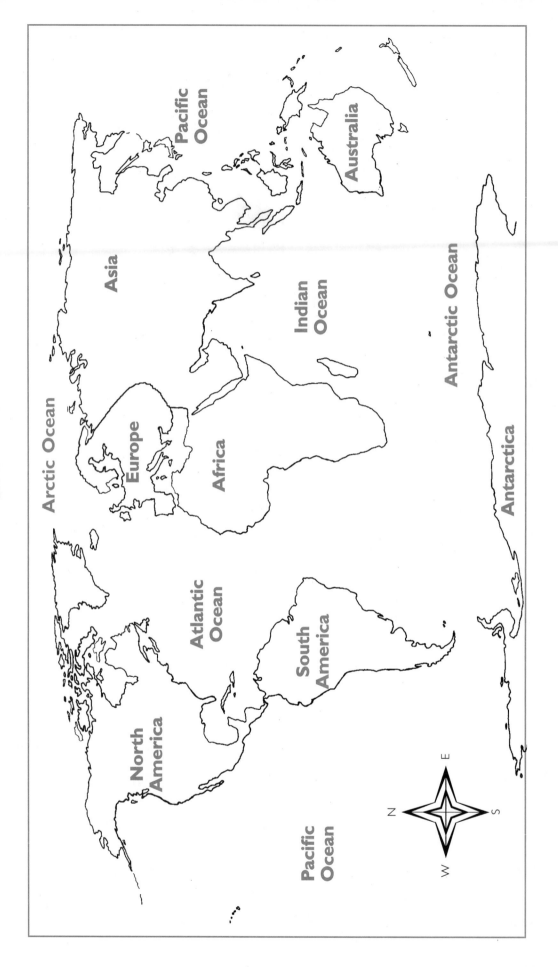

THE WORLD MAP

A. Read.

The world map has a compass rose.

The world map has seven **continents.**

The seven continents are **North America, South America, Europe, Africa, Asia, Australia,** and **Antarctica.**

Continents are **land.**

The world map has five **oceans.**

The five oceans are the **Arctic Ocean,** the **Pacific Ocean,** the **Atlantic Ocean,** the **Indian Ocean,** and the **Antarctic Ocean.**

Oceans are **water.**

B. • **Name** the seven continents.

1. North America
2. _____
3. _____
4. _____
5. _____
6. _____
7. _____

• **Name** the five oceans.

1. _____
2. _____
3. _____
4. _____
5. _____

C. Write the correct answer. Use the map on page 54.

1. Is North America **north** or **south**? _____north_____

2. Is Antarctica **north** or **south**? _____

3. Is the Arctic Ocean **north** or **south**? _____

4. Is South America **east** or **west**? _____

5. Is Asia **east** or **west**? _____

6. Is Australia **east** or **west**? _____

MATCHING

A. **Match** the letters to form the names of continents and oceans.

1.	Amer		ope
2.	Eur		lia
3.	Afri		arctica
4.	As		ia
5.	Austra		ific
6.	Ant		ica
7.	Atlan		ents
8.	Pac		eans
9.	contin		ca
10.	oc		tic

B. **Write** the words from part A.

1. America _____   6. _____

2. _____   7. _____

3. _____   8. _____

4. _____   9. _____

5. _____   10. _____

VOCABULARY PRACTICE

A. Write the words in ABC order.

map	1. _Africa_____
directions	2. _____
east	3. _____
west	4. _____
continents	5. _____
ocean	6. _____
North America	7. _____
South America	8. _____
Asia	9. _____
Europe	10. _____
✔ Africa	11. _____
Australia	12. _____
Antarctica	13. _____
land	14. _____
water	15. _____

B. Write the missing letters.

1. _A_ s i a
2. n ____ ____ t h
3. ____ o u t ____
4. c o n ____ i n e n ____
5. ____ c e a n
6. ____ a n d
7. ____ a t e ____
8. ____ a ____ t

9. A ____ e r i c ____
10. A ____ r i ____ a
11. ____ n t a ____ c t i ____ a
12. A u ____ t r a ____ i a
13. E u r o ____ e
14. w e ____ ____
15. ____ a p
16. ____ i ____ e c t i o n ____

MAP KEYS

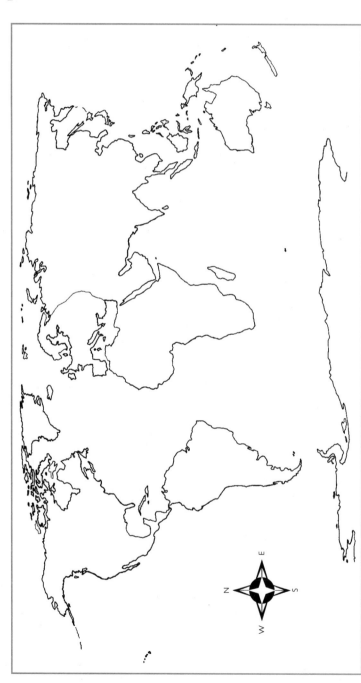

MAP KEY

☐ North America

☐ South America

☐ Europe

☐ Africa

☐ Asia

☐ Australia

☐ Antarctica

☐ Oceans

Map keys tell you where places on a map are.

● **Read** the directions.

● **Color** the places on the map and on the map key.

1. Color North America yellow.

2. Color South America orange.

3. Color Europe brown.

4. Color Africa green.

5. Color Asia red.

6. Color Australia purple.

7. Color Antarctica white

8. Color the oceans blue.

Name _____   **Date** _____

FROM HERE TO THERE

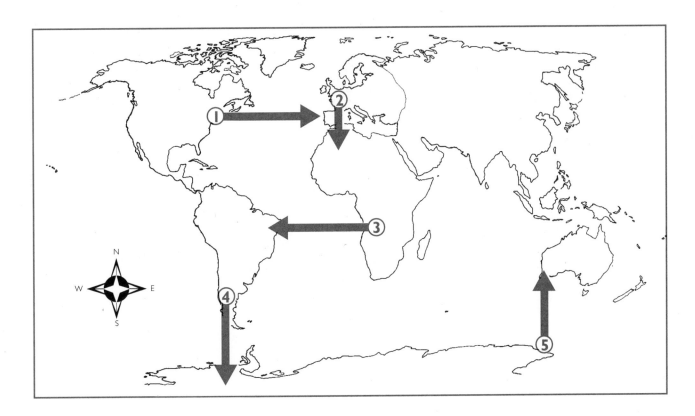

A. Write the directions.

1. Arrow 1 points from _____west_____ to _____east_____.

2. Arrow 2 points from _____ to _____.

3. Arrow 3 points from _____ to _____.

4. Arrow 4 points from _____ to _____.

5. Arrow 5 points from _____ to _____.

B. Write the names of the continents.

1. Arrow 1 points from ___North America___ to ___Europe___.

2. Arrow 2 points from _____ to _____.

3. Arrow 3 points from _____ to _____.

4. Arrow 4 points from _____ to _____.

5. Arrow 5 points from _____ to _____.

DIRECTIONS ON THE WORLD MAP

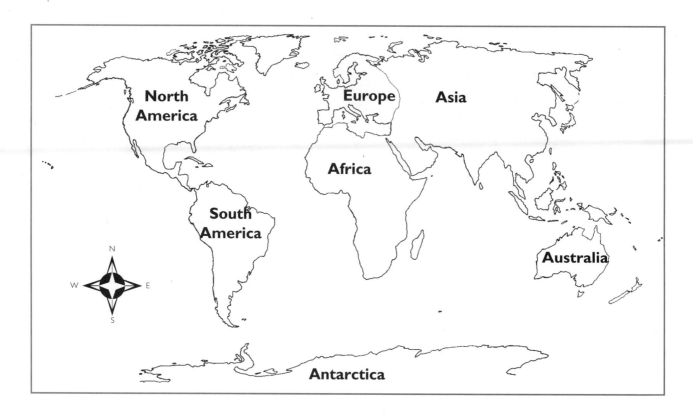

- **Write** the correct direction: north, south, east, or west.

1. North America is _north_____ of South America.

2. South America is _____ of North America.

3. Africa is _____ of Europe.

4. Africa is _____ of South America.

5. Europe is _____ of Asia.

6. South America is _____ of Antarctica.

7. Australia is _____ of Africa.

8. Europe is _____ of North America.

9. Asia is _____ of North America.

10. Antarctica is _____ of Africa.

THE EARTH AND THE GLOBE

A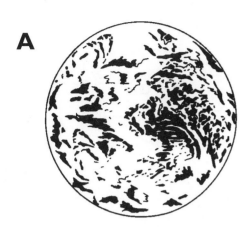

B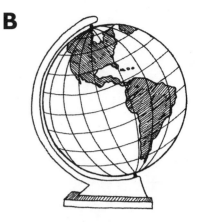

_____   _____

A. Read.

Picture A shows the Earth.

The Earth is round like a ball.

The Earth is not flat like a map.

Label the left picture: Earth

Picture B shows a globe.

The globe is round like the Earth.

Label the right picture: Globe

B. Answer "Yes" or "No."

1. Picture A shows the Earth.   _____Yes_____

2. The Earth is flat like a map.   _____

3. The Earth is round like a ball.   _____

4. Picture B shows a globe.   _____

5. The globe is flat like a map.   _____

6. The globe shows continents and oceans.   _____

BOTH SIDES OF THE GLOBE

A   North Pole

equator

South Pole

B _____

_____

A. Read.

This picture shows **both** sides of a globe.

The top of the globe is called the **North Pole.**

The bottom of the globe is called the **South Pole.**

The line around the **middle** of the globe is called the **equator.**

B.   **Follow** the directions.

1. **Label** the North Pole on the globe in Picture B.

2. **Label** the South Pole on the globe in Picture B.

3. **Label** the equator on the globe in Picture B.

4. **Draw** a red line on the equator in both pictures of the globe.

5. **Color** the oceans blue.

6. **Color** the land green.

WORLD MAP POSTER

- **Use** the materials your teacher gives you.

- **Work** with your group to make a world map poster.

- **Follow** the directions.

- **Check** (✔) the box after you finish each step.

✔ finished

1. **Color** the seven continents. ☐

2. **Label** the seven continents. ☐

3. **Cut out** the continents. ☐

4. **Paste** the continents on the poster in the correct position. ☐

5. **Color** the oceans blue. ☐

6. **Label** the oceans. ☐

7. **Draw** a compass rose on the map. ☐

8. **Draw** and **label** your country on the map. ☐

SUBTRACTION

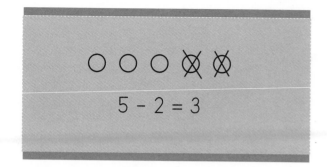

5 − 2 = 3

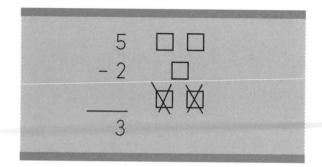

• **Solve** the problems.

1.

   7 − 4 = _____

2. ○ ○ ○ ○ ○ ○

   6 − 5 = _____

3. □ □ □ □ □
   □ □ □ □

   10 − 3 = _____

4. □ □ □ □ □ □ □
   □ □ □ □ □ □ □
   □ □ □ □ □ □ □

   24 − 10 = _____

5.   6
    − 4
   _____

6. 10
    − 5
   _____

7. 12
    − 8
   _____

8. 25
   − 10
   _____

Name _____   Date _____

PROBLEM SOLVING

- **Write** a subtraction problem to show how much change is left.
- **Solve** the problem.

1. How much is left?

   $\underline{5} - \underline{1} = $ _____ ¢

2. How much is left?

   _____ – _____ = _____ ¢

3. How much is left?

   _____ – _____ = _____ ¢

4. How much is left?

   _____ – _____ = _____ ¢

5. How much is left?

   _____ – _____ = _____ ¢

Name _____   **Date** _____

MATCHING

• **Write** the letter that matches.

<u>C</u> 1.

                                                    a. $ .25

____ 2.

                                                    b. $ 6.35

____ 3.

                                                    c. $ 1.50

____ 4.

                                                    d. $20.00

____ 5.

                                                    e. $30.30

____ 6.

                                                    f. $ 6.40

____ 7.

                                                    g. $16.05

3

In the Classroom

In this chapter, you will:

____ Identify things in your classroom.

____ Label a diagram of a classroom.

____ Find words in a dictionary.

____ Use and write words that describe where something is.

____ Identify and describe shapes.

____ Identify parallel lines.

____ Make a classroom map.

____ Measure length.

____ Measure perimeter.

____ Solve problems.

WHAT'S IN YOUR CLASSROOM?

• **Listen** to your teacher say the words.

• **Write** the missing letters.

1. c h a i ____

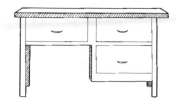

2. ____ e s k

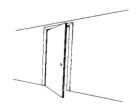

3. ____ o o r

4. ____ l a c k b o a r ____

5. b o o ____ s h e l ____

6. c ____ o c k

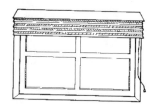

7. ____ i n ____ o w

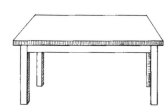

8. ____ a b ____ e

9. ____ a ____

10. c o m ____ u ____ e ____

IN THE CLASSROOM

- **Name** the things in the picture.
- **Write** the words on the lines.

1. door

2. _____

3. _____

4. _____

5. _____

6. _____

7. _____

8. _____

9. _____

10. _____

WORD FIND

- **Write** the words in capital letters.
- **Locate** and **circle** the words in the puzzle.

1. desk _____DESK_____
2. table _____
3. chair _____
4. door _____
5. map _____

6. computer _____
7. bookshelf _____
8. blackboard _____
9. window _____
10. clock _____

M	J	U	R	G	L	P	F	E	C
B	T	D	C	V	N	R	I	G	S
M	A	P	H	G	L	E	K	B	Q
A	D	T	A	J	Z	B	Y	L	P
C	C	W	I	N	D	O	W	A	V
C	Z	C	R	R	E	O	N	C	R
O	S	T	L	N	C	K	M	K	D
M	O	R	S	T	L	S	N	B	E
P	C	L	O	C	K	H	C	O	M
U	D	O	R	S	T	E	L	A	D
T	N	E	T	A	B	L	E	R	O
E	R	S	T	L	N	F	E	D	O
R	C	M	O	D	E	S	K	D	R

DICTIONARY AND SPELLING PRACTICE

A. • **Look up** each word in a dictionary.

   • **Write** the guide words from the top of the page.

1. _____ blackboard _____

2. _____ computer _____

3. _____ table _____

4. _____ window _____

5. _____ door _____

6. _____ bookshelf _____

7. _____ map _____

8. _____ clock _____

9. _____ desk _____

10. _____ chair _____

B. • **Listen** to your teacher say the words.

   • **Write** t or th.

1. _____ a b l e   6. _____ r a p e z o i d

2. _____ e   7. _____ i s

3. _____ i n g s   8. _____ e y

4. _____ r i a n g l e   9. _____ o

5. _____ o p   10. _____ r e e

WHERE IS THE BALL?

A. Read the words.

B. Write the correct word.

IN THE CLASSROOM

- **Complete** the paragraph describing the classroom on page 69.

- **Use** the words from the Word File. You can use each word more than one time.

Word File

in

on

under

over

next to

behind

A Classroom

This is a classroom. The table is (1) _next to_____ the door. The

computer is (2) _____ the table. The map is (3) _____

the computer. The clock is (4) _____ the door. The blackboard is

(5) _____ the door. The blackboard is (6) _____

the desk. The windows are (7) _____ the blackboard. The bookshelf

is (8) _____ the windows. The books are (9) _____ the

bookshelf.

DRAW IT

- **Read** the directions.
- **Complete** the picture.

Directions

1. Draw a cap on the dresser.

2. Draw a poster over the stereo.

3. Draw 5 books ▌▌▌▌▌ in the bookshelf.

4. Draw a football under the bed. ▭▭▭

5 Draw a lamp ⌼ next to the stereo on the bookshelf.

6. Draw a pillow ▱ behind the boy.

SHAPES

- **Name.**   • **Trace.**   • **Copy.**

1. circle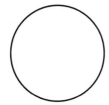

2. square

3. rectangle

4. triangle

5. trapezoid

SHAPES

A. Label each shape.

1. ___triangle___   2. _____   3. _____

4. _____   5. _____   6. _____

B. Draw and **color.**

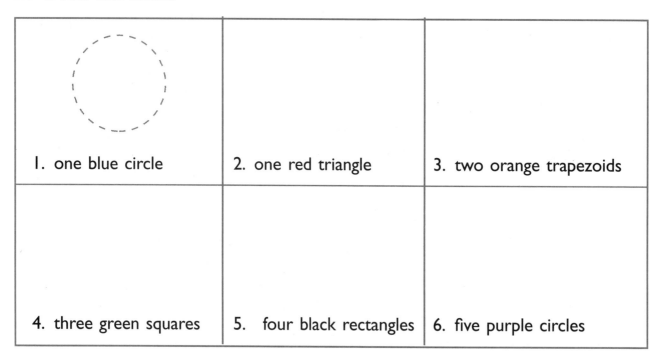

1. one blue circle	2. one red triangle	3. two orange trapezoids
4. three green squares	5. four black rectangles	6. five purple circles

C. Write the word your teacher says.

1. _____   2. _____   3. _____

4. _____   5. _____   6. _____

SHAPES

1. Color all ◯ red.

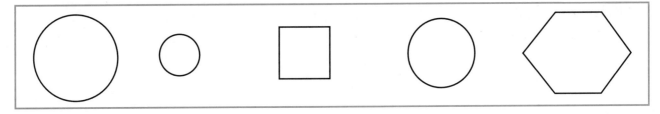

2. Color all ▢ blue.

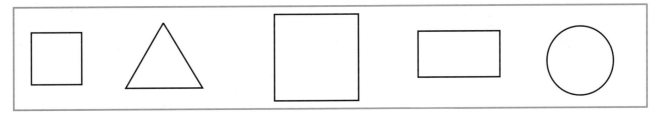

3. Color all ▭ yellow.

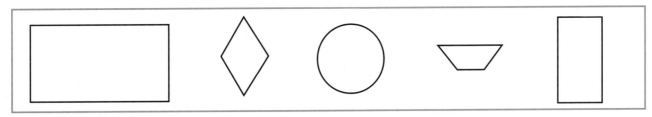

4. Color all △ green.

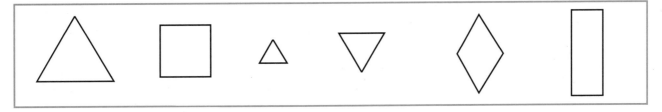

5. Color all ⬯ orange.

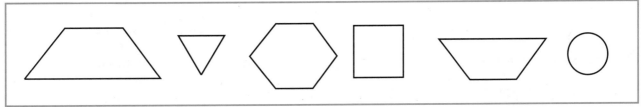

CLASSIFYING THINGS BY SHAPE

- **Name** the shape of things from your classroom.

- **Write** the words from the Word File in the column on the table that matches the shape.

Word File

blackboard	desk
clock	bookshelf
window	door
table	computer
flag	globe
map	

Circle ●	Square ■	Rectangle ▬
		blackboard

Do you see other things in your classroom that you can add to the table?

What shape do you find the most?

PARALLEL LINES

Parallel lines are straight lines.

Parallel lines never cross each other.

Parallel lines always stay the same distance apart.

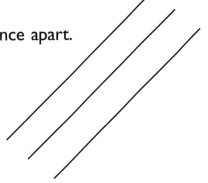

- **Circle** the letters that have parallel lines.
- **Put** an × over letters with no parallel lines.

A   E   F   H   I

K   L   M   N   T

V   W   X   Y   Z

DEFINING SHAPES

• **Read.**

1.    This is a circle. A circle is round.

2.    This is a square. A square has four sides. The sides are parallel. The sides are equal.

3.    This is a rectangle. A rectangle has four sides. The sides are parallel.

4. 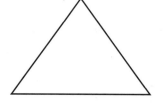   This is a triangle. A triangle has three sides. The sides are not parallel.

5.    This is a trapezoid. A trapezoid has four sides. Two sides are parallel. Two sides are not parallel.

MATCHING

• **Match** the definition to the shape.

1. _____ This is a trapezoid. A trapezoid has four sides. Two sides are parallel. Two sides are not parallel.

2. _____ This is a rectangle. A rectangle has four sides. The sides are parallel.

3. _____ This is a triangle. A triangle has three sides. The sides are not parallel.

4. _____ This is a circle. A circle is round.

5. _____ This is a square. A square has four sides. The sides are parallel. The sides are equal.

A.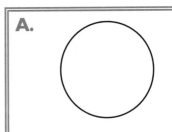

B.

C.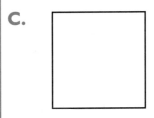

D.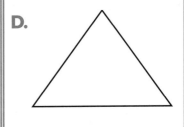

E.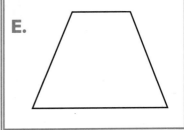

A CLASSROOM MAP

This is a classroom map.

- **Locate** each item from the map key on the map.
- **Write** the number of the item on the map.

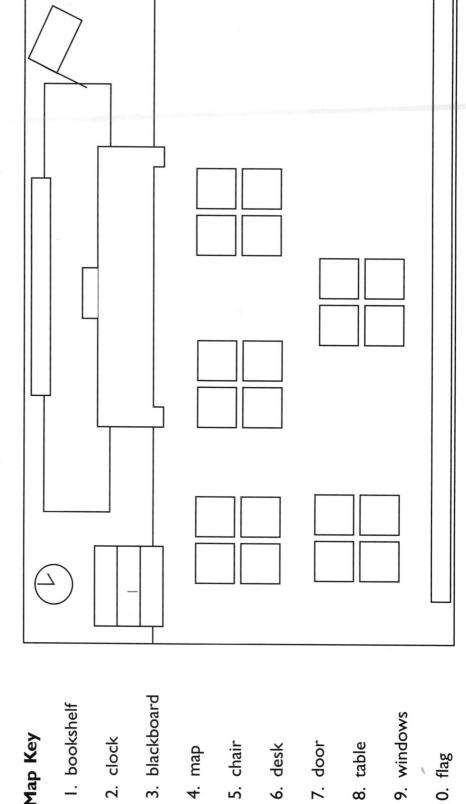

Map Key

1. bookshelf

2. clock

3. blackboard

4. map

5. chair

6. desk

7. door

8. table

9. windows

10. flag

Chapter 3

Name _____

Date _____

OUR CLASSROOM

• **Make** a map of your classroom.

• **Label** the map and the map key.

Map Key

1. _____
2. _____
3. _____
4. _____
5. _____
6. _____
7. _____
8. _____
9. _____
10. _____

MEASURING LENGTH

A. Read.

This is a ruler. A ruler is used to **measure** the **length** of something.
Length means how long something is.

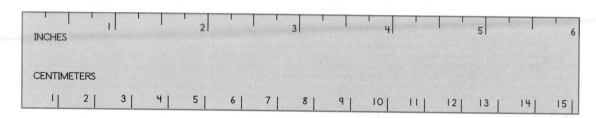

The top side of the ruler has **inches.** One inch (**1 in.**) is this long: ——————

The bottom side of the ruler has **centimeters.**
One centimeter (**1 cm**) is this long: ——

B. **Measure** the lines in inches.

1. _____ in. ——————

2. _____ in.

3. _____ in.

4. _____ in.

5. _____ in.

MEASURING LENGTH

A. Measure the lines in centimeters.

1. _____ cm

2. _____ cm

3. _____ cm ——

4. _____ cm

5. _____ cm

6. _____ cm

B. Draw the lines.

1. 1 in.

2. 5 in.

3. 2 in.

4. 3 cm

5. 10 cm

PERIMETER

Perimeter is the distance around something.

To find the **perimeter** of a shape, **add** all sides of the shape.

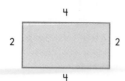

Perimeter = 2 + 4 + 2 + 4 = 12

Add the sides to find the perimeter of each shape.

1. P = _____ + _____ + _____ + _____ = _____

2. P = _____ + _____ + _____ + _____ = _____

3. P = _____ + _____ + _____ + _____ = _____

4. P = _____ + _____ + _____ = _____

5. P = _____ + _____ + _____ + _____ + _____ = _____

PROBLEM SOLVING

A. What is the distance around each shape?

- **Use** a ruler to measure the sides in centimeters (cm).

- **Add** the sides to find the perimeter.

1.

2.

P = 2 + 4 + 2 + 4 = _____ cm

P = _____ = _____

3.

4.

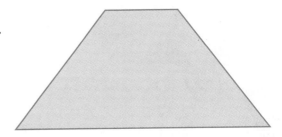

P = _____ = _____

P = _____ = _____

B. Measure length and perimeter.

1. What is the length of your pencil?   _____ in. _____ cm

2. What is the length of your ruler?   _____ in. _____ cm

3. What is the length of your shoe?   _____ in. _____ cm

4. What is the perimeter of a piece of paper? _____ in. _____ cm

5. What is the perimeter of this book?   _____ in. _____ cm

6. What is the perimeter of your desk or table? _____ in. _____ cm

4

In School

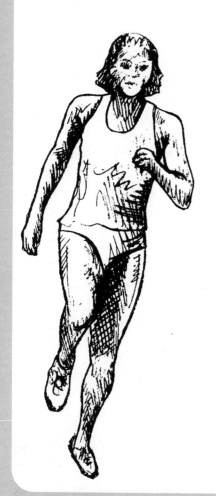

In this chapter, you will:

_____ Identify places on a school map.

_____ Talk and write about school activities.

_____ Identify horizontal, vertical, and diagonal lines.

_____ Find information about your school.

_____ Read and write ordinal words.

_____ Talk and write about school classes and schedules.

_____ Tell time.

_____ Say, read, and write numbers 100 to 1,000.

_____ Identify place value.

_____ Solve problems.

A MAP OF THE SCHOOL

- **Look** at the map of the school. **Point** to the rooms your teacher names. **Say** the names of the rooms.

- **Trace** the path with your finger to the rooms your teacher names.

- **Practice** giving and following directions with a partner.

A _____ B _____ C _____ D _____

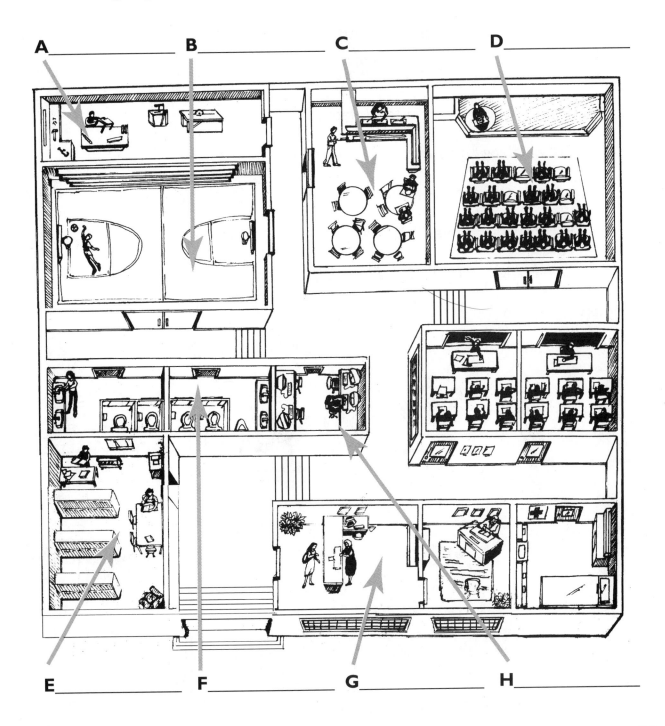

E _____ F _____ G _____ H _____

SCHOOL ACTIVITIES

A.
- **Match** the sentences to the rooms on the school map.
- **Label** the rooms on the map.

__B__ Marc is playing basketball. He's in the <u>gymnasium</u>.

_____ Zinat is getting a late pass. She's in the <u>office</u>.

_____ Marie is reading. She's in the <u>library</u>.

_____ Long is eating lunch. He's in the <u>cafeteria</u>.

_____ Amar is watching an assembly. He's in the <u>auditorium</u>.

_____ Ana is working on the computer. She's in the <u>computer lab</u>.

_____ Carlos is making a table. He's in the <u>shop</u>.

_____ Saba is washing her hands. She's in the <u>bathroom</u>.

B. Where does it belong?
- **Write** the name of the room where you might find these things.

cafeteria

Chapter 4

HORIZONTAL, VERTICAL, AND DIAGONAL LINES

A. **Trace** and **copy** the lines.

Horizontal	Vertical	Diagonal

B. **Use** a colored pencil to **trace** the lines in the letters.

1. **Trace** any horizontal lines.

F E H L T

2. **Trace** any vertical lines.

I L H P T

3. **Trace** any diagonal lines.

V A W N X

C. **Label** the lines horizontal, vertical, or diagonal.

1. — _____   3. X _____

2. / _____   4. I _____

5. ! _____   6. = _____

D. **Find** examples of the 3 kinds of lines in your classroom.

WORD FIND

- **Find** and **circle** the words from the Word File in the puzzle.

- **Look** for words that are **horizontal:** w o r d

vertical: w o r d   and **diagonal:**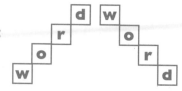

Word File

gymnasium	office	library
cafeteria	auditorium	bathroom
woodshop	computer lab	

g	o	n	k	o	p	u	f	s	x	b	j	m	l	o
b	y	i	p	k	m	b	g	r	e	s	u	z	t	a
a	c	m	c	a	f	e	t	e	r	i	a	b	r	w
t	f	e	n	t	m	y	p	i	s	b	b	v	v	o
h	r	o	l	a	r	q	z	o	a	n	s	x	p	o
r	b	o	r	a	s	d	t	i	f	w	d	s	c	f
o	r	t	r	p	m	i	z	a	k	f	i	o	n	s
o	k	b	p	o	d	e	u	m	a	r	i	s	v	h
m	i	e	r	u	s	t	u	m	o	r	d	c	i	o
l	r	t	a	s	o	p	o	a	k	n	q	s	e	p
a	s	t	e	c	o	m	p	u	t	e	r	l	a	b
h	f	e	p	t	m	l	p	i	a	b	w	d	b	s

MATCHING

- **Underline** the words that end with **-ing.**
- **Match** each sentence to the correct picture.

1. _d_ He's reading a book.

2. ____ She's writing a report.

3. ____ They're running.

4. ____ He's drawing a picture.

5. ____ He's erasing the blackboard.

6. ____ They're eating pizza.

7. ____ She's washing her hands.

8. ____ They're watching a movie.

9. ____ She's working on the computer.

WRITING PRACTICE

- **Write** a sentence about each picture.
- **Use** the Word File to make your sentences.

1.

2.

3.

4.

5.

6.

1. _____ They're watching T.V. _____.

2. _____.

3. _____.

4. _____.

5. _____.

6. _____.

Word File

	playing	a sentence
He's	reading	T.V.
	writing	ice cream
She's	drawing	a book
	eating	basketball
They're	watching	a picture

KNOW YOUR SCHOOL

- **Work** with a partner or group.
- **Find** the information about your school.
- **Write** the answers.

1. What is the name of your school district? _____

2. What is the name of your Principal? _____

3. What is the name of your Vice Principal? _____

4. What is the name of the school librarian? _____

5. How many secretaries work in the office? _____

6. How many English or ESL teachers are in your school? _____

7. What is the school's mascot? _____

8. How many floors does your school have? _____

9. How many bathrooms does your school have? _____

10. How many exit doors does your school have? _____

Number correct: _____

ORDINAL NUMBERS AND WORDS

A.

- **Look up** "Ordinals" in the Reference section.

- **Write** the ordinal number.

1. first _____1st_____

6. sixth _____

2. second _____

7. seventh _____

3. third _____

8. eighth _____

4. fourth _____

9. ninth _____

5. fifth _____

10. tenth _____

B. Write the ordinal word.

1. 4th _____fourth_____

6. 10th _____

2. 8th _____

7. 7th _____

3. 6th _____

8. 5th _____

4. 1st _____

9. 9th _____

5. 3rd _____

10. 2nd _____

C. Order the pictures from first to fourth.

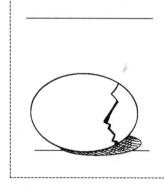   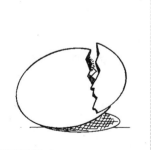

ORDINAL WORDS

A. Write the ordinal word.

1. C is the ___third___ letter of the alphabet.

2. F is the _____ letter of the alphabet.

3. I is the _____ letter of the alphabet.

4. B is the _____ letter of the alphabet.

5. D is the _____ letter of the alphabet.

6. H is the _____ letter of the alphabet.

7. G is the _____ letter of the alphabet.

B. Write the student's name.

Marc   Marie   Amar   Zinat   Carlos

Saba   David   Ana   Mina   Long

1. ___Marc_____ is first in line.

2. _____ is third in line.

3. _____ is seventh in line.

4. _____ is fifth in line.

5. _____ is last in line.

6. _____ is sixth in line.

7. _____ is ninth in line.

Name _____ **Date** _____

SCHOOL SUBJECTS

A.

• **Listen** and **point** to the school classes your teacher names.

• **Say** the names of the classes with your teacher.

English

math

science

social studies

computers

physical education (P.E.)

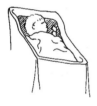

child development

music

art

vocational ed.

home ec.

shop

B. **Write** the names of the classes you take now.

1. _____   2. _____

3. _____   4. _____

5. _____   6. _____

7. _____   8. _____

ZINAT'S CLASS SCHEDULE

Period	Class	Time	Room
1st	math	8:30	212
2nd	English	9:20	204
3rd	P.E.	10:10	gymnasium
4th	science	11:00	111
5th	lunch		cafeteria
6th		12:40	
7th			

A.

- **Read** Zinat's class schedule.
- **Complete** the sentences.

1. Zinat's first class is _____math_____.

   She has math at 8:30 in Room _____212_____.

2. Zinat's second class is _____.

   She has English at _____ in Room 204.

3. Zinat's _____ class is P.E.

   She has P.E. at 10:10 in the _____.

4. Zinat's fourth class is _____.

   She has science at 11:00 in _____ 111.

B.

- **Read** the sentences.
- **Complete** Zinat's schedule.

1. Zinat's fifth class is lunch. She has lunch at 11:50 in the cafeteria.

2. Zinat's sixth class is social studies. She has social studies at 12:40 in Room 109.

3. Zinat's seventh class is art. She has art at 1:30 in Room 201.

YOUR CLASS SCHEDULE

A. **Complete** your class schedule.

Period	Class	Time	Room
1st			

B.

• **Answer** the questions in complete sentences.
• **Write** a . at the end of each sentence.

1. What is your first class?

    My first class is _____

2. What is your second class?

    _____

3. What is your third class?

    _____

4. What is your fourth class?

    _____

5. At what time is your fifth class?

    _____

6. At what time is your sixth class?

    _____

7. At what time is your seventh class?

    _____

TELLING TIME

It's 2:00.   It's 5:00.   It's 10:00.   It's 12:00.

• **Circle** the correct time.

5:00			
11:00			
3:00			
	12:00	6:00	5:00
	7:00	12:00	8:00

WHAT TIME IS IT?

It's 2:00.   It's 2:15.   It's 2:30.   It's 2:45.

A. Write the correct time.

1.    2.    3.   4.

It's 3:00. _____   _____   _____   _____

5.    6.   7.   8.

_____   _____   _____   _____

B. Draw the hands on the clock.

1.   2.    3.   4.

It's 4:00.   It's 2:30.   It's 11:15.   It's 9:45.

NUMBERS 100–1,000

A.

• **Look up** "Numbers" in the Reference section.

• **Write** the word.

1. 100   one hundred   6. 600   _____

2. 200   _____   7. 700   _____

3. 300   _____   8. 800   _____

4. 400   _____   9. 900   _____

5. 500   _____   10. 1,000 _____

B. Underline the number your teacher says.

1. 20   200   202   6. 909   9,009   99

2. 350   35   305   7. 88   8,888   888

3. 100   1,000   110   8. 660   666   606

4. 145   154   1,045   9. 550   555   5,050

5. 402   432   4,320   10. 700   7,000   70

C. Write the number your teacher says.

1. _____   5. _____   9. _____

2. _____   6. _____   10. _____

3. _____   7. _____   11. _____

4. _____   8. _____   12. _____

Name _____ **Date** _____

PLACE VALUE

257 = 2 (hundreds) 5 (tens) 7 (ones)   3,961 = 3 (thousands) 9 (hundreds) 6 (tens) 1 (ones)

A. Circle the correct place value.

1. Circle the **ones.**   4 3 (9)   How many tens? _____3_____
2. Circle the **tens.**   8 2 1   How many ones? _____
3. Circle the **hundreds.** 9, 0 5 7   How many thousands? _____
4. Circle the **thousands.** 6, 9 4 2   How many ones? _____
5. Circle the **ones.**   3, 7 8 0   How many hundreds? _____

B. Write the number.

1. 1 hundred   _____129_____
    2 tens
    9 ones

2. 8 hundreds _____
    4 tens
    0 ones

3. 1 thousand _____
    9 hundreds
    8 tens
    6 ones

4. 3 thousands _____
    6 hundreds
    0 tens
    7 ones

5. 0 thousands _____
    2 hundreds
    5 tens
    9 ones

6. 7 thousands _____
    3 hundreds
    9 tens
    3 ones

PROBLEM SOLVING

- **Match** the numbers.

1. __d__   This number has
3 hundreds and 0 thousands.   a. 9,393

2. _____   This number has 7 ones
and no hundreds.   b. 99

3. _____   This number has 9 tens
and 9 thousands.   c. 730

4. _____   This number has 7 ones,
3 hundreds, and no tens.   ✔ d. 370

5. _____   This number has 3 tens
and 7 hundreds.   e. 907

6. _____   This number has
9 thousands and 9 hundreds.   f. 1,007

7. _____   This number has 9 tens
and 9 ones.   g. 9,933

8. _____   This number has 7 ones
and 9 hundreds.   h. 3,307

5
The Calendar

In this chapter, you will:

____ Read a calendar.

____ Say, read, and write the months of the year.

____ Say, read, and write the days of the week.

____ Complete a True / False test.

____ Answer questions with **How many?**

____ Complete a crossword puzzle.

____ Read and construct a bar graph.

____ Say, read, and write dates.

____ Read and write fractions.

____ Solve problems.

THE CALENDAR

- **Read.**

Months of the Year

This is a page from a **calendar.** The calendar shows the **months** of the **year.** There are twelve months in one year. The twelve months of the year are **January, February, March, April, May, June, July, August, September, October, November,** and **December.** This page shows the month of October. The year is 1996.

Days of the Week

The calendar shows the **days** of the **week.** There are seven days in one week. The seven days of the week are **Sunday, Monday, Tuesday, Wednesday, Thursday, Friday,** and **Saturday.** There are 31 days in October. Not all months have 31 days. Some months have 30 days. February has only 28 or 29 days.

October						1996
Sunday	Monday	Tuesday	Wednesday	Thursday	Friday	Saturday
Sun.	Mon.	Tues.	Wed.	Thurs.	Fri.	Sat.
	1	2	3	4	5	6
7	8	9	10	11	12	13
14	15	16	17	18	19	20
21	22	23	24	25	26	27
28	29	30	31			

Chapter 5

READING CHECK

- **Answer** the questions in complete sentences.

1. How many months are there in one year?

   There are twelve months in one year. _____

2. How many days are there in one week?

   There are _____

3. How many days are there in the month of October?

   There _____

4. What are the first six months of the year?

   The first six months of the year are _____

   _____

   _____

5. What are the last six months of the year?

   _____

   _____

   _____

6. What are the seven days of the week?

   _____

   _____

   _____

7. What is the day today?   Today is _____.

8. What is the month?   The month is _____.

9. What is the year?   The year is _____.

TRUE OR FALSE?

A.

- **Circle** "True" if the sentence is correct.
- **Circle** "False" if the sentence is not correct.

1.	October is a month.	(True)	False
2.	There are twelve months in one year.	True	False
3.	January is a month.	True	False
4.	May is a year.	True	False
5.	October has 31 days.	True	False
6.	All months have 31 days.	True	False
7.	There are 12 days in one week.	True	False
8.	Friday is a day.	True	False
9.	December is a day.	True	False
10.	Monday is a month.	True	False

B. Write Yes, it is or No, it isn't.

1. January is the first month of the year. _____Yes, it is._____

2. Sunday is the first day of the week. _____

3. December is the last day of the year. _____

4. December is the last month of the year. _____

5. Thursday is the second day of the week. _____

6. Wednesday is in the middle of the week. _____

7. Today is Friday. _____

8. The year now is 1997. _____

Chapter 5

HOW MANY ARE THERE?

How many people **are there** in your class?

There are 21 students in our class.

There is 1 teacher in our class.

• **Answer** the questions in complete sentences.

1. How many **students** are there in your class today?

   There are _____ _____ students in our class today. _____

2. How many **teachers** are there in your class?

   There _____ _____ _____ _____ in our class. _____

3. How many **boys** are there in your class?

   _____

4. How many **girls** are there in your class?

   _____

5. How many **computers** are there in your classroom?

   _____

6. How many **chairs** are there in your classroom?

   _____

7. How many **principals** are there in your school?

   _____

8. How many **people** in your class are wearing blue today?

   _____

CROSSWORD PUZZLE

- **Complete** the sentences.
- **Write** the words in the spaces in the puzzle.

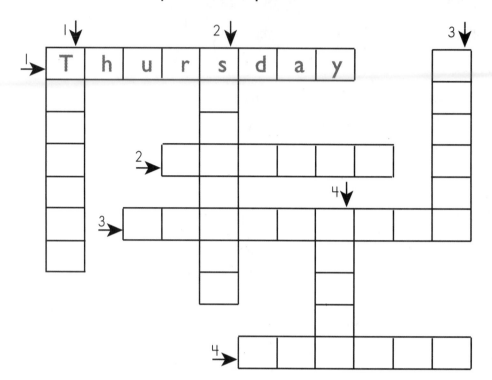

ACROSS ⟶

1. The fifth day of the week is _____Thursday_____.

2. The first day of the week is _____.

3. _____ is the fourth day of the week.

4. _____ is the second day of the week.

DOWN ⬇

1. The third day of the week is _____.

2. _____ is the seventh day of the week.

3. _____ is the sixth day of the week.

4. There are _____ days in one week.

READING A BAR GRAPH

Amar is selling magazines to raise money for the school's basketball team. This bar graph shows how much money Amar made in one week.

Amar's Sales for the Basketball Team

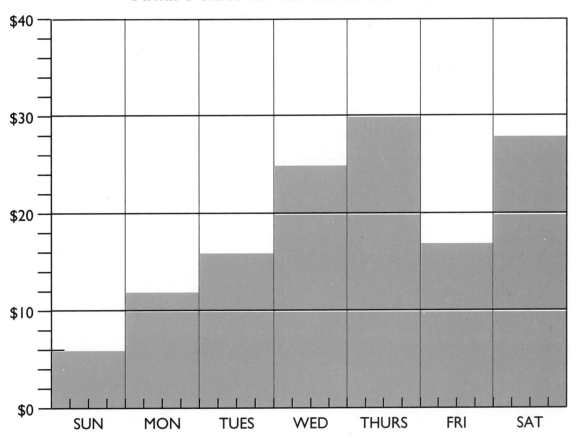

- **Read** the graph and **answer** the questions.

1. What is the title of the graph? _____

2. How much money did Amar make on Monday? $ _____

3. How much money did Amar make on Friday? $ _____

4. On what day did Amar make the most money? _____

5. On what day did Amar make the least money? _____

6. How much did Amar make for the whole week? _____

MAKING A BAR GRAPH

The table below shows how much money Linda made in one week of selling magazines for the basketball team.

A. **Use** the data from the table to **complete** the bar graph.

Linda's Sales for the Basketball Team

SUN	MON	TUE	WED	THU	FRI	SAT
$0	$7.00	$32.00	$20.00	$15.00	$28.00	$8.00

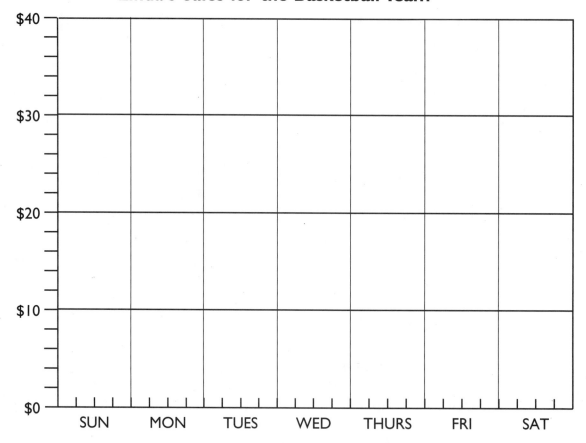

Linda's Sales for the Basketball Team

B. **Answer** the questions.

1. How much money did Linda make for the whole week? _____

2. Did Linda make more money on Tuesday or Friday? _____

3. Who made more money, Linda or Amar? _____

ALL MIXED UP!

A. **Order** the letters in each word to spell the names of the 12 months.

GSUUAT   <u>AUGUST</u>

CARHM   _____

CDMERBEE   _____

AYM   _____

NUEJ   _____

FRUBEYAR   _____

RMOVNBEE   _____

LYUJ   _____

PSMETEBRE   _____

REBCTOO   _____

RPALI   _____

UANYAJR   _____

B. **Write** the months in the correct order on the calendar.

WRITING DATES

You can write dates in the long form: (month) (day) (year)

        May 2, 1996   January 1, 1997

        October 31, 1982   July 4, 1776

You can write dates in the short form: (month number) (day) (year)

        7 / 4 / 95   or   7 - 4 - 95

        10 / 23 / 82   or   10 - 23 - 82

- **Write** the dates in the long form.

1. 4 / 31 / 95   April 31, 1995 _____

2. 11 / 2 / 93   _____

3. 12 / 25 / 99   _____

4. 10 / 31 / 96   _____

5. 1 / 1 / 25   _____

6. 3 - 15 - 02   _____

7. 6 - 5 - 99   _____

8. 7 - 31 - 97   _____

9. 2 - 12 - 86   _____

10. 5 - 23 - 23   _____

WRITING DATES

A. Write the dates in the short form.

1. May 28, 1929   5 – 28 – 29

2. December 1, 1995   _____

3. August 15, 1988   _____

4. September 4, 1990   _____

5. February 14, 1975   _____

6. March 17, 1945   _____

7. January 5, 1962   _____

8. April 10, 1933   _____

9. July 4, 1970   _____

10. November 18, 1990   _____

B. Write the dates in the long and short forms.

	Long	**Short**
1. Today is	_____	_____
2. Yesterday was:	_____	_____
3. Tomorrow will be:	_____	_____
4. My birthday is:	_____	_____
5. I came to this country:	_____	_____

MAKING DATES

JANUARY						1997
Sun.	Mon.	Tues.	Wed.	Thurs.	Fri.	Sat.
		1 No school today	2	3 Dance class	4	5
6 Visit Grandma	7	8	9	10	11	12
13	14	15	16	17 Dance class	18	19
20	21 Soccer game	22	23	24	25 English test	26
27	28	29	30	31 Dance class		

PARTNER A: This is Saba's calendar.

- **Ask** your partner the questions.
- **Write** the missing dates on the calendar.

PARTNER B:
Go to page 119.

Ask:

1. When does Saba have a math test?

2. When does Saba go to a birthday party?

3. When does Saba go to the movies?

4. When does Saba go to dance class?

5. When does Saba go to the doctor?

Write:

Math test

Birthday party

Go to movies

Dance class

Doctor appt. 2:30

MAKING DATES

JANUARY						1997
Sun.	Mon.	Tues.	Wed.	Thurs.	Fri.	Sat.
		1	2	3	4	5 Go to movies
6	7	8	9	10 Dance class	11	12
13	14	15 Math test	16	17	18	19
20	21	22	23	24 Dance class	25	26 Birthday party
27	28 Doctor appt. 2:30	29	30	31		

PARTNER B: This is Saba's calendar.

- **Ask** your partner the questions.
- **Write** the missing dates on the calendar.

Ask: **Write:**

1. When does Saba have an English test?   English test

2. When does Saba have a soccer game?   Soccer game

3. When does Saba visit her grandma?   Visit Grandma

4. When does Saba go to dance class?   Dance class

5. When does Saba have no school?   No school today

FRACTIONS

A fraction shows a part of something. All the parts must be equal:

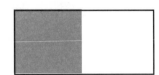

1 out of 2 parts = $\frac{1}{2}$ or 1/2   3 out of 5 parts = $\frac{3}{5}$ or 3/5

- **Write** the fraction to show the colored parts.

1. $\frac{1}{2}$

2. _____

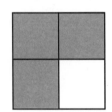

3. _____

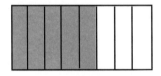

4. _____

5. _____

6. _____

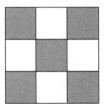

7. _____

8. _____

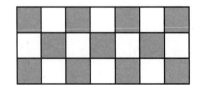

9. _____

Name _____   Date _____

FRACTIONS

A. Show the fraction.

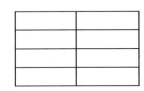

1. $\frac{1}{2}$

2. $\frac{3}{4}$

3. $\frac{5}{8}$

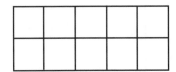

4. 5/10

5. 2/3

6. 3/3

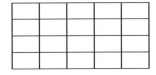

7. 15/20

8. 1/12

9. 1/1

B. Write a fraction for each sentence.

1. 2 out of 3 parts. $\frac{2}{3}$

2. 1 out of 2 parts.   _____

3. 5 out of 6 parts.   _____

4. 11 out of 15 parts.   _____

5. You go to school 5 out of 7 days a week.   _____

6. You go to school 10 out of 12 months a year.   _____

7. Carlos works 3 out of 7 days a week.   _____

Chapter 5

121

PROBLEM SOLVING

 = =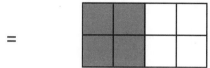

$$\frac{1}{2} \qquad\qquad \frac{2}{4} \qquad\qquad \frac{4}{8}$$

• **Draw** and **write** a fraction that shows the same amount as the first.

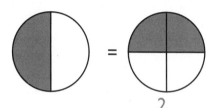

1.   1/2   = $\frac{2}{4}$

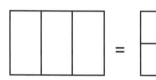

2.   2/3   =   _____

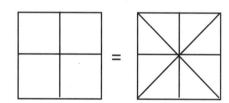

3.   3/4   =   _____

4.   1/3   =   _____

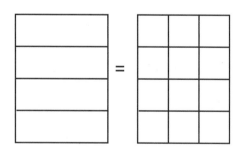

5.   1/4   =   _____

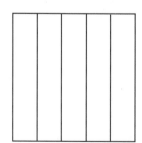

6.   4/5   =   _____

WRITING FRACTIONS

A. **Match** the fraction to the word.

1. one-half   a. 3/5

2. one-fourth   b. 1/2

3. two-thirds   c. 7/10

4. three-fifths   d. 1/4

5. seven-tenths   e. 3/4

6. one-twentieth   f. 9/10

7. two-sixths   g. 5/16

8. nine-tenths   h. 1/20

9. three-fourths   i. 2/3

10. five-sixteenths j. 2/6

B. • **Write** the fraction.   • **Write** the word.

1. one-half $\frac{1}{2}$ 1. 1/4 _____

2. one-third   _____   2. 3/5 _____

3. two-ninths   _____   3. 7/8 _____

4. five-sixths   _____   4. 2/9 _____

5. three-fourths _____   5. 8/10 _____

6

The Weather

In this chapter, you will:

_____ Describe the weather and the four seasons.

_____ Classify hot, warm, cool, and cold.

_____ Talk and write about the clothes you wear.

_____ Complete a "Multiple Choice" test.

_____ Measure temperature.

_____ Read and construct line graphs.

_____ Read and complete tables.

_____ Conduct a science experiment.

_____ Solve problems.

THE WEATHER

1. It's hot.

2. It's warm.

3. It's cool.

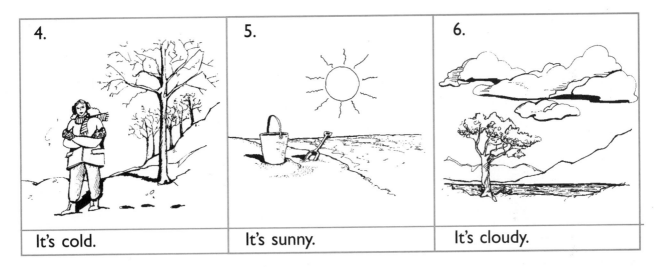

4. It's cold.

5. It's sunny.

6. It's cloudy.

7. It's windy.

8. It's rainy.

9. It's snowy.

HOT, WARM, COOL, OR COLD?

- **Look** at the pictures.
- **Decide** if something is hot, warm, cool, or cold.
- **Cut** each picture and glue it on the chart.

Hot	Warm	Cool	Cold

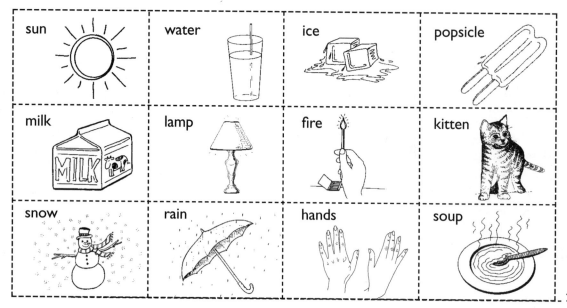

WEATHER REPORT

What's the weather like today?

- **Write** a sentence about the weather in the picture.

1. It's _____cold_____ and _____rainy_____ .

2. It's _____ and _____ .

3. It's _____ and _____ .

4. It's _____ and _____ .

5. It's _____ and _____ .

6. Today it's _____ and _____ .

CLOTHES YOU WEAR

- **Read** the weather report for each day.

- **Circle** the clothes that are good to wear on that day.

1. Today is hot and sunny.

2. Today is cold and windy.

3. Today is cool and cloudy.

4. Today is warm and rainy.

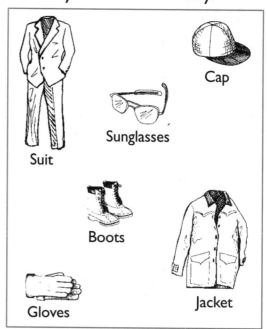

WHAT ARE THEY WEARING?

A.

- **Complete** the paragraphs.

1. It is a cool and cloudy day. Ana is
   wearing a _____skirt_____. Ana is also
   wearing a black _____.
   She has on _____ shoes.

2. It is a warm and sunny day. Long is
   wearing _____.
   Long is also wearing _____.
   He has on _____
   and _____.

B. What is the weather like today? What are you wearing today?

- **Write** a paragraph.

   ____It is a____ _____ and _____ day. Today I am wearing _____

   _____

   _____

   _____

THE FOUR SEASONS

- **Read** pages 130 and 131.

- **Color** the pictures.

The Four Seasons

There are four seasons every year. The four seasons are **spring, summer, fall,** and **winter.** In many parts of the world, the weather changes with each season.

Marie lives in New York state. **Spring** is usually warm and rainy in New York. In spring, Marie's apple tree grows pink flowers and little green leaves.

In New York, **summer** is hot and sunny. The leaves on Marie's apple tree are big and green. Little green apples begin to grow on the tree.

THE FOUR SEASONS (continued)

Fall is cool in New York. Sometimes it is windy. The apples on Marie's apple tree are now big and red. Marie can pick and eat them. The leaves on the tree turn red, yellow, orange, and brown. The leaves fall to the ground.

Winter is cold and snowy in New York. White snow falls on the apple tree and on the ground. The tree has no leaves or apples. New leaves and apples will grow again in spring.

Seasonal Calendar

Season	Begins	Ends
Spring	March	June
Summer	June	September
Fall	September	December
Winter	December	March

READING CHECK: MULTIPLE CHOICE

- **Circle** the correct word(s) to complete the sentence.

1. The title of the reading on pages 130 and 131 is _____.

    a. Spring

    b. The Apple Tree

    c. The Four Seasons

2. There are _____ seasons every year.

    a. four

    b. two

    c. five

3. In spring, the apple tree grows pink _____.

    a. leaves

    b. flowers

    c. apples

4. In New York, summer is _____ and sunny.

    a. rainy

    b. cool

    c. hot

5. In fall, the apples on the tree are _____.

    a. growing

    b. little

    c. big

6. Winter is _____ in New York.

    a. cold and snowy

    b. cold and sunny

    c. hot and snowy

TEMPERATURE

Temperature tells us if something is hot, warm, cool, or cold. You can measure the temperature of things with a **thermometer.** Some thermometers show the temperature in **degrees Celsius.** Some thermometers show the temperature in **degrees Fahrenheit.**

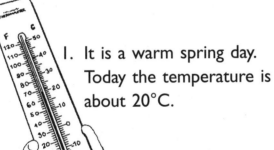

degrees Fahrenheit = °F   **degrees Celsius = °C**

Amar and Zinat live in Toronto. They use a thermometer to measure the air temperature during the year.

1. It is a warm spring day. Today the temperature is about 20°C.

2. It is a hot summer day. Today the temperature is about 30°C.

3. It is a cool fall day. Today the temperature is about 15°C.

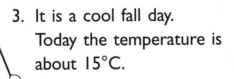

4. It is a cold winter day. Today the temperature is about −12°C.

THE THERMOMETER

• **Label** the missing numbers on the thermometer.

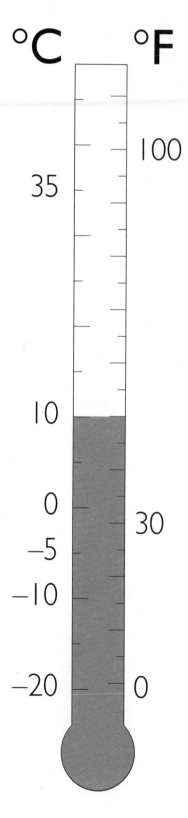

MEASURING TEMPERATURE

A. Write the temperature in degrees Fahrenheit (°F).

1. _____ °F   2. _____ °F   3. _____ °F   4. _____ °F

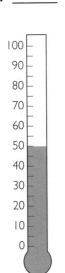 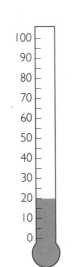 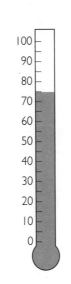 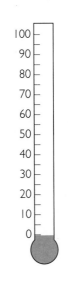

B. Write the temperature in degrees Celsius (°C).

1. _____ °C   2. _____ °C   3. _____ °C   4. _____ °C

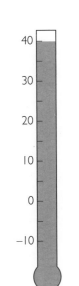 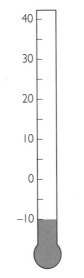

READING A LINE GRAPH

This is a line graph. It shows the average monthly temperatures in Washington, D.C. for the first six months of the year.

• **Complete** the sentences using the graph.

1. The title of the graph is _____.

2. The graph shows the temperature for the months of _____,
   _____, _____, _____, _____, and _____.

3. The average temperature in March was _____.

4. The average temperature was 67°F in the month of _____.

5. The hottest month was _____. The temperature was _____.

6. The coldest month was _____. The temperature was _____.

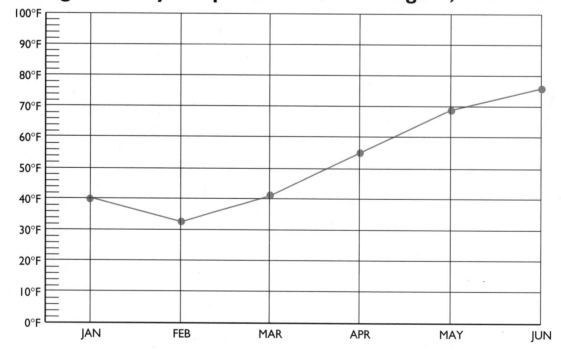

Average Monthly Temperatures in Washington, D.C.: 1993

TABLES AND GRAPHS

A. Complete the table of average monthly temperatures for January to June using the line graph on page 136.

Month	JAN	FEB	MAR	APR	MAY	JUN
Temp.						

B. Complete the line graph "Average Monthly Temperatures in Washington, D.C. 1993" for the months of July to December. **Use** the information from the table.

Month	JUL	AUG	SEP	OCT	NOV	DEC
Temp.	83°F	80°F	71°F	58°F	49°F	38°F

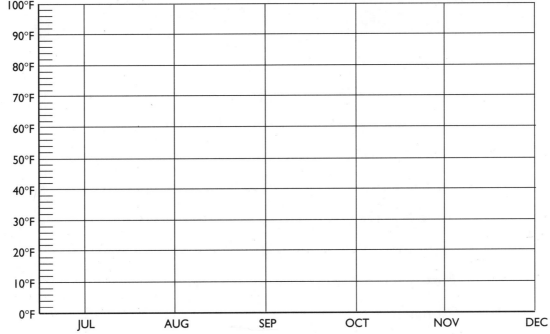

Average Monthly Temperatures in Washington, D.C.: 1993

SCIENCE EXPERIMENT

Color and Heat

Problem:	What is the question we want to answer?

Which colors absorb more heat,

light colors or dark colors?

Hypothesis:	What do you think is the answer to the question?

a) Light colors absorb heat more than dark colors.

b) Dark colors absorb heat more than light colors.

c) Light and dark colors absorb the same amount of heat.

Materials:	What things do we need?

1. 4 pieces of felt or cloth:

    1 white, 1 yellow, 1 green, and 1 black.

2. 4 thermometers

3. tray

4. clock

Procedure:	What are the steps we follow?

1. Cut cloth into equal-size squares.

2. Place the squares on a tray.

    Order the colors from lightest to darkest.

3. Place a thermometer under each square and record the
    temperature in degrees **Fahrenheit** on the table at
    Time = 0 minutes.

4. Place the tray in a sunny place.

5. Measure the temperature of each square every 5 minutes, for
    20 minutes.

SCIENCE EXPERIMENT

Data: **What information can we gather?**

Table: **Temperature of the color squares**

Time	White	Yellow	Green	Black
0 minutes				
5 minutes				
10 minutes				
15 minutes				
20 minutes				

Line Graph: Change in Temperature for 4 Colors

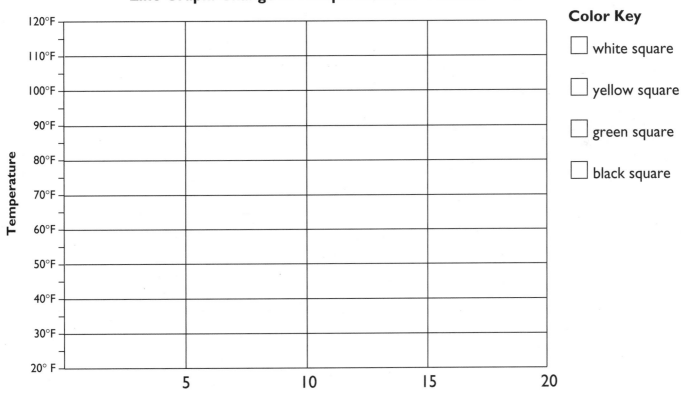

Color Key

☐ white square

☐ yellow square

☐ green square

☐ black square

SCIENCE EXPERIMENT

Conclusion: What did we learn?

- **Answer** these questions in complete sentences in your conclusion paragraph.

1. Was your hypothesis correct or incorrect?

2. What was the correct answer to the problem?

3. Which color absorbed the most heat?

4. Which color absorbed the least heat?

5. How much heat did the other colors absorb?

_____

_____

_____

_____

_____

_____

_____

_____

_____

_____

PROBLEM SOLVING

A.

- **Answer** the following questions based on your conclusions from the science experiment.
- **Write** complete sentences.

1. On a hot and sunny day, is it better to wear dark or light clothes?

   _____

2. On a cold day, is it better to wear dark or light clothes?

   _____

3. On a hot day, is it best to wear white, yellow, green, or black?

   _____

4. On a cold day, is it best to wear white, yellow, green, or black?

   _____

B. Match the words to their meanings.

1. _____ problem   a. the steps we follow

2. _____ hypothesis   b. what we learn

3. _____ materials   c. the question we want to answer

4. _____ procedure   d. the information we gather

5. _____ data   e. what we think is the answer to the question

6. _____ conclusion   f. the things we need

7
Families

In this chapter, you will:

_____ Read and talk about different kinds of families.

_____ Name and write about the people in your family.

_____ Write sentences using possessive **'s**.

_____ Read and construct a family tree.

_____ Count with tally marks.

_____ Read and talk about where families live.

_____ Take a class poll.

_____ Read and construct a circle graph.

ALL KINDS OF FAMILIES

This is Ana's **family.** Ana has a **father,** a **mother,** a **brother,** and a **sister.** Ana also has a **grandmother** and a **grandfather.**

This is Marc's family. Marc lives with his mother and his two sisters. Marc does not live with his father. His mother and father are not **married** now. They are **divorced.**

This is Long's family. Long has an **adopted** mother and father. Long's first **parents** died when he was 5 years old. Long's adopted family became his new family. Long doesn't have any brothers or sisters.

This is Marie's family. Marie lives with a **foster** family. She has a foster mother, a foster father, a foster brother, and a foster sister. Marie will live with her foster family until a family **adopts** her.

READING CHECK

- **Answer** each question with a sentence from the Word File.

Word File

Yes, she does.	No, she doesn't.
Yes, he does.	No, he doesn't.

1, Does Ana have a sister? _____ Yes, she does. _____

2. Does Ana have a brother? _____

3. Does Ana have a grandmother? _____

4. Does Marc have brothers? _____

5. Does Marc live with his father? _____

6. Does Marc live with his mother? _____

7. Does Long have adopted parents? _____

8. Does Long have any brothers? _____

9. Does Long have any sisters? _____

10. Does Marie have adopted parents? _____

11. Does Marie live with a foster family? _____

12. Does Marie have a foster sister? _____

FAMILY PICTURES

A. Read.

I am Ana Lopez. This is a picture of my family. We are celebrating my 14th birthday. I am in the middle. I am trying to hit the piñata.

My mother and my father are in front of me. My father is holding the rope to make the piñata go up and down. My mother is holding my baby sister, Luisa. She is 8 months old. My older brother is behind me. His name is Carlos. He is 16 years old.

My grandmother and grandfather are next to Carlos. They are my father's parents.

B. Label the people in the picture.

1. Ana
2. Ana's father
3. Ana's mother
4. Ana's sister

5. Ana's brother
6. Ana's grandmother
7. Ana's grandfather

ANA'S FAMILY TREE

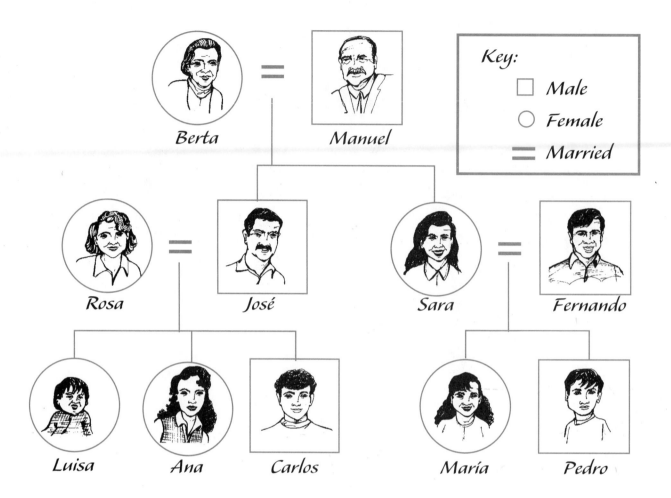

- **Complete** the sentences about Ana's family tree.

1. José is Ana's _____ father _____.

2. Luisa is Ana's _____.

3. Rosa is Ana's _____.

4. Manuel is Ana's _____.

5. Berta is Ana's _____.

6. Ana's father has a sister named _____ Sara _____. She is Ana's **aunt.**

7. Ana's aunt is married to _____. He is Ana's **uncle.**

8. Ana's aunt and uncle have a daughter named _____ and a

   son named _____. They are Ana's **cousins.**

PEOPLE IN YOUR FAMILY

A. **Complete** the missing letters. Use these letter pairs:

nd   th   br   gr   cl   st   nt   th

1. fa t h e r

2. m o _ _ e r

3. s i _ _ e r

4. _ _ o t h e r

5. _ _ a n d m o t h e r

6. g r a _ _ f a t h e r

7. a u _ _

8. u n _ _ e

B. **Rewrite** the sentences using 's.

1. Ana has a sister named Luisa.   Luisa is Ana's sister.

2. Ana has a brother named Carlos.   Carlos is Ana's _____

3. Ana has a grandfather named Manuel.   Manuel is _____ _____

4. Ana has a cousin named María.   _____

5. Maria has a brother named Pedro.   _____

6. Maria has a father named Fernando.   _____

7. Fernando has a wife named Sara.   _____

8. Rosa has a husband named José.   _____

9. José has a son named Carlos.   _____

10. Rosa has a daughter named Ana.   _____

YOUR FAMILY

A. Complete the table.

1. In the first column, **write** the names of people in your family.

2. In the second column, **write** their relationship to you (mother, father, or . . .).

3. In the third column, **write** F for female or M for male.

For example:

NAME	RELATIONSHIP	F or M
Rosa Lopez	mother	F

NAME	RELATIONSHIP	F or M

B. Answer the questions with **Yes, I do.** or **No, I don't.**

1. Do you have any brothers? _____

2. Do you have any sisters? _____

3. Do you have any cousins? _____

4. Do you have any aunts? _____

5. Do you have any uncles? _____

6. Do you have a grandmother? _____

7. Do you have a grandfather? _____

MY FAMILY TREE

- **Make** your own family tree using the table on page 148.

1. **Write** the names of males in a ☐.

2. **Write** the names of females in a ○.

3. **Write** = if two people are married.

Key
☐ Male
○ Female
= Married

MY FAMILY

- **Write** a paragraph about your family. **Use** sentences like these:

> There are five people in my family.
>
> I have a father and a mother.
>
> I have one brother named Carlos. Carlos is 16 years old.
>
> I have a sister named Luisa.
>
> Luisa is 8 months old. I am 14 years old.

There are _____ people in my family. I have _____ brothers and _____ sisters.

_____

_____

_____

_____

_____

_____

_____

_____

_____

_____

_____

_____

_____

_____

_____

COUNTING WITH TALLY MARKS

You can use tally marks to count. One tally mark looks like this: $|$.

- **Cross** tally marks in groups of five:

$1 = |$	$5 = \cancel{||||}$	$15 = \cancel{||||}\ \cancel{||||}\ \cancel{||||}$
$4 = ||||$	$10 = \cancel{||||}\ \cancel{||||}$	$18 = \cancel{||||}\ \cancel{||||}\ \cancel{||||}\ |||$

A. **Count** the tally marks

1. $|||$	= __3__	6. $\cancel{||||}\ \cancel{||||}$	= ____
2. $||||$	= ____	7. $\cancel{||||}\ \cancel{||||}\ ||||$	= ____
3. $\cancel{||||}$	= ____	8. $\cancel{||||}\ \cancel{||||}\ \cancel{||||}$	= ____
4. $\cancel{||||}\ ||$	= ____	9. $\cancel{||||}\ \cancel{||||}\ \cancel{||||}\ \cancel{||||}$	= ____
5. $|$	= ____	10. $\cancel{||||}\ \cancel{||||}\ \cancel{||||}\ \cancel{||||}\ ||$	= ____

B. **Write** the tally marks

1. 2 = __$||$__	7. 15 = _____
2. 4 = _____	8. 17 = _____
3. 5 = _____	9. 20 = _____
4. 8 = _____	10. 23 = _____
5. 10 = _____	11. 30 = _____
6. 12 = _____	12. 34 = _____

WHERE FAMILIES LIVE

Where do you live?

in a **house**   in a **townhouse**   in an **apartment**

Take a poll in your class to find out where people live.

- **Ask** each student: **"Where do you live?"**
- **Record** the number of students in each group **with tally marks.**

Type of home	Number of students who live here
house	
townhouse	
apartment	
other: _____	

SHOWING YOUR RESULTS

A. **Explain** the results of your poll.

1. How many students live in a house? _____

2. How many students live in a townhouse? _____

3. How many students live in an apartment? _____

4. Most students live in ____ _____.

5. Where else do people live? _____

B. • **Show** the results of your poll on a bar graph.

  • **Label** the numbers on the left side of the graph.

Where Students in Our Class Live

House   **Townhouse**   **Apartment**   **Other**

CIRCLE GRAPHS

Carlos took a class poll in his class to find out where students live. He made a **circle graph** to show the results of his poll.

Where Students Live

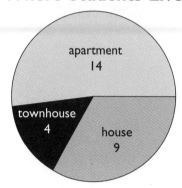

A. **Answer** the questions about Carlos' circle graph.

1. What is the title of Carlos' circle graph? _____

2. How many students in Carlos' class live in an apartment? _____

3. How many students in his class live in a house? _____

4. How many students in his class live in a townhouse? _____

5. How many students are in Carlos' class altogether? _____

B. **Show** the results of **your** poll on a circle graph.

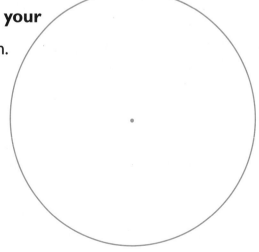

Chapter 7

PROBLEM SOLVING

Saba took a class poll to find out what foods students like best. She then made a circle graph, but she fogot to label the parts of the graph.

- Help Saba **complete** her poll results and **label** her graph.

Poll Results	**Fractions**
13 out of 30 students like pizza.	13/30
3 out of 30 students like chicken.	_____
8 out of 30 students like hamburgers.	_____
6 out of 30 students like spaghetti.	_____

Favorite Foods

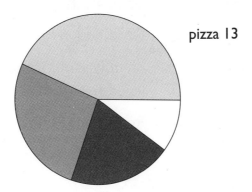

pizza 13

8
Communities

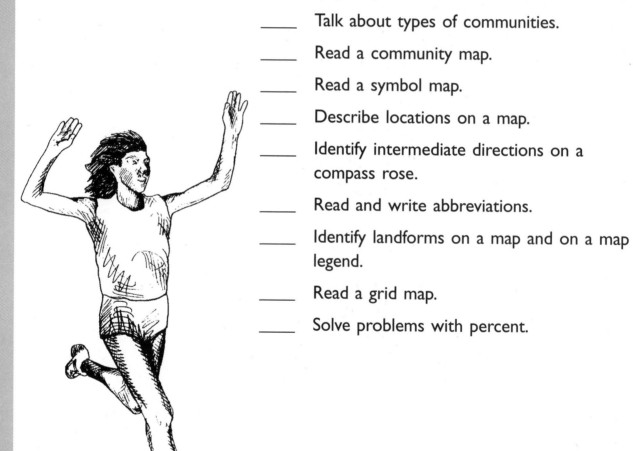

In this chapter, you will:

_____ Talk about types of communities.

_____ Read a community map.

_____ Read a symbol map.

_____ Describe locations on a map.

_____ Identify intermediate directions on a compass rose.

_____ Read and write abbreviations.

_____ Identify landforms on a map and on a map legend.

_____ Read a grid map.

_____ Solve problems with percent.

COMMUNITIES

What is a community? A community is a place where people live. A community has many people and places. What type of community do you live in? Do you live in a **city**, in the **suburbs**, in a **town**, or in the **country**?

I live in _____ .

City

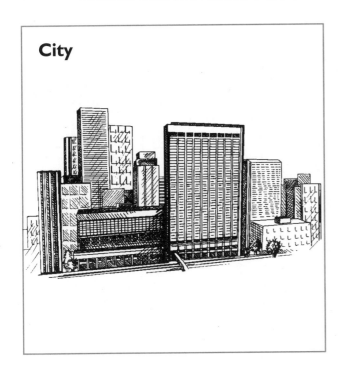

Suburbs

Town

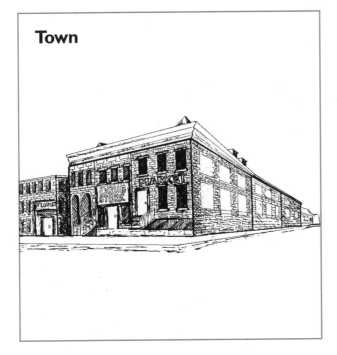

Country

PLACES IN YOUR COMMUNITY

Marie lives in a town called Northfield.

- **Look** at the map of Northfield. What places do you see in Northfield? What places are in your community also?

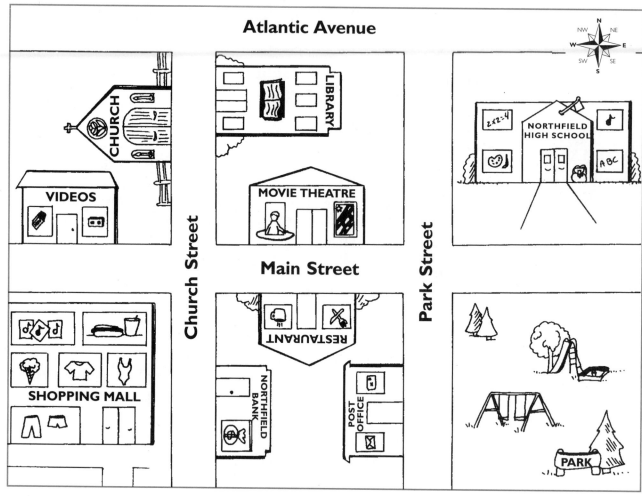

- **Write** the name of each street from the map.
- **Write** if the street runs north–south or east–west.

1. _____   _____

2. _____   _____

3. _____   _____

4. _____   _____

READING A SYMBOL MAP

This is a symbol map of Northfield. The symbols are pictures of things on the map.

- **Name** symbols on the map of Northfield. Use the map on page 158.
- **Label** the symbols on the map legend.

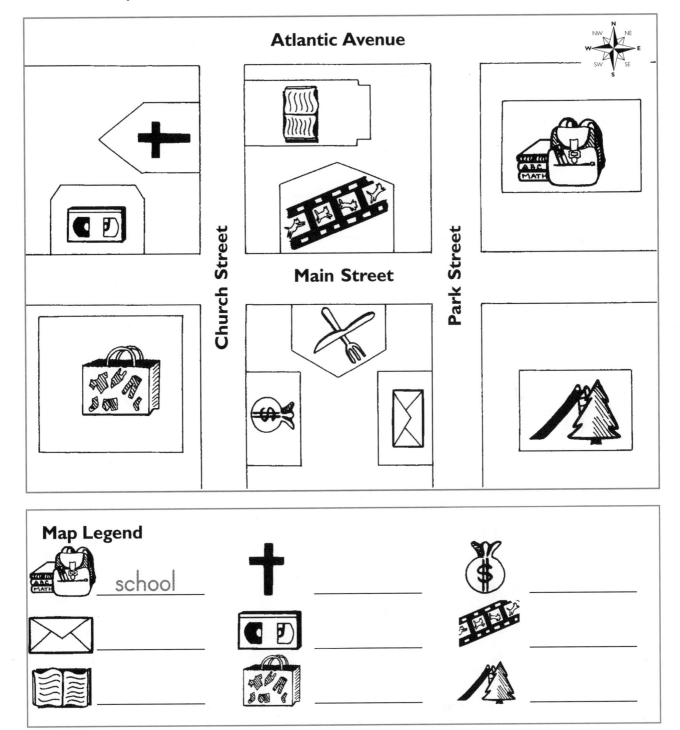

DESCRIBING LOCATIONS ON A MAP

A. **Complete** the sentences. Use the map on page 159.

1. The school is on the corner of _____ Street and _____ Street.

2. The park is on the corner of _____ Street and _____ Street.

3. The library is on the corner of _____ Street and _____ Avenue.

B. **Complete** the sentences. Use the map on page 159.

1. The restaurant is on Main Street, across from the _____ .

2. The bank is on Church Street, across from the _____ .

3. The church is on Church Street, across from the _____ .

4. The post office is across from the _____

FOLLOWING DIRECTIONS

- **Read** the directions to find the locations on the map of Northfield.
- **Circle** the name of the location.

1. It's on Main Street, across from the shopping mall.
   a. the movie theater
   b. the video store
   c. the bank

2. It's on Main Street, across from the restaurant.
   a. the school
   b. the movie theater
   c. the bank

3. It's on the corner of Church Street and Atlantic Avenue, across from the library.
   a. the church
   b. the movie theater
   c. the bank

4. It's on the corner of Park Street and Main Street, across from the post office.
   a. the school
   b. the movie theater
   c. the park

5. It's on Park Street, across from the park.
   a. the post office
   b. the school
   c. the restaurant

INTERMEDIATE DIRECTIONS

The compass rose has four **cardinal directions**. The cardinal directions are **north**, **south**, **east**, and **west**.

The compass rose also has four **intermediate directions**. The four intermediate directions are **northeast**, **northwest**, **southeast**, and **southwest**.

Intermediate means in the middle or **between**. The intermediate directions are between the cardinal directions. Northeast is between north and east. Northwest is between north and west. Southeast is between south and east. Southwest is between south and west.

A. Name the four cardinal directions:

_____north_____   _____   _____   _____

B. Name the four intermediate directions:

_____   _____   _____   _____

C. Label the intermediate directions on the compass rose:

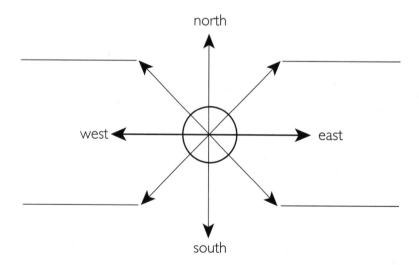

ABBREVIATIONS

Abbreviations are short ways to write words.

You can write abbreviations for directions.

A. • **Read** the abbreviations on the compass rose.

   • **Write** the direction word next to the abbreviation.

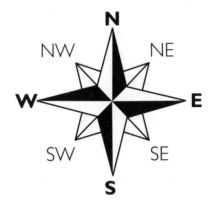

1. N _____north_____   5. SW _____

2. E _____   6. NE _____

3. W _____   7. NW _____

4. S _____   8. SE _____

B. • **Match** the word to the abbreviation. Look at the first letters in each word.

1. ___c___ New York   a. B.C.

2. _____ Los Angeles   b. U.S.

3. _____ United States   c. N.Y.

4. _____ British Columbia d. m.p.h.

5. _____ post office   e. P.O.

6. _____ miles per hour   f. L.A.

7. _____ compact disc   g. CD

MAP LEGENDS

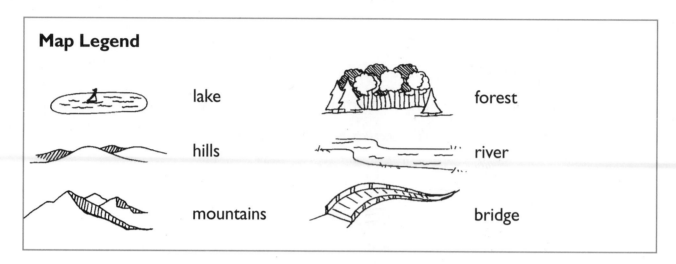

Map Legend

lake   forest

hills   river

mountains   bridge

This is a map legend for the map of Green County on page 165.

• **Match** each picture to a symbol on the map legend.

• **Label** the pictures.

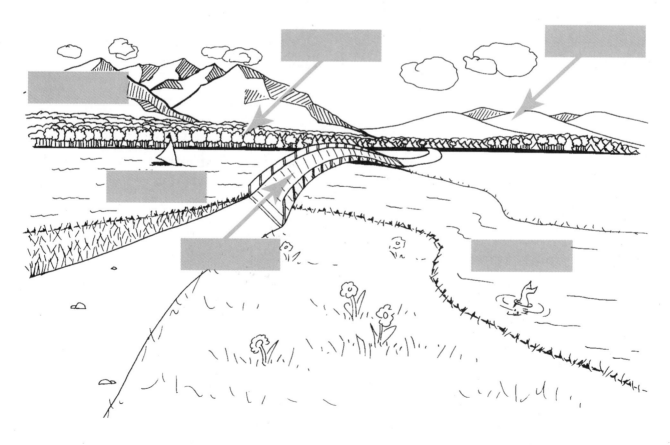

GREEN COUNTY

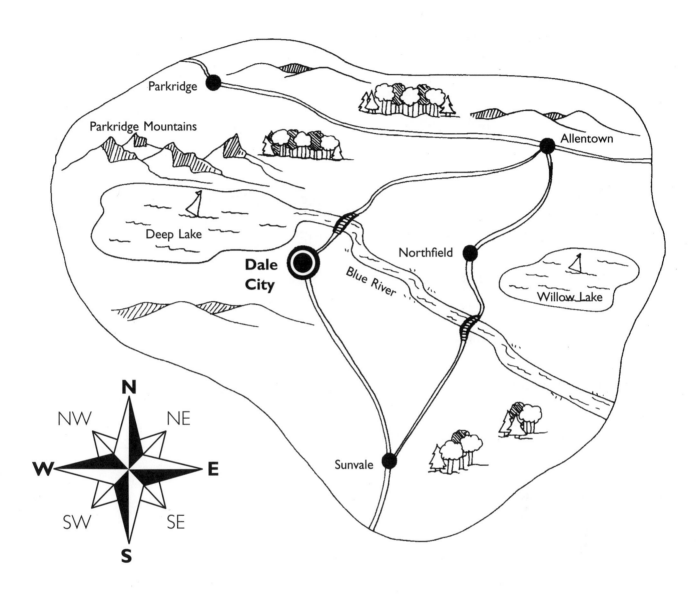

Parkridge

Parkridge Mountains

Deep Lake

Dale City

Blue River

Northfield

Allentown

Willow Lake

Sunvale

N
NW   NE
W   E
SW   SE
S

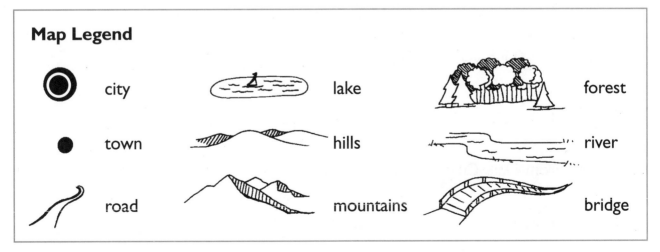

Map Legend

◉ city

🚣 lake

🌲 forest

● town

⛰ hills

〜 river

〰 road

⛰ mountains

🌉 bridge

READING A MAP

A. **Circle** the correct direction.

1. Sunvale is:	N	(S)	E	W
2. Willow Lake is:	N	S	E	W
3. Deep Lake is:	NE	NW	SE	SW
4. Allentown is:	NE	NW	SE	SW
5. The Parkridge Mountains are:	NE	NW	SE	SW
6. Blue River runs from Deep Lake to the:	NE	NW	SE	SW

B. **Write** the correct direction.

1. The road between Parkridge and Allentown runs east– _____.

2. The road between Dale City and Sunvale runs north– _____.

3. The road between Dale City and Allentown runs southwest– _____.

4. Blue River runs northwest– _____.

5. To drive from Parkridge to Allentown, you go _____.

6. To drive from Allentown to Sunvale, you go _____.

7. To drive from Sunvale to Dale City, you go _____.

8. To drive from Dale City to Allentown, you go _____.

9. To drive from Northfield to Allentown, you go _____.

MAKE A MAP

- **Follow** the directions for making a map of Blake County.
1. **Label** the compass rose.
2. **Complete** the map legend.
3. **Draw** a lake east of Georgetown.
4. **Draw** a forest northeast of Riverdale.
5. **Draw** hills south and southeast of Munville.
6. **Draw** a river from the lake to the northwest corner of the map.
7. **Draw** mountains in the southwest corner of the map.
8. **Draw** roads between the towns and the city.
9. **Write** the title of the map.

King City

Riverdale

Georgetown

Munville

Map of _____

Map Legend

city   _____   _____

town   _____   _____

road   _____   _____

READING A GRID MAP

This map shows the city of Vancouver. The map has a **grid** pattern. A grid pattern has horizontal and vertical lines that make squares. The horizontal squares make **rows**. Each row has a letter. The vertical squares are called **columns**. Each column has a number.

To read the grid map, use the letters and numbers to find a square. Square **A-2** is located in row A and column 2. What place is inside square A-2?

A. • **Listen** to your teacher name a square.
   • **Find** the square on the map of Vancouver.

B. • **Find** each place on the map.
   • **Write** the square number for each place on the map index.

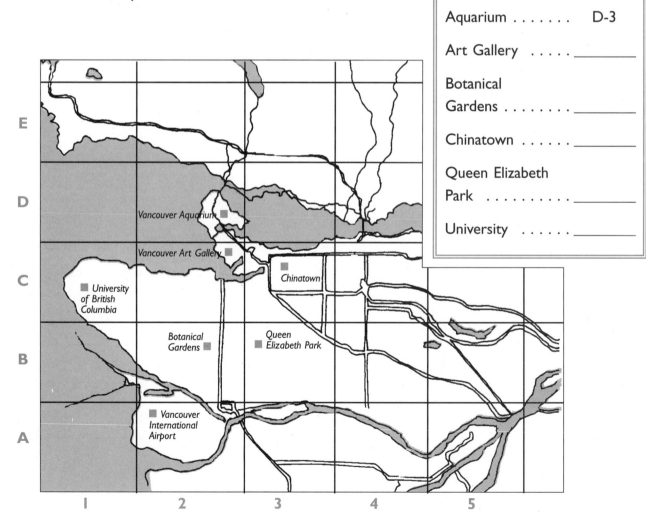

Vancouver
Map Index

Airport A-2

Aquarium D-3

Art Gallery . . . . . _____

Botanical
Gardens . . . . _____

Chinatown . . . . . . _____

Queen Elizabeth
Park . . . . _____

University . . . . . . _____

PERCENT

% is a symbol that means **percent.**

Percent shows how many out of 100. Percent is a fraction out of 100 parts.

$$50 \text{ out of } 100 \ = \ \frac{50}{100} \ = \ 50\%$$

$$15 \text{ out of } 100 \ = \ \frac{15}{100} \ = \ 15\%$$

A. **Write** the percent.

1. $\dfrac{40}{100}$ = _40%_

2. $\dfrac{75}{100}$ = _____

3. $\dfrac{10}{100}$ = _____

4. $\dfrac{20}{100}$ = _____

5. $\dfrac{15}{100}$ = _____

6. $\dfrac{90}{100}$ = _____

7. 60/100 = _____

8. 35/100 = _____

9. 17/100 = _____

10. 80 out of 100 = _____

11. 5 out of 100 = _____

12. 19 out of 100 = _____

13. 100 out of 100 = _____

B. **Write** the fraction.

1. 10% = _____

2. 70% = _____

3. 85% = _____

4. 27% = _____

5. 100% = _____

6. 99% = _____

7. 33% = _____

8. 81% = _____

9. 56% = _____

PROBLEM SOLVING

Mr. Wood is grading his class's math tests.
The test has 100 questions. These are the students' test scores.

Carlos got 90 out of 100 correct.   Sharifa got 97 out of 100 correct.
Gloria got 80 out of 100 correct.   Mei Ling got 65 out of 100 correct.
Rashid got 70 out of 100 correct.   Eric got 58 out of 100 correct.
Junichi got 81 out of 100 correct.

A. **Write** the *percent* of test questions each student got correct
   in Mr. Wood's grade book.

Student	Test Score	Grade
Carlos	90%	A
Gloria		
Rashid		
Junichi		
Sharifa		
Mei Ling		
Eric		

B. • **Use** the grade key to find each student's grade on the math test.

   • **Write** the grade in Mr. Wood's grade book.

Grade Key	
A = 90% – 100%	D = 60% – 69%
B = 80% – 89%	F = 59% or less
C = 70% – 79%	

References

COLORS

☐	red	☐	brown
☐	orange	☐	green
☐	yellow	☐	blue
☐	white	☐	purple
☐	black	☐	pink

DAYS OF THE WEEK

Sunday	Sun.
Monday	Mon.
Tuesday	Tue.
Wednesday	Wed.
Thursday	Thu.
Friday	Fri.
Saturday	Sat.

MONTHS OF THE YEAR

January	Jan.	July	Jul.
February	Feb.	August	Aug.
March	Mar.	September	Sep.
April	Apr.	October	Oct.
May	May	November	Nov.
June	Jun.	December	Dec.

GRAPHS

picture graph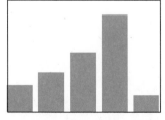

line graph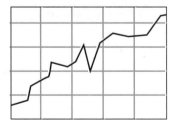

bar graph

circle graph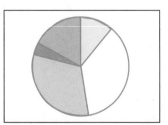

NUMBERS

0	zero			
1	one	30	thirty	
2	two	40	forty	
3	three	50	fifty	
4	four	60	sixty	
5	five	70	seventy	
6	six	80	eighty	
7	seven	90	ninety	
8	eight			
9	nine	100	one hundred	
10	ten	101	one hundred one	
		110	one hundred ten	
11	eleven	125	one hundred twenty-five	
12	twelve	150	one hundred fifty	
13	thirteen			
14	fourteen	200	two hundred	
15	fifteen	300	three hundred	
16	sixteen	400	four hundred	
17	seventeen	500	five hundred	
18	eighteen	600	six hundred	
19	nineteen	700	seven hundred	
20	twenty	800	eight hundred	
		900	nine hundred	
21	twenty-one			
22	twenty-two	1,000	one thousand	
23	twenty-three	10,000	ten thousand	
24	twenty-four	100,000	one hundred thousand	
25	twenty-five	1,000,000	one million	
26	twenty-six	10,000,000	ten million	
27	twenty-seven	100,000,000	one hundred million	
28	twenty-eight	1,000,000,000	one billion	
29	twenty-nine			

.1	one-tenth
.01	one-hundredth
.001	one-thousandth

LETTERS

Aa Bb Cc
Dd Ee Ff
Gg Hh Ii
Jj Kk Ll
Mm Nn Oo
Pp Qq Rr
Ss Tt Uu
Vv Ww Xx
Yy Zz

Aa Bb Cc
Dd Ee Ff
Gg Hh Ii
Jj Kk Ll
Mm Nn Oo
Pp Qq Rr
Ss Tt Uu
Vv Ww Xx
Yy Zz

ORDINAL NUMBERS

1st	first	11th	eleventh		
2nd	second	12th	twelfth		
3rd	third	13th	thirteenth	30th	thirtieth
4th	fourth	14th	fourteenth	40th	fortieth
5th	fifth	15th	fifteenth	50th	fiftieth
6th	sixth	16th	sixteenth	60th	sixtieth
7th	seventh	17th	seventeenth	70th	seventieth
8th	eighth	18th	eighteenth	80th	eightieth
9th	ninth	19th	nineteenth	90th	ninetieth
10th	tenth	20th	twentieth	100th	one hundredth
		21st	twenty-first		
		22nd	twenty-second		

PUNCTUATION MARKS

.	period	*The boy ran to his mother.*
?	question mark	*What is your name?*
!	exclamation point	*Wow! She runs fast!*
,	comma	*I study math, English, and science.*
-	hyphen	*He ate one-half of the cake.*
"	quotation marks	*"Can you help me?" Toni asked.*

MONEY

¢ = cent $ = dollar

Coins

penny = 1¢

nickel = 5¢

dime = 10¢

quarter = 25¢

fifty cents = 50¢

dollar = $1.00 (Canada)

Bills

one dollar = $1.00 (U.S.)

five dollars = $5.00 (U.S.)

ten dollars = $10.00 (U.S.)

twenty dollars = $20.00 (U.S.)

fifty dollars = $50.00 (U.S.)

one hundred dollars = $100.00 (U.S.)

ROMAN NUMERALS

I	1		XV	15
II	2		XX	20
III	3		XXV	25
IV	4		L	50
V	5		C	100
VI	6		D	500
VII	7		M	1,000
VIII	8			
IX	9			
X	10			

SHAPES

 circle

 oval

 square

 polygon

 rectangle

 sphere

 triangle

 cube

 cylinder

 trapezoid

 cone

 pyramid

References

MATH SYMBOLS

+	add (plus)		$\frac{1}{2}$ or 1/2	fraction
−	subtract (minus)			
× or •	multiply (times)		angle	angle
÷ or ⟌	divide (divided by)		%	percent
=	equals		•	decimal
>	greater than			
≥	greater than or equal to			
<	less than			
≤	less than or equal to			

MEASUREMENTS

Measuring length or distance

mm	millimeter
cm	centimeter (1 cm = 10 mm)
m	meter (1 m = 100 cm)
km	kilometer (1km = 1,000 m)

Measuring volume

ml	milliliter
L	liter (1 L = 1,000 ml)
fl. oz.	fluid ounce
pt.	pint (1 pt. = 16 fl. oz.)
qt.	quart (1 qt. = 2 pt.)
gal.	gallon (1 gal. = 4 qt.)

Measuring weight

oz.	ounce
lb.	pound (1 lb. = 16 oz.)
g	gram
kg	kilogram (1 kg = 1,000 g)

Measuring temperature

°C	degrees Celsius
°F	degrees Fahrenheit

0°C = 32°F

MULTIPLICATION TABLE

X	1	2	3	4	5	6	7	8	9	10
1	1	2	3	4	5	6	7	8	9	10
2	2	4	6	8	10	12	14	16	18	20
3	3	6	9	12	15	18	21	24	27	30
4	4	8	12	16	20	24	28	32	36	40
5	5	10	15	20	25	30	35	40	45	50
6	6	12	18	24	30	36	42	48	54	60
7	7	14	21	28	35	42	49	56	63	70
8	8	16	24	32	40	48	56	64	72	80
9	9	18	27	36	45	54	63	72	81	90
10	10	20	30	40	50	60	70	80	90	100

SIGHT WORDS

the	in	you	for	was
of	is	his	from	are
and	it	he	on	as
a	I	they	at	be
to	this	that	with	have

Healing Power of Coconut

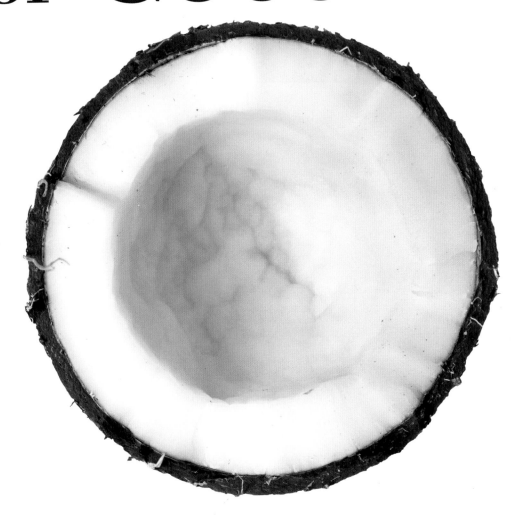

Publications International, Ltd.

Written by Jacqueline B. Marcus, MS, RDN, LDN, CNS, FADA, FAND

Photography from Shutterstock.com

The publisher would like to thank the Dole Food Company, Inc. for the use of their recipes and photographs in this publication.

Louis Weber, CEO
Publications International, Ltd.
8140 Lehigh Avenue
Morton Grove, IL 60053

Permission is never granted for commercial purposes.

ISBN: 978-1-64030-102-3

Manufactured in China.

8 7 6 5 4 3 2 1

Table of Contents

Introduction

Most people wouldn't recognize the term "*Cocos nucifera*." But the fruit of the palm *Cocos nucifera*—the incredible coconut—is a multidimensional and tremendously useful member of the plant kingdom. It can help you to prevent and treat some common health problems, nourish your body and groom your hair and nails, supercharge your metabolism, and much more.

Coconuts provide concentrated energy in their "meat," refreshing hydration in their water, hardy fibers for household necessities like brushes and twine, and a hard shell that can be converted into charcoal or used for various handcraft applications—and all these uses come in one compact and economical package!

Coconut Origins

Coconut palms may have originated in Malaysia. This conclusion is based on the number of species of insects around the world that are associated with coconut palms, but botanists do not fully agree.

A broader viewpoint is that coconuts originated somewhere in tropical Asia. Part of what makes their origin so difficult to pinpoint is that coconuts are so hardy. It is speculated that coconut seeds probably floated to different parts of the globe before humans transported them to different cultures.

Some early evidence of coconut use comes from the Marquesans, who have lived on a group of small islands located in the South Pacific a few degrees south of the equator since around AD 300. Coconuts were thought to have been consumed in a variety of ways throughout the Marquesas. Immature coconuts were cut open and their creamy interiors were used to nourish children. Coconut "cream" was extracted from freshly grated coconut meat, which was also

The coconut has been a staple in the diet of many cultures for thousands of years. They primarily grow between the fronds at the crown of large treelike palms that exceed 100 feet in tropical climates.

combined into other dishes. Marquesan men grated coconuts with an apparatus that looked like a sawhorse. The coconut blossom was also a favorite food source. Its sap, called *jekamai*, was heated to prevent fermentation and the sweet syrup of the blossom was used to flavor dishes.

While the coconut was reportedly mentioned in ancient eastern Indian documents, the Asian geography that is west of India is not truly suitable for its growth—nor is the south of China. Excursions by sailors and tradesmen both north and south brought coconuts into new lands.

Europeans first recognized the existence of coconuts in the Middle Ages, though Arab traders might have introduced coconuts to eastern Africa much earlier. The explorer Marco Polo (above), a Venetian merchant traveler and explorer who engaged in an epic round-trip Asian journey that lasted 24 years, is said to have discovered coconuts in Java and the Nicobar Islands in Southeast Asia.

During pre-Columbian times in Central America, the earliest Spanish invaders are said to have found coconuts growing along the western coast of Panama. They subsequently introduced it to Puerto Rico.

The Portuguese explorer Vasco da Gama (above), who was the first European to reach India by sea and link Europe and Asia by an ocean route, located coconuts on an island off Mozambique in the 15th century. Then Portuguese explorers introduced coconuts to Brazil in the 16th century. However, it wasn't until the 19th century that cultivation spread throughout Florida.

Today, the main areas growing and exporting coconuts are Brazil, the Caribbean, India, Indonesia, Malaysia, Mexico, Papua New Guinea, the Philippines, Sri Lanka, and East and West Africa.

Coconut Geography

Coconut palms thrive along seascapes. Coconut palms are usually tall and prefer light, salty, and sandy conditions with airy soil, achieved by the ebb and tide of the neighboring seawater. The tree has shallow, widely spread roots that allow the coconut palms to gently sway, while the huge leaves (often 20 feet long with massive midribs for stability) also provide needed shade from the penetrating tropical sun for the coconut palms.

> Hawaii, India, Indonesia, the Philippines, and parts of South America produce more than 20 billion coconuts each year.

Harvesting and Using Coconuts

The coconut is the world's largest—and some say the most important and useful—nut. It is not just humans who think so: When not harvested by humans, coconuts may be picked by local monkeys right off of the palm trees.

In modern coconut plantations where dwarf cultivars of coconuts are grown, coconuts may be harvested directly from the ground with hooked knives attached to bamboo poles.

The coconut requires a sharp strike of force to split it open for its meat and water. A spike or machete is traditionally used to strike the end of the coconut and remove the husk. The coconut husk contains useful fibers known as *coir* that are used for coconut matting, among other purposes.

The "meat" or *copra*, located within the interior of the coconut, is firm and creamy white in texture and snowy white in appearance.

Also inside of the coconut is a hollowed center that is filled with a sweet, watery liquid called coconut water. Coconut water is sometimes referred to as coconut "milk," but it is really a thin liquid. If the nut is "green" or young, once it is pried open, then the refreshing coconut water is released. A sharp instrument is generally pierced into the coconut "eyes" to enable the coconut water to be poured out or for a straw to be inserted. Once mature, the dried coconut meat (copra) may yield some additional coconut water.

In addition to coconut "meat" and coconut water, coconuts produce a wide array of products that include coconut "cream," coconut "milk," and coconut "oil." Coconuts provide nourishment both as a food and as a beverage, fuel for cooking, and a vessel for serving. Coconuts also produce basket materials, chemicals, medicines, textile fibers, thatching, timber, and other useful and valued products that are described in more detail in chapter 10.

A Nutritional Nut

Aside from their most notable taste and aroma, coconuts have been valued for centuries for their nutrients—particularly for their fats with energy and health-enhancing benefits. The calories contained within coconuts from fats, carbohydrates, and proteins are impressive.

One medium coconut (397 grams) contains about 1,405 calories, with:

- 133 grams of total fat (204 percent of the Daily Value [DV] based on a 2,000 daily calorie diet)
- Zero cholesterol
- 60 grams of carbohydrates (144 percent of the Daily Value)
- 36 grams of dietary fiber
- 25 grams of naturally occurring sugars
- 13 grams of protein (26 percent of the Daily Value)

What is particularly impressive about the nutrients in coconuts are the types of fats. Within 133 grams of total fat, one medium coconut contains about 118 grams of saturated fats (590 percent of the Daily Value), 1.5 grams of polyunsaturated fats, and 6 grams of monounsaturated fats. While these amounts may seem high, there are good explanations about these fats and why they are considered to be so important for diet and health. A thorough explanation of dietary fats and cardiovascular disease and weight control are found in chapters 4 and 5.

While it is rare that a person consumes an entire medium coconut at one time, even in smaller amounts coconuts provide a proportional array of these nutrients.

Other nutrients in one medium coconut include:

- Calcium (5 percent of the Daily Value)
- Vitamin C (21 percent of the Daily Value)
- Iron (53 percent of the Daily Value)
- Vitamin B-6 (10 percent of the Daily Value)
- Magnesium (31 percent of the Daily Value)

What You'll Find in This Book

Healing Power of Coconut celebrates the coconut, from its long and varied history and multiple, universal uses to its countless health and wellness applications and other virtues.

People have bad hair or skin days depending on where they live, their diet, and lifestyle—even their genes. Weight loss and weight maintenance, cardiovascular and brain health, and anti-aging are ongoing concerns. An array of products and procedures in today's real and virtual marketplaces promise better health, transformation, and longevity. Fine-looking skin, hair, and nails, improved defense against disease, and a youthful demeanor are on many wish lists—not to mention the satisfaction of getting these things through tasty foods and beverages.

The media extolls the next-best manufactured personal care products, and the public eagerly tries one solution after another. But Mother Nature has packaged an array of impressive beauty and health-enhancing benefits into natural foods and beverages—the coconut being one of her finest examples.

More than that, the coconut is incredibly versatile—it supplies materials for countless uses, from simple brushes to strong ropes, furniture and car polish, and even serving bowls. How many delicious tasting foods or beverages can boast all of these attributes?

In this book you'll learn about many more fascinating ways that coconuts come to the rescue every day for home, work, and health. Tips and recipes are scattered throughout the book, with an additional section of coconut recipes at the back. You'll soon want to savor its goodness, sample its many benefits, and discover more of its uses on your own.

Here's a taste of what's to come:

Chapter 2: Coconut Basics

Is the coconut is a fruit, nut, seed, or all of these classifications? The unique categorization of coconuts will be featured in this chapter. You'll learn that coconuts have been staples in the diets of many cultures for thousands of years, why they were so popular, and how they are used throughout the world today.

This chapter introduces some of the many different people from around the globe who consider the coconut as a staple in their diet, including the Veddas of Sri Lanka and native Hawaiians. Could their lower incidences of heart disease be related to their coconut consumption?

The different forms of coconut, including coconut meat, milk, oil, and water are featured, along with the processes that are involved in each of these products. The differences in types of coconut oil, including cold-pressed, expeller-pressed, refined, unrefined, virgin and extra-virgin, are also highlighted, as well as whether or not any of these types of coconut oil have advantages over the others.

The spelling *cocoanut* is an archaic form of the word coconut. The more modernized word coconut is derived from the 15th century Portuguese and Spanish word *coco* that was used by seamen and translates to goblin, head, monkey, or skull. This is because the markings on the stem end of coconuts are said to resemble facial features. The embryo of a coconut is buried within one of the eyes of the face of the stem end. It grows through it when it sprouts!

Carl Linnaeus (above), the Swedish botanist, physician, and zoologist who formalized the modern system of naming organisms called binomial nomenclature, dubbed the coconut tree *cocos* in the 18th century. Linnaeus was also thought to have considered the word *coccus* or berry in Latin.

You could even call the coconut the "coker-nut," which is an old variation of the word coconut that was used commercially in the Port of London.

Chapter 3: How Do Coconuts Help Health?

We're taught that saturated fats are bad, which might make us want to steer clear of the coconut. But this chapter describes how the saturated fats in coconuts are different than some other saturated fats. Some dietary fats are essential to the human body and diet—contrary to the past low-fat diet craze.

Dietary fats are essential for normal physiological activities such as brain function, energy production, and a healthy immune system, but eating the right types of dietary fats and the total amount of fat in one's diet matter.

The medium-chain triglycerides (MCTs) that are found in coconuts are considered to be healthy fats. In this chapter, you'll learn why they're thought to be more beneficial than some other types of fats.

The digestive process of different kinds of fats will be simplified in this chapter to help illustrate why the medium-chain triglycerides that are found in coconuts and other foods such as some butters, cheese, and yogurts may have advantages over other types of dietary fats.

Chapter 4: I Heart Coconuts

This chapter focuses on examples that demonstrate the cardiovascular benefits of coconuts. Some research has shown that the dietary fats that are found in coconuts do not contribute to cardiovascular disease; rather, they may protect the heart and prevent cardiovascular disease. Once again, the medium-chain triglycerides in coconuts are central to this discussion.

Coconuts are thought to increase the levels of high-density lipoproteins (HDLs, or "good" cholesterol) and lower the levels of low-density lipoproteins (LDLs, or "bad" cholesterol) in the human body and they may also help to lower blood pressure. All three measures are considered to be heart-healthy. The roles that coconuts play in reaping these heart-healthy benefits will be discussed—especially in comparison to populations where coconut consumption is prominent and heart disease in particular is lower than in the U.S.

Chapter 5:
Fat to Fight Fat?

Even with their higher-fat content, coconuts have been shown to aid weight loss. This chapter details the various ways that coconuts may help to fight fatness that is rapidly becoming a universal epidemic. For example, the medium-chain triglycerides that are found in coconut oil may actually help to burn stored fat and boost metabolism. Using coconut oil in cooking instead of other fats and oils may actually result in

a *thermogenic* effect, in that it may help to increase energy and accelerate metabolism.

Coconut has been shown to help break down excess abdominal fat that is an established risk factor for cardiovascular disease and diabetes. Additionally, the consumption of coconuts may lead to satiety, or a feeling of fullness, and to reduced appetite. In turn, this may result in fewer calories consumed with greater enjoyment.

While the fats in coconut may help with weight loss and management, it is important to recognize that these fats contain about the same number of calories per gram (9 calories/gram) as any other fat or oil, so they should still be consumed in moderation. You'll hear about smart ways to incorporate coconuts and their healthy fats into diets without being too excessive.

This chapter also examines some of the properties of coconut water. Unlike coconut oil, coconut water is fat-free. It is also lower in calories and higher in many nutrients such as magnesium, potassium, and vitamin C. Coconut water can be used for hydration, especially as a substitute for sugary and caloric sports drinks. Like other forms of coconut, tasty coconut water is also reported to have cardiovascular protective benefits.

Chapter 6:
Use Your Brain

Some past and evolving research about coconuts involves the possible links between coconut oil and decreased risks of dementia and epilepsy. Much of the research surrounds the *ketogenic* diet, which is higher in fat and lower in carbohydrates than a typical U.S. diet. Ketogenic diets tend to encourage the human body to burn fat for energy instead of carbohydrates, the body's preferred fuel.

This chapter describes the ketogenic diet in detail, how coconuts may conform with ketogenic diets, and why ketogenic diets may be beneficial for certain disorders affecting the brain.

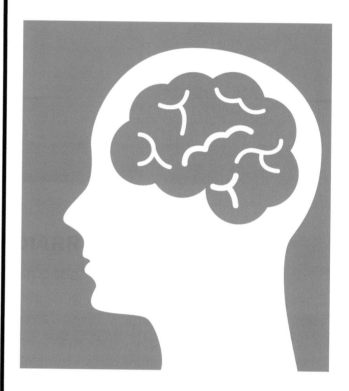

For example, the effectiveness of ketogenic diets in reducing the seizures of children with epilepsy has been demonstrated. This promising discovery has prompted scientists to theorize that coconut oil's medium-chain triglycerides may be useful for people with Alzheimer's disease and other forms of dementia.

This chapter will delve into this provocative research and pose some food for thought. It will also describe ways that coconuts may nourish the aging brain and possibly provide protection to it in order to help protect your mind and memory.

Chapter 7:
Things That Go Bump

This chapter explores the many various ways that coconut can be used for host of maladies, including minor bumps and bruises. The antimicrobial properties in coconuts will be described and how they may be beneficial for a multitude of minor ailments.

For instance, coconut oil may be used to soothe bee stings, bug bites, and simple scrapes and scratches. It can be applied as an insect repellent and has been used to prevent and treat lice infestation.

When ingested, the antibacterial and antiviral properties of coconuts may protect against common colds and strengthen the immune system. The many practical and economical uses of coconuts and solutions for common ailments are featured in this chapter—some ancient, others more modern.

Chapter 8:
Coconut the Beautiful

Coconut oil, like some other tropical oils, has been used for various beauty rituals for centuries. This chapter explains how the unique properties of coconut oil make it very versatile and useful for a myriad of beauty and hygienic practices.

Coconut oil helps to hydrate the skin, may delay aging skin with its supply of antioxidants, has antibacterial and antifungal properties, and conveys a pleasant fragrance.

Due to its versatility, coconuts can be used as a body moisturizer, hair conditioner, lip balm, makeup remover, manicure aid, moisturizer, shave lotion, and many more applications. Coconut oil can also be used for acne since its antibacterial properties are reported to help clear up the skin without clogging the pores. Coconut oil has an SPF of about 4, so it may be used as a mild, natural sunscreen.

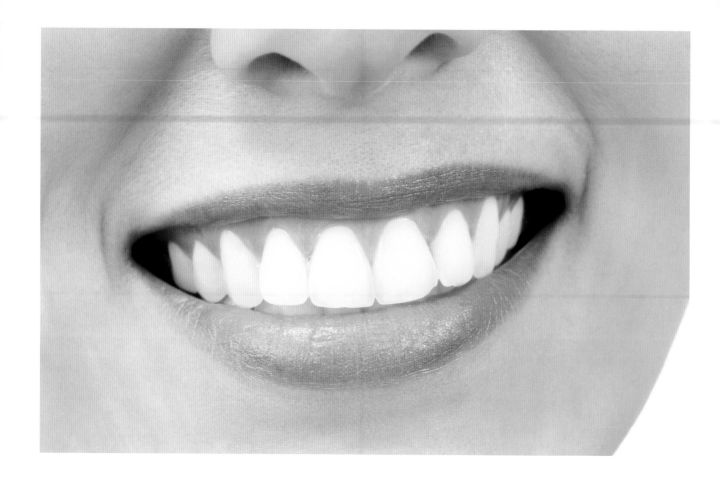

Chapter 9:
Oil-Pulling: Yea or Nay?

One of the more unusual uses of coconuts is the ritual of oil-pulling, which has been practiced for thousands of years in some parts of the world and has recently become more popularized in Western countries.

Practitioners of oil-pulling swish coconut oil in their mouths for several minutes (sometimes as long as 20 minutes). This practice is said to improve gum health, kill bacteria, prevent cavities, and strengthen teeth.

However, the American Dental Association does caution against this oil-pulling because it has not been researched in depth and many who have attempted it say they have not noticed improvements in their overall mouth health. Nevertheless, the practice of oil-pulling coconut oil will be explored in this chapter, along with the pros and cons, to help you to formulate your own opinion.

Chapter 10:
A Natural Alternative

While the coconut contributes impressive health benefits, there are many other unexpected ways that versatile coconuts can be used in daily life. It can be used as a natural product in cleaning and maintaining household items.

Chapter 11:
Protecting Your Pet

Don't keep the health benefits of coconut to yourself—share them with your furry friends! This chapter explores how to use the coconut's healing and protective properties to help your pets.

Chapter 12:
Putting It All Together

We'll give you with some tips for coconut use, as well as tips for buying, storing, toasting, and cracking coconuts. The coconut is Mother Nature's one-stop beauty counter, hardware store, pantry, and pharmacy all packaged into one fruit, nut, and seed. Incredible coconuts help to add flavor, texture, and nourishment to foods and beverages, beautify and nourish the hair and skin, prevent and treat common health problems, supercharge the metabolism, take care of your car and home, and more.

Chapter 13:
Additional Recipes

This chapter contains additional recipes that incorporate coconut in its various forms. You will find recipes for smoothies and shakes, breakfast foods and breads, scrumptious soups and side dishes, delicious main dishes, and decadent desserts. Some of the dozens of recipes include: Banana Chai Smoothie, Green Power Smoothie, Piña Colada Milkshake, Blueberry Coconut Flour Muffins, Pumpkin Granola, Loaded Banana Bread, Chickpea and Orange Squash Soup, Coconut-Lime Sweet Potatoes with Walnuts, Baked Fish with Thai Pesto, Herbed Lamb Chops, Coconut-Macadamia Shrimp, Dark Chocolate Coconut Cake, Amaretto Coconut Cream Pie, and many more.

Date-Nut Granola

⅓ **cup melted coconut oil**
2 **cups old-fashioned oats**
2 **cups barley flakes**
1 **cup sliced almonds**
⅓ **cup honey**
1 **teaspoon vanilla**
1 **cup chopped dates**

1. Preheat oven to 350°F. Grease 13x9-inch baking pan.

2. Combine oats, barley flakes, and almonds in large bowl. Combine oil, honey, and vanilla in small bowl; mix well. Pour honey mixture over oat mixture; stir until blended. Spread in prepared pan.

3. Bake about 25 minutes or until toasted, stirring frequently after first 10 minutes. Stir in dates while mixture is still hot. Cool completely; store in airtight container.

Makes 6 cups

To whet your appetite for what's to come, enjoy this tasty recipe for Date-Nut Granola. It combines melted coconut oil with old-fashioned oats, barley flakes, almonds, honey, vanilla, and dates for wholesome goodness. For a vegan version, the honey can be replaced with agave nectar or maple syrup. For a "coconutty" touch, dried coconut "meat" can be added to the mixture before baking. Eat and enjoy!

Coconut Basics

What is basic about the coconut? Hardly anything at all! Coconuts are very simple, yet very complex in character. Understanding the inner workings of coconuts is key to appreciating their impressive characteristics and benefits.

Unique Classification

Coconuts are uniquely classified as a seed, fruit, and nut. This is because a coconut is the stone or seed of a *drupe*, or fleshy fruit (the seed-bearing structure of a flowering plant), that is capable of reproducing. The word "drupe" is derived from the Latin word *drũpa* or *druppa*, which translates to overripe olive.

The fruit grows on the *Cocos nucifera*, treelike palms that are part of the Arecaceae palm family and the only species of the Cocos genus. These palms are more closely related to grasses than they are to nut trees. However, the coconut is also considered a nut, which is a fruit that is composed of a hard, tough shell that encapsulates an edible kernel.

Structure

Coconuts are encircled by a smooth, deep tan hard outer covering that encloses the husk and a thick and fibrous layer of fruit and milk. The outside husk of a coconut is called the *exocarp*, or outer layer. The exocarp is smooth and very strong. It is green to reddish brown in color, and grays as a coconut matures. In some varieties of coconuts, the exocarp is ivory in color. The husk has three indented "eyes" at one end of the coconut.

The husk is lined with a thin brown skin called the *testa* that firmly adheres to the hollow kernel that is filled with coconut water. The *mesocarp* (fleshy middle layer) is thick and filled with coarse brown fibers. Within the hairy husk is the *endocarp* (a hard, woody layer that surrounds the seed) that is filled with coconut meat and milk.

Development

Coconuts originate and develop over the course of a year. A coconut is filled with liquid after about four months and attains its full size around five months when its meat becomes jellylike.

Immature coconuts are about five to seven months old and are filled with sweet coconut water that contains about two percent sugars. Immature coconuts also contain fragile, gelatinous, moist meat that is composed of sugars and other carbohydrates and water.

Coconuts are considered to be mature after about 11 to 12 months of growth. They may weigh about 2 to 5 pounds and contain about 15 percent water, with one-quarter of their total weight composed of creamy, gelatinous, textured coconut meat. As coconuts continue to age, the meat becomes more solid and lightly fibrous.

As the coconut meat develops its fatty, firm, and white characteristics, the coconut liquid becomes less plentiful than within immature coconuts. At this stage of development, mature coconut meat is comprised of about 45 percent water, 35 percent fat, 10 percent carbohydrates, and 5 percent protein. The liquid provides a sweet and refreshing drink—often called coconut juice or simply coconut water.

Tall, Dwarf, and Hybrid

Coconuts differ in the regions where they grow throughout the world, which also determines their size, shape, and edible and usable qualities.

In general, coconuts can be classified as tall, dwarf, or hybrid.

Tall coconut palm trees include the Jamaican Tall, Panamanian Tall, West African Tall, and the Mancapuno coconuts from the Philippines. Tall coconut palms are also found in India, Indonesia, Malaysia, New Guinea, Sri Lanka, and Tahiti.

Tall coconut palm trees are generally long-lived palm trees: to an age of about 80 to 90 years. They attain an average height of about 49 to 59 feet (15 to 18 meters). Tall coconut palm trees thrive well under different soil conditions and grow well at an altitude of about 3,000 feet above sea level. They begin to bear fruit about 8 to 10 years after planting and are fairly resistant to diseases and pests.

The coconuts from tall coconut palm trees are medium-to-large in size and they vary from spheroid to linear-oblong in shape, in colors that range from green, yellow, and orange to brown. About 6,000 of these coconuts yield about a ton of copra.

Dwarf coconut palm trees include the *Cocos Niño* of the Philippines and the Dwarf Malay Golden and Dwarf Malay Green of the Caribbean. Dwarf coconut palm trees can also be found in Brazil, Fiji, India, Malaysia, Sri Lanka, and Thailand.

In contrast to tall coconut palm trees, dwarf coconut palm trees are smaller in stature (16 to 23 feet, or 5 to 7 meters) and bear fruit earlier than tall coconut palm trees. On the average, dwarf coconut palm trees flower as early as three years after planting and bear their fruit in the ninth year of their average life span of 40 to 50 years. They produce green, orange, and yellow nuts that are small in size, ovoid or round in shape, and susceptible to drought. The coconuts from dwarf coconut palm trees weigh about 3 ounces and have about 65 percent coconut oil content.

Hybrid coconut palm trees are the result of a cross between two structurally different forms of coconut. They are generally produced by two methods: with tall coconut palm trees as the female parent and dwarf coconut palm trees as the male parent (tall x dwarf), or with dwarf coconut palm trees as the female parent and tall coconut palm trees as the male parent (dwarf x tall).

Hybrid coconut palm trees tend to flower early and have increased yield and better quality of copra and coconut oil when compared to their parental varieties. They also tend to grow well with the proper nutrient management and irrigation.

Worldwide Coconut Development

Humans have been transporting and cultivating coconuts around the world for ages. Coconuts were probably first cultivated in the Pacific and Indian Ocean basins, according to DNA analysis of coconuts that were collected around the world. In the Pacific Ocean basin, coconuts were likely first cultivated in Southeast Asian islands, including Indonesia, Malaysia, and the Philippines, and perhaps on the Asian mainland. In the Indian Ocean basin, the southern border of India, including Sri Lanka, the Maldives, and the Laccadives, were likely the centers of coconut cultivation.

Coconuts from the western Indian Ocean, specifically Madagascar and the Comoros Islands, are an exception to the theories about Pacific Ocean and Indian Ocean basin cultivation. These coconuts are a genetic mixture of the Indian Ocean basin and Pacific basin coconuts and were probably first introduced and cultivated during pre-Columbian times by ancient Austronesians (from continental Asia, Madagascar, Maritime Southeast Asia, and the islands of the Pacific Ocean). The Austronesians then established trade routes that connected and transported Southeast Asia to Madagascar and coastal East Africa. Their descendants are still living in Madagascar today. It has been reported that some coconut trees on Madagascar are genetic mixtures of the Pacific and Indian varieties.

Western Coconut Expansion

During the Spanish Colonial Era (about 1521 to 1898), the Spanish brought coconuts from the Pacific Ocean basin

Ra Ramon coconuts from the Philippines bear the largest known coconuts. King Coconuts from Sri Lanka are known for their liquid with high sugar content. Maldivian Coconuts from the Maldives may contain the smallest of fruits, as they are no larger than eggs.

(especially from the Philippines) to the Pacific coast of Mexico that was governed for a period of time on behalf of the king of Spain. Some coconuts also appear to have been transported there during pre-Columbian times by the ancient Austronesians who traveled east rather than west. In Mexico today, the genetic diversity of coconut palms between ecotypes of different origins has evolved from these early introductions to its shores.

The Indian Ocean basin coconuts were transported to the New World by European explorers probably during the Age of Exploration from about the end of the 15th century to the 18th century. For example, Portuguese explorers transported coconuts from the Indian Ocean basin to the west coast of Africa where that were later carried to the Caribbean and coastal Brazil.

This is why you may find Pacific-type coconuts on the Pacific coast of Central America and Indian-type coconuts on the Atlantic coast. The coconuts that are found in Florida today are largely the Indian Ocean basin type, in the *niu kafa* form, although several cultivars of coconut palms are grown. Niu kafa coconuts are ancestral, naturally evolved, wild coconuts that are scattered by floating. They are angular and elongated and up to six inches in diameter, with a small egg-shaped nut that is encased by a thick husk. Niu kafa coconuts are desirable for their endosperm (meat and milk).

Dietary Staple

Coconuts have been a staple food and beverage in the diets of many cultures for thousands of years, in Polynesia, Hawaii, and Sri Lanka.

Polynesians

The Pukapuka and Tokelau of Polynesia, who live on atolls near the equator, consume diets that are high in saturated fat, but low in dietary cholesterol and sucrose. Coconut is their main source of calories. Vascular disease is uncommon among these Polynesians and there is little evidence of their high saturated fat intake having harmful effects.

There are two distinctively different forms of coconuts that are consumed in Polynesia: the *niu kafa* and *niu vai*, Samoan names for these Polynesian varieties.

In the late 1700s, Captain William Bligh of the British Royal Navy allegedly pitched coconuts overboard while sailing in the South Pacific. Reportedly, the historic event of the "Mutiny of the Bounty" on April 28, 1789, was prompted by Captain Bligh's harsh punishment of the mutineers for the theft of coconuts from the ship's store.

The niu kafa coconuts of Polynesia (as the coconuts that made their way to Florida) are triangular and oblong with large fibrous husks. This is in comparison to the niu vai coconuts that are rounded and brightly colored green, red, or yellow when unripe, with plenty of sweet coconut water inside.

Hawaiians

The first Hawaiian Island settlers who arrived from the Marquesas Islands around AD 300 to 400 are thought to have been of Polynesian descent. They likely brought *Niu*, the coconut that was elevated from just an ordinary food to a sacred tree in the Hawaiian Islands.

Niu is depicted in mythical art and verbal lore as a magical tree that is an image of *Ku*, the Hawaiian ancestor and the link to their heritage and life itself. Niu was valued cargo since it was considered to be the most useful plant of the tropics. There are stories of Hawaiian Islanders who survived months of drought by consuming coconut water. Ancient Hawaiians were said to be strong and sturdy from their native diet, which was considered one of the best in the world for the time.

Sri Lankans

The Veddas, or "Forest People," are indigenous people of Sri Lanka. The majority of Sri Lankans are of the Sinhalese race that migrated from India around two thousand years ago.

Coconut palms were very important to the Veddas for their steady source of food and drink, as well as materials that were used for building fires, eating utensils, rope, and tools.

The majority of dietary fat in the traditional Vedda diet was derived from coconuts and wild game that are both high in saturated fats. In the 1980s the Veddas were studied to determine how their high-fat diet affected their health. Their rate of cardiovascular disease was very low. Heart disease and stroke were also virtually nonexistent in Kitava, Papua New Guinea, where coconuts, fish, fruit, and tubers are the main dietary staples.

While these indigenous populations survived and thrived on coconut meat and coconut water, it is important to note that their lifestyles were very different from typical North American lifestyles today, with much more activity and a less-processed diet without many of the stresses of modern society. While it is easy to make correlations between coconut consumption and decreased or absent diseases of affluence (such as cardiovascular disease, diabetes, or hypertension), one needs to keep the isolation and location of population groups such as the Veddas in mind. Still, the low cardiovascular disease rate despite the high saturated fat consumption of the Veddas is an impressive trait worth studying.

Coconut Forms and Processes

The majority of people around the world do not cultivate their own coconuts today; rather, they purchase them whole, cracked, or dried, or as coconut oil or coconut water. What follows are some of the products on the market today.

Cocolait is commercially produced coconut milk that has been nutritionally configured to resemble cow's milk.

Coconut cream is a coconut-flavored liquid that contains less water than coconut milk, which results in a more concentrated consistency and flavor. Coconut cream may also be solid and require reconstitution with warm to hot water.

Coconut gelatin (*nato de coco*) is a moist, translucent mass of cellulose or linked sugars. It is produced by a vinegar bacterium (*Acetobacter xylinum*) on the surface of coconut water that ferments.

Coconut gelatin has a crunchy texture and little flavor. Once its vinegary flavor is removed, flavor is then added and it is packed in sugar syrup to be consumed as a sweet. Coconut gelatin produced in this manner is popular in the Philippines. It is often not exported due to its unusual consistency.

Coconut ice is usually an English confection that is prepared with grated *desiccated* (dried, grated, unsweetened) coconut, condensed milk, and sugar. The mixture forms a solid, soft candy with a chewy, slightly grainy, and soft texture. In the U.S., chocolate is sometimes added to coconut ice.

Coconut meat (*or copra*) is the edible, white "meat" of coconuts that can be consumed raw or is often shredded. Coconut meat is high in fiber, calories, and fat, mostly from saturated fats. Coconut oil is extracted from the coconut meat.

Coconut milk is a sweet, coconut-flavored liquid that is produced by pouring boiling water over shredded coconut, then cooling and straining the mixture. Coconut milk of normal thickness is produced by using twice-as-much water by volume as the amount of grated coconut. A thicker coconut milk can be made with half-as-much water. The coconut pulp can be reused in the process for culinary applications. It should be covered and refrigerated.

Coconut milk is popular in southern Indian and Southeast Asian cuisines. Since it is an emulsion (its fat droplets are dispersed within the coconut water), coconut milk is a handy ingredient for thickening. Coconut milk contains less protein and more fat than cow's milk, but a lower-fat variety of coconut milk is available. If the fat rises to the surface of coconut milk, it can then be removed and used as coconut oil.

Coconut oil is pressed from copra, the dried meat of coconuts, but it can also be made with fresh coconuts. Coconut oil contains natural lecithin, an emulsifier and lubricant. Lecithin is an excellent cooking oil for commercial frying because it prevents spattering and provides even frying.

Coconut oil contains a higher proportion of saturated fatty acids than some polyunsaturated oils such as canola, which makes it more resistant to rancidity (the deterioration of a fat or oil that leads to unpleasant odor or flavor). Coconut oil is also used as an ingredient in some candies, cookies, and pies, as well as cosmetics, margarines, and soaps.

Coconut palm heart is a vegetable that is harvested from the growing buds and inner cores of certain palm trees that include the coconut palm tree (*Cocos nucifera*). Palm hearts may also be harvested from the Açaí, Palmito Juçara, Pejibaye, Pupunha, and Sabal palm trees.

Coconut pearls are sometimes discovered inside coconuts and may be the result of arrested germination. For this reason, coconut pearls are said to have magical and medicinal powers. Their sizes range from the equivalent of an oyster pearl to a cherry. Coconut pearls are white or blue in color and are filled with calcium carbonate, which is also found in calcium supplements.

Coconut flour is a nutritious gluten-free flour; it's high in fiber, a good source of protein, and relatively lower in carbohydrates than other flours. In fact, the majority of the carbohydrate content in coconut flour comes from fiber, which aids in digestive health. Coconut flour is made from coconut meat that has been dried, defatted, and finely ground. Because it is made from coconuts, it provides a unique, natural sweet flavor when used in baking. The Blueberry Coconut Flour Muffins recipe in chapter 13 uses coconut flour.

Coconut aminos is made from the sap of the coconut palm, which is dried and blended with sea salt. This dark, salty sauce contains 17 amino acids. Coconut aminos doesn't have a pronounced coconut flavor and is often used as a substitute for soy sauce in paleo recipes because it does not contain soy. Use coconut aminos in stir-fries, dressings, and wherever you would use soy sauce. This bottled product can be found in health food and vitamin stores, some grocery stores, or online.

Coconut roots are composed of a fibrous root system that is often ground to produce tea for drinking and treating minor ailments, such as skin conditions.

Coconut shells, wood, and leaves are often used in furniture making, hut walls and roofs, and tools and flooring materials, most often in areas where coconuts are grown.

Coconut water is the liquid that is contained within the shell of fresh coconuts. It is sometimes clear and sometimes cloudy, depending upon its nutrient content, with a slightly nutty and sweet taste. Coconut water was a popular drink of the ancients and still is popular today for its reported medicinal value.

Young (baby) coconuts (*Coquitos* in Chilean) are about the size of acorns and are generally sold without husks. They are often harvested early and may still have their brown hairy husks.

White coconuts are young coconuts that have the brown hairy husks removed. This process exposes their hard inner white shell.

Whole coconuts are the stones of coconut fruit that have their husks removed. This process decreases the weight of coconuts and eases shipping and handling.

Thai Veggie Curry

- **2** tablespoons coconut oil
- **1** onion, quartered and thinly sliced
- **1** tablespoon Thai red curry paste (or to taste)
- **1** can (about 13 ounces) unsweetened coconut milk
- **2** red or yellow bell peppers, cut into strips
- **1½** cups cauliflower and broccoli florets
- **1** cup pea pods
- **1** package (about 14 ounces) tofu, pressed* and cubed

  Salt and pepper
- **¼** cup slivered fresh basil

  Hot cooked jasmine rice

Tip: Make sure to buy unsweetened coconut milk, which is usually sold in the Asian section of the supermarket. Other coconut products cannot be substituted.

*To press tofu, cut in half horizontally. Place tofu between layers of paper towels. Place flat, heavy object on top for 10 to 30 minutes.

1. Heat oil in wok or large skillet over medium-high heat. Add onion; cook and stir 2 minutes or until softened. Add curry paste; cook and stir to coat onion. Add coconut milk; bring to a boil, stirring to dissolve curry paste.

2. Add bell peppers, cauliflower, and broccoli; simmer over medium heat 4 to 5 minutes or until crisp-tender. Stir in snow peas; simmer 2 minutes. Gently stir in tofu; cook until heated through.

3. Season with salt and pepper. Sprinkle with basil; serve with rice.

Makes 4 to 6 servings

Thai Vegetable Curry combines coconut oil and coconut milk with onions, bell peppers, broccoli, cauliflower, pea pods, and tofu for a mouth-watering mixture to serve over rice.

Commercially Available Coconut

Dessicated coconut is produced from the white section of the coconut kernel after the thin brown layer of skin is removed. It is generally sterilized, mixed with water into a moist pulp, and sieved for different "grades"—the finest grade referred to as "macaroon." Fine grade desiccated coconut is smaller in particle size than medium grade or coconut shreds. Desiccated coconut is typically then dried, flaked, or grated. It is unsweetened and has about 3 percent moisture content.

Dried coconut meat (or copra) or dried coconut kernel can be pressed for its oil for use in cooking and soap making.

Fresh coconut meat is available all year; however, its peak season is considered to be October through December. Fresh coconuts are best when they are heavy for their size and sound full of liquid when shook. Fresh coconut "eyes" should not be damp, as coconut water might be leaking and lead to spoilage.

Depending upon their degree of ripeness, fresh coconuts may last about 6 months if left untouched at room temperature. Once the thin juice is removed through the eyes, then the meat can be grated or chopped. Freshly grated coconut should be tightly covered and refrigerated. Then it may last up to 4 days and be frozen up to 6 months.

Packaged and canned coconut is available in bags or cans, sweetened or unsweetened, flaked or shredded, and dried, moistened, or frozen. Unopened coconut in bags may last about 6 months. Unopened canned coconut may last up to about 18 months at room temperature. Once opened, both types of coconut must be sealed and refrigerated or frozen since its high fat content may promote rancidity.

Coconut honey is made in a similar fashion as coconut syrup: by blending and heating coconut milk and invert sugar (a mixture of the two simple sugars glucose and fructose) until the mixture is a golden syrup. Golden honey contains a little of the coconut's brown rind and is cooked longer.

Coconut palm sugar is the crystallized form of coconut palm syrup, or jaggery. It has a low Glycemic Index value. (Carbohydrates with a low GI value are more slowly digested, absorbed, and metabolized by the human body, which results in a slower rise in blood glucose and insulin levels.) Coconut palm sugar is popular in Indonesia. In the U.S., coconut palm sugar may be mixed with cane sugar.

Coconut jaggery is the strained, unfermented coconut sap that is boiled, crystallized, and transferred into molds. Semisolid coconut jaggery then solidifies into a crystallized hard substance that is used as a sweetening agent.

Coconut syrup is made by blending and heating coconut milk and invert sugar (a mixture of simple sugars glucose and fructose). This process yields "golden syrup" that is similar to pure invert sugar. It is less prone to crystallization, moist, sweet, and valued by bakers.

Coconut toddy is an alcoholic beverage that is made by tapping the coconut tree by cutting off the tips of the flowing stems. Once fermented, this beverage can be consumed raw or distilled to produce *arak* (a Levantine alcoholic spirit that is anise-flavored, clear, colorless, and unsweetened). It can also be used as a source of yeast in bread making or it can be fermented further into vinegar.

Types and Advantages of Coconut Oil

Coconut oil is generally liquid at room temperature, though this characteristic may change depending upon its country of origin. However, it solidifies at temperatures below that, so refrigerated or frozen coconut oil will look quite dense.

After processing, coconut oil is almost tasteless, so it is commonly used in baked goods, confections, cooking oils, and margarines for its great versatility.

There are several types of coconut oil, mostly distinguished by the types or lack of processing.

Unrefined coconut oil, also called "pure" or "virgin" coconut oil, is made from fresh coconut meat instead of dried. The coconut oil is extracted by either a quick-dry method or through a wet-milling process.

Quick drying dries the coconut meat rapidly; then the coconut oil is pressed out mechanically. *Wet milling* first processes the coconut meat into coconut milk. Then the coconut milk is separated from the coconut oil by boiling, centrifuging, fermenting, straining, or by the use of enzymes.

Because both of these extraction methods are quick, the coconut oil does not require additives or bleaching. Both processes also retain more flavor since they do not expose the coconut oil to high temperatures.

Virgin coconut oil is derived from the expeller pressing of coconut oil from dried (desiccated) coconut. It is not distinguished by an industry standard, much like in the olive oil industry; however, it is considered to be unrefined.

Refined coconut oil is made from dried coconut meat, or copra. (Some copra-based refined coconut oils are referred to as "RBD oils" since they are **r**efined, **b**leached, and **d**eodorized.) The coconut meat is bleached (generally not by a chemical process, but by filtration) and treated to reduce any bacteria. However, the drying process itself may produce contaminants.

A high heat process is then used to extract the coconut flavor and aroma. Sometimes chemicals are used to extract as much oil as possible. Sodium hydroxide may be added to increase shelf life. Refined coconut oil is sometimes partially hydrogenated, but this process may produce trans fats, which are disallowed in United States manufacture by the U.S. Food and Drug Administration (USFDA).

Extra-virgin coconut oil, similar to virgin coconut oil, bears little distinction to extra-virgin olive oil or any oil with an "extra-virgin" designation. It implies that this type of coconut oil has the highest quality and retains the original chemical composition and nutritive values of coconuts. Unlike olive oil there is no industry standard definition.

Cold-pressed coconut oil is produced at low temperature from fresh, dried coconut flakes. It has a stronger coconut flavor than expeller-pressed coconut oil and may contain tiny traces of soluble components that are extracted from the dried coconut meat. Cold-pressed coconut oil is considered as "raw" coconut oil. Since it is not exposed to high heat, many of its nutrients may be retained so it may be preferable to other choices.

Expeller-pressed coconut oil is produced through a mechanical extraction process that does not rely upon solvent extracts or other chemical processes. Expeller-pressed coconut oil has less of a coconut taste than cold-pressed coconut oil, but it has a higher smoke point that makes it desirable for cooking.

Centrifuge-extracted coconut oil is made from freshly pressed coconut milk that is chilled and separated by centrifugal force. Like cold-pressed coconut oil, centrifuge-extracted coconut oil is considered as a raw coconut oil because it retains mostly all of its nutrients during processing. It has a light coconut flavor and may be quite expensive, likely due to its nutrient retention and subtle taste and aroma.

Organic coconut oil should be produced under organic standards, unrefined, and pressed at low heat to retain its antioxidants and *phenols*, biologically active compounds. Select unhydrogenated organic coconut oil without trans fats (which must appear on the nutrition label). Refrigerate after opening.

Some refined coconut oils, especially those that are used in chocolate production and commercial baking, may be partially hydrogenated.

Coconut Cost

Coconuts are relatively inexpensive in cost—that is, if one lives in India, Indonesia, Mexico, or Thailand. Because coconuts have become so popular, prices have soared and are continuing their upward trend. In particular, the sale of coconut water is a rising industry.

The coconut plantations in the Caribbean have experienced a shortage and those in the Philippines have faced natural disasters, raising prices. Still, coconuts are relatively economical in their natural state.

In Hawaii, a coconut may cost about $2.00, but once it is opened and processed, then the price may escalate (one pound of organic coconut shreds could cost as much as $10.00 a bag). A metal coconut opener may be pricy, but a stake of some kind should be able to poke open a coconut through one of its "eyes."

Coconut milk and coconut water may range in price depending upon the size and type of packing and manufacturer. Pricy coconut water is fashionable, but the cost per nutrient may not make sense.

Bottom line: Coconuts may require some "elbow grease" to pry open; still, they are economical for all of their benefits.

Availability

If one lives in the southeast or southwest and along the coastlines, then coconut palms may be familiar sights. Coconuts may be so abundant that they drop off their branches onto the ground to be scooped up for cracking, munching fresh coconut meat, or sipping refreshing coconut water.

Around the world coconuts, coconut milk, coconut water, and other forms of coconuts may be instantly purchased and promptly delivered. Mass food markets now sell coconuts and coconut products to meet consumer demand for coconut's beauty, culinary, health, and home usages. Due to their popularity, the accessibility makes coconuts different than some other hard-to-purchase foods or beverages. It's easy to access the benefits of coconuts!

How Do Coconuts Help Health?

In this chapter, we'll look at five notable features of the incredible coconut that point to its healing properties.

1. Saturated Fats

The word is that fat is bad for us, and saturated fat especially, so how are the saturated fats in coconut different than other saturated fats in foods and beverages? This chapter discusses how, contrary to what the diet industry has the public believing, fat is needed in our daily diets. This nutrient is essential for processes such as brain function, energy production, and immune protection. Still, it is vital to consume the right kinds of fats and in the right amounts.

The "medium-chain triglycerides" (MCTs) that are found in coconuts (and discussed in many chapters throughout this book—particularly in chapters 4, 5, and 6) are considered to be more beneficial than some other kinds of fats and for good reason.

For instance, medium-chain triglycerides are more easily digested and immediately converted to energy, whereas "long-chain triglycerides" (LCTs), which make up the majority of the fat in our diets, are carried by the bloodstream and are not necessarily burned for energy. This chapter will distinguish among these types of fats and more to illustrate why the coconut is a cut above other foods of its kind.

Chemically speaking, saturated fats are fat molecules that are saturated with hydrogen molecules. Practically speaking, saturated fats are fats that are filled to capacity and are difficult for the body to disengage.

Saturated fats have been on the nutrition and health radar for years due to their relationship to cardiovascular disease. The reason why saturated fats are discouraged is that they tend to raise the level of cholesterol in the bloodstream, which in turn may increase a person's risk of cardiovascular disease and stroke.

Saturated fats occur naturally in foods and beverages. The majority of saturated fats are derived from animal sources, particularly meats and dairy products. Beef fat (tallow), butter, cheese, and other dairy products that are made with two percent or whole milk, fatty beef, lard, lamb, pork, and poultry with skin are examples of animal products that contain saturated fats.

Conversely, replacing foods and beverages that are higher in saturated fats with those that are lower in saturated fats may lower serum (blood) cholesterol, improve lipid profiles in the blood, and conceivably even reduce the risks of cardiovascular disease and stroke. The *lipid profile* is a panel of blood tests that provides a screening tool for blood lipids that include cholesterol and triglycerides.

Polyunsaturated fats are fat molecules that have openings in their structures without hydrogen molecules. They tend to be lighter fats and are thought to be health enhancing. Polyunsaturated fats are sometimes made into saturated fats through the process of *hydrogenation*, as discussed in chapter 4. Hydrogenation adds more hydrogen to fat molecules to make them more stable.

Consider canola oil. Through hydrogenation, canola oil could become hydrogenated into canola oil-based margarine, transformed from tub to stick. In the process, artificial trans fats are formed, which have been deemed unsafe by the U.S. Department of Agriculture.

Currently the American Heart Association (AHA) offers recommendations that Americans should aim for a dietary pattern that contains five to six percent of calories from saturated fat. If a person consumes 2,000 calories daily (the figure that the U.S. Food and Drug Administration uses to determine the Daily Values [DVs] of different nutrients), then this means that no more than about 120 calories or 13 grams of saturated fats should be consumed daily.

Also according to the American Heart Association, a daily diet pattern should emphasize fruits, vegetables, whole grains, low-fat dairy products, poultry, fish, and nuts, and limit red meats and sugary foods and beverages. The AHA also suggests that foods with high monounsaturated and/or polyunsaturated fatty acids should replace foods that are higher in saturated fatty acids.

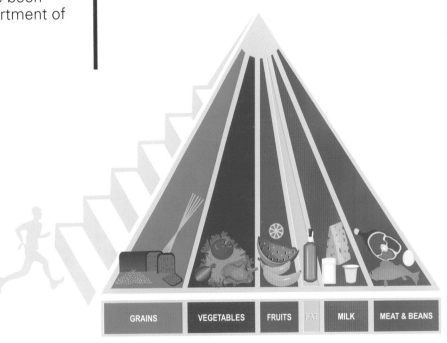

GRAINS | VEGETABLES | FRUITS | FAT | MILK | MEAT & BEANS

Some plant-based oils such as coconut oil, palm oil, and palm kernel oil do not contain cholesterol (a fatty substance that is also a risk factor in cardiovascular disease and stroke), but they do primarily contain saturated fats.

Coconuts, Saturated Fats, Health, and Heart Disease

What might be considered as an enigma to this discussion about the relationship between saturated fats and cardiovascular disease and stroke is the relationship of coconuts and cardiovascular and brain health that will be described more fully in later chapters.

Out of the 133 grams of total fat in one medium coconut, 118 grams or roughly 88.7 percent is from saturated fats. This is approximately 590 percent of the Daily Value that is based on a 2,000 daily calorie diet. In comparison, the amount of polyunsaturated fat is only 1.5 grams and the amount of monounsaturated fat is only 6 grams.

Also in comparison, the amount of saturated fat in butter is about 64 percent of total calories and the amount of saturated fat in beef fat is about 40 percent of total calories, or about the same amount as in lard.

What is different about the saturated fats in coconut oil is that these fats tend to increase high-density lipoprotein cholesterol (or HDL—the "good" cholesterol). This is based on short-term studies that examined the affects of coconut oil on serum cholesterol levels. As of last year, the exact mechanisms by which coconut oil affects cardiovascular disease were not confirmed.

The saturated fat in coconut oil is mostly comprised of medium-chain triglycerides (MCTs). These medium-chain triglycerides are handled differently in the body than the longer-chain fatty acids that are found in dairy products, fatty meals, and liquid vegetable oils. This distinction is the next notable feature of coconuts.

Coconut Curry Chicken Soup

- 3   cups chicken broth
- 8   boneless skinless chicken thighs
- 1   cup chopped onion, divided
- 1   teaspoon salt, divided
- 4   whole cloves
- 1   tablespoon coconut oil
- 2   tablespoons curry powder
- 1¼ cups coconut milk
- ¼   cup plus 1 tablespoon chopped fresh mint, divided
- 3   tablespoons crystallized ginger
- ¼   teaspoon ground cloves
- 1½ cups half-and-half
- 3   cups cooked rice
  Lime wedges (optional)

1. Bring broth to a boil in large saucepan over high heat. Add chicken, ½ cup onion, ½ teaspoon salt, and whole cloves. Return to a boil. Reduce heat to low; cover and simmer 40 minutes or until tender. Remove chicken; set aside. Strain cooking liquid; reserve 1 cup.

2. Melt coconut oil in same skillet over medium-high heat. Add remaining ½ cup onion; cook and stir 4 minutes or until onion is translucent. Sprinkle curry powder over onions; cook 20 seconds or just until fragrant, stirring constantly.

3. Add coconut milk, 1 tablespoon mint, ginger, ground cloves, and reserved cooking liquid to saucepan. Cover; simmer 10 minutes. Add chicken; cover and simmer 15 minutes. Stir in half-and-half and remaining ½ teaspoon salt. Shred chicken slightly, pressing down with spoon. Cook 1 minute or until heated through. Sprinkle with remaining ¼ cup mint. Spoon rice over each serving and garnish with lime wedges.

Makes 4 servings

Coconut Curry Chicken Soup uses chicken broth, skinless chicken thighs, onions, cloves, coconut oil, curry powder, coconut milk, fresh mint, crystalized ginger, and half-and-half along with cooked rice and fresh lime for a mouth-watering and tempting synthesis of tastes.

2. Medium-Chain Triglycerides

Triglycerides are the most common type of fat in the body. They come from food; the human body also makes triglycerides. Once the triglycerides in foods and beverages are consumed and digested, they travel through in the blood and supply energy or are stored for future use. Foods and beverages that are higher in cholesterol and saturated fats tend to elevate serum (blood) triglyceride levels. High levels of blood triglycerides are frequently seen in people with heart problems, have diabetes, or are overweight.

There are different types of triglycerides that are differentiated according to the number and types of fatty acids, whether they are saturated or unsaturated, and their degree of unsaturation. Triglycerides are designed as short, medium, or long in length.

Short-chain triglycerides: Short-chain triglycerides are triglycerides that are generally about 2 to 5 carbon atoms in length. They are primarily absorbed through the portal vein during lipid digestion, much like medium-chain triglycerides are.

Medium-chain triglycerides (MCTs): Medium-chain triglycerides are triglycerides that are generally about 6 to 12 carbon atoms in length. The fatty acids in medium-chain triglycerides are generally broken off from their triglyceride structure without the need of bile (an alkaline fluid that aids in fat digestion) from the liver. Then the MCTs are "shuttled" via the portal artery directly to the liver without the use of chylomicrons (small, lipoprotein particles) for transport. This attribute makes medium-chain triglycerides desirable for their relatively quicker source of energy compared to long-chain triglycerides with less dependency upon the liver.

Long-chain triglycerides (LCTs): Long-chain triglycerides are triglycerides that are generally about 14 to 22 carbon atoms in length. Long-chain triglycerides usually require both bile and lipases (fat-digesting enzymes) to be emulsified and broken down into individual fatty acids in the small intestine. Then these fatty acids are reassembled and carried through the blood or lymph, used by the body as needed, or stored. The process is lengthier than medium-chain triglyceride digestion, absorption, and utilization and is dependent upon bile and lipases.

What makes the types of fat in coconuts different than the fats that are found in other foods and beverages is that practically all of the fat in coconuts are medium-chain triglycerides (MCTs), while the majority of fats that are consumed by humans are long-chain triglycerides (LCTs). This factor is responsible for the unique character and healthful properties of coconut oil and has many implications.

Medium-chain triglycerides are used in hospital formulas to feed very young infants, people who are critically ill, and those who may have digestive problems. This is because MCTs are easily digested, absorbed, and utilized to nourish the human body. Because of their quick conversion into energy, medium-chain triglycerides are also used by athletes, for weight management, and in the treatment of *epilepsy* in children. Epilepsy is a neurological disorder that is designated by recurrent episodes of sensory disturbances. When medium-chain triglycerides are used in conjunction with a prescribed ketogenic diet, symptoms appear to decrease. Later chapters describe the ketogenic diet in more detail.

What makes the medium-chain triglycerides in coconuts different is that most of the fatty acids are saturated. Other than treating epilepsy, the critically ill, those with digestive disorders, and young infants, the medium-chain triglycerides in coconuts have shown effectiveness in cardiovascular risk prevention and health promotion. These attributes are opposite to the effects that other saturated fats may have on the human body and health.

This leads to another feature of the coconut that makes it different in good ways: the lauric acid content.

3. Lauric Acid

Lauric acid, a component of triglycerides, is saturated fatty acid with a 12-carbon chain, so it is considered to be a medium-chain fatty acid. Lauric acid comprises about one-half of the fatty acids in coconut milk and coconut oil (49 percent of total fat). It is also found in cow's milk (2.9 percent of total fat), goat's milk (3.1 percent of total fat), and human breast milk (6.2 percent of total fat).

Lauric acid increases total serum cholesterol due to its favorable increase in high-density lipoprotein cholesterol (HDL, or "good" cholesterol) that correlates with decreased risks of *atherosclerosis* (hardening of the arteries) and cardiovascular disease.

A fairly recent animal study demonstrated the ability of lauric acid to reduce blood pressure, heart rate, and oxidative stress in the arteries and the kidneys.

Both lauric acid and monolaurin also have demonstrated antimicrobial activity against some bacteria, fungi, and viruses. This is why, along with vascular disease, lauric acid may be used to treat a host of other conditions that include the avian flu, cold sores, the common cold, fever blisters, genital herpes and warts, the swine flu, and viral infections including influenza. And this is also why coconut oil, with its high percentage of lauric acid, is valued by some for its antibacterial, antifungal, and antiviral properties.

4. Coconut's Nutritional Value

Some foods and beverages boast that they are Mother Nature's perfect food. While no food or beverage is 100 percent perfect, the incredible coconut provides its share of nutrients in one convenient package.

First consider coconut meat, the edible white interior of coconuts.

- It is a storehouse of energy providing 283 calories per one cup of raw, shredded coconut meat.

- It provides carbohydrates with 12 tasty grams of carbohydrates per one cup.

- It is a high source of dietary fiber with 7 grams of dietary fiber per one cup.

- It has 27 grams of total fat with 24 grams of saturated fat and no cholesterol per one cup of raw, shredded coconut meat.

- It provides 3 grams of protein per one cup.

- It is low in sodium with only 16 milligrams of sodium per one cup.

> The medium-chain triglycerides that are found in coconuts are also found in human breast milk.

Berry Coconut Milk Smoothie

1   cup unsweetened coconut milk

2   cups berries (blueberries, raspberries, and/or strawberries)

4 to 5 whole ice cubes

1   tablespoon coconut oil (optional)

Cinnamon (optional)

1. Place the first three ingredients into a blender.
2. Blend at low speed until smooth.
3. Dribble with coconut oil, if desired.
4. Blend at medium speed until well blended.
5. Top with sprinkle of cinnamon, if desired.

Makes 2 cups

Next consider coconut milk.

- It is a storehouse of energy with 552 calories per one cup of raw coconut milk.
- It provides carbohydrates with 13 grams of carbohydrates per one cup.
- It is a good source of dietary fiber with 5 grams of dietary fiber per one cup.
- It contains 57 grams of total fat with 51 grams of saturated fat and no cholesterol.
- It provides protein with 5 grams of protein per one cup.
- It is low in sodium with only 36 milligrams of sodium per one cup.

Then consider coconut water.

- It is low in calories with only 46 calories per one cup of coconut water.

- It provides carbohydrates with 9 grams of carbohydrates per one cup of coconut water.

- It provides dietary fiber with 3 grams of dietary fiber per one cup.

- It contains zero grams of total fat, saturated fat, or cholesterol.

- It provides protein with 2 grams of protein per one cup.

- Note that it is higher in sodium at 252 milligrams per one cup.

This equates to plenty of energy from the calories in fats, carbohydrates, and proteins, plus dietary fiber and relatively little sodium with plenty of essential and supportive vitamins and minerals (to be discovered throughout this book). What other foods or beverages can boast all of these nutrients in these levels that are encapsulated into just one incredible coconut?

5. Body Benefits

What other fruit, nut, or seed has so many beauty properties that can be used in such a variety of different hygiene and beauty applications? Coconut oil can be used as a body oil, body lotion, body scrub, breath freshener, cuticle oil, make-up remover and make-up brush cleanser, dandruff treatment, deep conditioner, deodorant, frizz tamer, itch reliever, leave-in conditioner, lip balm, massage oil, night cream, under eye cream, shaving cream, stretch mark cream, and teeth whitener, among many other usages.

A mixture of apple cider vinegar and coconut oil when combed through hair may be effective in ridding and preventing head lice. Just ask any parent of school-aged children who have been infested with head lice: they may agree that delousing the hair with a natural product such as coconut oil may be the alternative to harsh chemical treatments.

In comparison, avocadoes are technically classified as fruit since they are large berries that contain single seeds. Like coconuts, avocadoes have a host of beauty benefits. Avocadoes contain antioxidants carotenoids that include alpha- and beta-carotene, cryptoxanthin, zeaxanthin, and lutein. These antioxidants help to protect the skin from environmental damage from oxygen-free radicals, which may contribute to visible signs of aging, such as fine lines or wrinkles.

Plus, avocadoes contain vitamin C—also for healthy skin. Vitamin C is needed to create elastin and collagen that helps to bind the skin and maintain the firmness and structure of skin cells.

Another antioxidant that is found in avocadoes is vitamin E, which also helps to prevent free radical damage and may be protective against excessive sun exposure.

One of the biggest beauty benefits of avocadoes is their composition of monounsaturated fatty acids from their high oleic acid content. Monounsaturated fatty acids help to moisturize the epidermal layer of the skin to keep it hydrated and soft in appearance and are said to help decrease inflammation.

However, a virgin coconut oil-enriched diet was also shown to have a beneficial role in improving antioxidant status and preventing lipid and protein oxidation, or breakdown. Plus, the saturated fat content of coconuts has shining benefits.

The inherent saturated fats in coconuts reportedly help to strengthen the underlying tissues of the skin and remove excessive dead cells on the skin's surface, leaving it smooth and devoid of roughness and flakiness. Also, the medium-chain triglycerides act as antibacterial, antifungal, and antiviral agents to protect the skin and scalp from these menacing invaders. Lastly, coconut water with its light and refreshing coconut aroma is refreshing and hydrating for needy skin.

So while other foods and beverages may have their beauty benefits, the coconut is different: it scores threefold as a fruit, nut, and seed in the beauty world.

Not Just for Health

The benefits of coconut don't end with your health. Let's take a quick look at some of the other uses and benefits of the amazing coconut.

• One surprising use of coconuts and what makes them a standout in the plant kingdom is their use to both whiten and shine the body and the home. Who would imagine that a natural substance such as coconut oil could whiten the stains on tooth enamel *and* shine leather shoes? Or that coconut oil may moisten and shine lips *and* polish wooden floors and furniture to a warm glow? Or that coconut oil may lighten simple bruises and scrapes *and* brighten cast-iron pans?

• It is difficult to walk into a bakery or perfumery without sensing the pleasantly sweet and tropical scent of coconuts. Likewise, the taste of coconuts is so distinct that it is hard not to identify the taste of coconuts in savory or sweet foods or beverages. This can be advantageous and disadvantageous. The scent and taste of coconut are so distinct that some may either have a love or dislike for these sensations. Some subtler smelling fruits, nuts, and seeds are too difficult to detect so assertively as coconuts.

• Coconut has many culinary applications in cooking and baking. The coconut meat, milk, and water are exceptionally versatile in appetizers, breakfasts, desserts, main dishes, side dishes, smoothies, soups, and stews. Coconut meat, milk, and water add aroma, fat, moisture, taste, and texture in common and surprising ways. For example, when shredded coconut is used in baked goods the flavor is full-bodied, moist, and tropical. And when toasted coconut tops fruit or curries, browning brings out the fatty, nutty coconut taste.

I Heart Coconuts

This chapter focuses on all the ways that the coconut has been shown to protect the heart. Contrary to past thinking, research has shown that the fat in coconuts does not contribute to heart disease and on the contrary, may protect the heart and prevent heart disease.

The coconut is thought to increase levels of high-density lipoproteins (HDL, or "good" cholesterol) and lower levels of low-density lipoprotein (LDL, or "bad" cholesterol) and may also help to lower blood pressure.

In this chapter the roles that the coconut plays in reaping heart-healthy benefits are discussed.

Cardiovascular Disease

For more than 50 years cardiovascular disease has been one of the major causes of death in the United States. The underlying cause of cardiovascular disease is atherosclerosis, which is a condition that is characterized by plaque, or fatty deposits that are lodged within the arterial walls. Plaque interferes with blood flow to the heart and brain that may lead to a heart attack or stroke.

Diet is a modifiable cardiovascular and cerebral risk factor, meaning that when one's diet is heart-healthy then risks decrease.

Heart Disease: Terms to Know

Angina pectoris is a condition that is marked by severe chest pain and/or discomfort that often spreads to the neck and shoulders. It is frequently due to insufficient blood flow to the heart muscle that results from obstruction or spasm within the coronary arteries.

Risk factors, such as age, gender, and genetics are fixed and may either compound or reduce various cardiovascular risks. As an example, an older man with a family history of heart disease may have greater cardiovascular and cerebral risks than a younger woman without cardiovascular family incidents.

Ischemic heart disease is characterized by reduced blood supply to the heart due to narrowing of the arteries and less blood and oxygen delivered to the heart muscle. Ischemic heart disease is the most common cause of death in Western countries.

A heart attack is sometimes referred to as a myocardial infarction. It occurs when one or more regions of the heart have severe oxygen debt. This may be the result of blood clots that block the flow of blood through coronary arteries to the heart muscle.

The average age for a first heart attack in the U.S. is 65 years old. However, it has been estimated that four to ten percent of U.S. men aged 45 years or younger experience a heart attack and that **atherosclerosis**, or hardening of the arteries, starts in youth.

The risk factors for heart attacks include age, autoimmune disease, diabetes, family history of heart attack, high blood cholesterol or triglyceride levels, high blood pressure, illegal drug use, lack of physical activity, obesity, preeclampsia, stress, and tobacco use.

A stroke occurs when the blood supply to the brain is either blocked or a blood vessel within the brain ruptures. In either instance, brain tissue may die and brain health may be compromised or this may lead to death.

A stroke is considered a medical emergency and treatment is needed very quickly. It is the fifth leading cause of death in the U.S.

There are three main types of strokes: ischemic, hemorrhagic, and mini-strokes (transient ischemic attacks). An ischemic stroke is the result of an obstruction within a blood vessel that supplies blood to the brain. A hemorrhagic stroke occurs when a weakened blood vessel ruptures. A transient ischemic attack occurs when the blood supply to the brain is briefly blocked.

In comparison to a heart attack, the risks for having a stroke of any kind doubles each decade after the age of 55 years, though strokes may occur at any age. In fact, almost one-fourth of strokes occur in the U.S. to people under 65 years of age, especially when they have risks factors that include alcohol consumption, gender (women more than men), oral contraceptive use, post-menopausal hormone therapy, race (Asian, African American, and Hispanic in particular), tobacco use, and past heart attacks or strokes.

Coconut Consumption

Let's examine populations around the world with higher coconut consumption than in the United States and see what we can learn from these populations in terms of coconuts in history, cardiovascular disease, health, and longevity. There is a rich history of coconut consumption for nutrition, health, and well-being in countries around the world where coconuts have thrived for centuries.

Kitavans

The Kitavans who reside on the Trobriand Islands, Papua New Guinea, consume a significant amount of coconuts and report-edly exhibit excellent health. A subsistence lifestyle is still followed by Kitavan islanders. Dietary staples include coconuts, fish, fruit, and tubers. Stroke and ischemic heart disease appear to be absent in this population.

In a study that was conducted in the 1990s, when the frequencies of aphasia, exertion-related chest pain, hemiparesis, sudden imbalance, or spontaneous sudden death were assessed in Kitavan islanders, no cases that corresponded to angina pectoris, stroke, or sudden death was reported.

Pukapukas and Tokelauans

The Pukapukas and Tokelauans from the southern Pacific Ocean are also sizeable coconut consumers. Over 60 percent of their daily calorie intake is from coconuts and they reportedly have the largest saturated fat consumptions in the world with the absence of heart disease.

The diets of the atoll dwellers near the equator from both Pukapuka and Tokelau are high in saturated fats but low in dietary cholesterol and sucrose. Coconut is the main source of energy for both of these population groups.

A study from the 1980s showed that Tokelauan people acquire a higher percentage of energy (calories) from coconuts than people from Pukapuka: 63 percent compared to 34 percent, with a higher intake of saturated fat. In comparison, the serum cholesterol levels in Tokelauans were 35 to 40 milligrams higher than in the Pukapukans.

The difference in serum cholesterol level was attributed to the higher saturated fat intake of the Tokelauans due to the high lauric acid (12:0) and myristic acid (14:0) content. In both populations vascular disease is uncommon and there is no evidence of high saturated fat intake having detrimental health effects in these populations.

In order to truly understand the cardiovascular and brain benefits that the coconut consumption provides for these indigenous populations, an examination of heart-healthy diets and the heart disease process is warranted.

Heart-Healthy Diets

In the 1950s the connection between saturated fats and cardiovascular disease was widely circulated throughout the U.S. and lower-fat diets were developed and promoted for cardiovascular disease protection.

Then, in the 1980s, the first set of U.S. Dietary Guidelines were established by the Departments of Agriculture (USDA) and Health and Human Services (HHS). These new guidelines recommended that all Americans avoid eating too much total fat, saturated fat, and cholesterol. The U.S. Dietary Guidelines were revised every five years and Americans were advised, among other recommendations, to continue to follow lower total fat, lower saturated fat, and lower cholesterol diets.

In the 1990s, while the recommendtions for dietary fats generally remained the same, the recommendation for dietary carbohydrates instructed that Americans, "Choose a diet with plenty of grain products with vegetables and fruits."

Some dietary fats in foods and beverages were replaced by carbohydrates and often by sugars. This led to recommendations to "Choose a variety of grains daily, especially whole grains; choose a variety of fruits and vegetables daily; choose beverages and foods to moderate your intake of sugars and choose a diet that is low in saturated fat and cholesterol and moderate in total fat."

These guidelines may have been misinterpreted by the U.S. public, who thought that carbohydrates could be freely consumed—as long as they were healthy whole grains. As a result, higher carbohydrate diets were popular at the close of the twentieth century.

Concurrently, fats such as butter and lard were replaced with manufactured margarines, most with trans fatty acids (which have a relationship to increased cardiovascular disease).

In conjunction with these 50 years of U.S. Dietary Guidelines, after peaking around 1968, the age-adjusted rates from cardiovascular disease were reduced in half by the year 2000. Two factors mainly contributed to this reduction: substantial decreases in elevated total cholesterol, high blood pressure, and tobacco use (major cardiovascular risk factors) and new treatments for established cardiovascular disease. These include angioplasty, bypass grafting, stents, enzyme (ACE) inhibitors, statins, and thrombolysis. Deaths from strokes also declined over this same period of time. However, the prevalence of both diabetes and obesity has alarmingly increased.

Today saturated fatty acids, such as those that are found in coconuts, are looked at differently than before for their relationship to cardiovascular disease prevention and health enhancement. An examination of differences among fatty acids helps to sort out which are healthier by today's standards and why and how coconuts fit into the total cardiovascular picture.

Lentil Vegetable Stew

3   **tablespoons coconut oil (refined)**
1   **large onion, coarsely chopped**
1   **can (28 ounces) crushed tomatoes**
2   **cups water**
1   **tablespoon curry powder**
1   **tablespoon cider vinegar**
1½ teaspoons salt
1½ teaspoons ground cumin
1½ teaspoons ground coriander
1   **teaspoon ground ginger**
1¼ cups dried lentils, rinsed
2   **cups cauliflower florets**
1   **cup chopped red bell pepper**
1   **cup chopped yellow squash**

Lentil Vegetable Stew combines coconut oil with cauliflower, onions, red bell pepper, tomatoes, and yellow squash with lentils for a filling, savory, and nourishing soup or entrée.

1. Heat oil in large saucepan over medium heat. Add onion; cook and stir 5 minutes or until softened. Stir in tomatoes, water, curry powder, vinegar, salt, cumin, coriander, and ginger. Stir in lentils; bring to a boil. Reduce heat to medium-low; simmer 35 to 45 minutes or until lentils begin to soften.

2. Add cauliflower, bell pepper, and squash; cook 30 to 40 minutes or until vegetables and lentils are tender.

Makes 8 servings

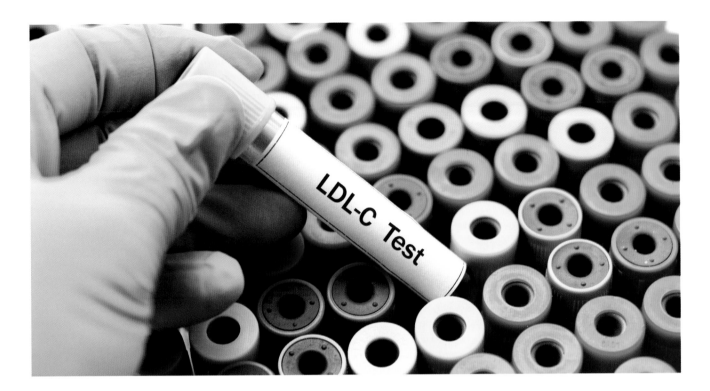

A Fat Primer

Cholesterol is a fatty substance that occurs in only animal foods and products. Organ meats, high-fat dairy products, and some seafood are higher in cholesterol. Cholesterol is a contributing factor in cardiovascular disease, but non-dietary factors may also raise cholesterol and increase one's predisposition to cardiovascular disease. There are primarily three types of serum cholesterol that are considered predictive of cardiovascular disease:

• **High-density lipoproteins (HDL-cholesterol)**: known as the "good cholesterol" because it proportionally carries more protein than cholesterol from the blood to the liver to be recycled or for disposal. HDL-cholesterol is affected more by a person's activity level, gender, obesity, and smoking than diet.

• **Low-density lipoproteins (LDL-cholesterol)**: known as the "bad" cholesterol because it mainly carries cholesterol and is associated with increased risk of cardiovascular disease.

Dietary cholesterol, saturated fat intake, total dietary fat, trans fat, and excess calories are some of the dietary factors that are thought to increase LDL-cholesterol, in addition to the lifestyle factors of obesity, inactivity, and smoking.

• **Very-low density lipoproteins (VLDL-cholesterol)**: is also known as the "bad" cholesterol. It is produced by the liver and released into the blood to supply triglycerides (see below). High VLDL-cholesterol is associated with plaque development on artery walls that narrows and restricts blood flow. By exercising and losing weight and avoiding sugary foods and alcohol, the body's serum (blood) triglyceride level may be decreased.

Lipids are a family of fats, oils, phospholipids (such as lecithin), and sterols (such as cholesterol) that are found in plants or animals, or sometimes both. Cholesterol is only found in animals.

Sometimes lipids are inadvertently called "fats," but they really contain many more substances.

Fats are lipids that are solid at room temperature. Animal fats include bacon, butter, lard, the skin of poultry, and the fat that runs though meats. Generally speaking, the more solid the fat, the more difficult it is for the body to break down.

Hydrogenation is the process of converting unsaturated fatty acids into saturated fatty acids through a method of trans bonds. As a result, these fatty acids are very difficult for the body to break down and they may contribute to cardiovascular disease.

Partially hydrogenated means that some fatty acid bonds are "partially" hydrogenated or filled, which makes them somewhat easier to digest. Instead of risky trans bonds, partially-hydrogenated fatty acids have different linkages, or cis bonds. Some frostings, margarines, and shortenings are all foods with partially-hydrogenated products.

Phospholipids are similar in structure to triglycerides, but they also contain phosphorus. They also provide the major structural components of membranes. Lecithin is a phospholipid that naturally occurs in animals, plants (in soybeans), and eggs, among other foods. Lecithin is used as an emulsifier by the body and by the food industry.

Phospholipids in the form of lecithin are found in egg yolks, liver, peanuts, and wheat germ. They are also found in milk, soybeans, and lightly cooked meats. The human body can synthesize lecithin if there is sufficient choline in the diet from dairy foods, eggs, fish, meats, poultry, pasta, or rice.

Oils are lipids that are liquid at room temperature. They include such oils as avocado, canola, coconut, olive, peanut, and safflower. While coconut oil is semi-solid at room temperature (due to its saturated fat), it is referred to as an oil.

Monounsaturated fatty acids are unsaturated at one point in their fatty acid structures where they can be broken down, so they are considered to be healthier. Monounsaturated fatty acids are primarily found in canola, olive, peanut, safflower, and sesame oils, as well as in avocadoes, peanut butter, and many nuts and seeds.

Essential fatty acids must be consumed by the body and are essential for its normal functioning. There are two essential fatty acids (EFAs) that cannot be synthesized by the body: *linoleic* and *alpha-linolenic*. These must be obtained by food. These two essential fatty acids are used to build omega-3 fatty acid and omega-6 fatty acid, both important in normal body functioning (see below). Salmon, herring, mackerel, hemp, flax, walnuts, almonds, dark leafy green vegetables, olive oil, whole grains, and eggs are good sources of essential fatty acids. The human body can generally produce non-essential fatty acids from other substances.

Omega-3 fatty acids (Omega 3's) are essential fatty acids that are associated with heart health and disease prevention. Omega 3-fatty acids may help to decrease cholesterol and platelet clotting and inflammatory and immune reactions. They are primarily found in chia seeds, fatty fish, fish oil, flaxseeds and flax oil, seafood, soybeans, spinach, and walnuts.

Omega-6 fatty acids (Omega 6's) are essential fatty acids that have a number of body functions. Along with omega-3 fatty acids, omega 6-fatty acids play a critical role in healthly brain function and normal growth and development. While omega-3 fatty acids tend to decrease inflammation, omega-6 fatty acids tend to promote it and may play a role in complex regional pain syndrome.

Ideally the body should have a 1:1 ratio of omega-3 and omega-6 fatty acids from the diet. Omega-6's are found in eggs, cereals, fried foods, meats, poultry, and some vegetable oils, including corn, grape seed, soybean, sunflower, and wheat germ oil.

Phytosterols are plant sterols with structures that are similar to cholesterol and in fact, inhibit the intestinal absorption of cholesterol and serum cholesterol. They have protective and disease-fighting benefits. Foods with the highest concentration of phytosterols include almonds, Brussels sprouts, canola oil, corn oil, macadamia nuts, olive oil, peanuts, rice bran oil, rye bread, sesame oil, wheat bran, and wheat germ.

Saturated fatty acids are fully saturated, which means that their bonds are filled. This feature normally makes them difficult for the body to break down, or metabolize. Generally saturated fatty acids are found in animal foods and beverages; however, coconut and palm oils are noted for their saturated fatty acid content.

Polyunsaturated fatty acids have many bonds that are unsaturated so they can easily be broken down by the body. This is not always a good feature since this may lead to instability, particularly when they are located within cellular membranes. Foods with higher amount of polyunsaturated fats include corn oil, fish (such as albacore tuna, herring, mackerel, salmon, and trout), safflower, soybean, and sunflower oils, and walnuts.

Sterols (also known as steroid alcohols) are a type of steroid that occur naturally in animals (such as cholesterol), fungi, and plants (such as phytosterols that are found in soy foods). Cholesterol is vital to animal cell membranes. It also functions as a precursor for making fat-soluble vitamins (vitamins A, D, E, and K) and steroid hormones. Dietary cholesterol also contributes to increased risks of cardiovascular disease when it is elevated in blood cholesterol. Phytosterols, or plant sterols, have been shown to block cholesterol absorption and help to reduce serum cholesterol.

Trans fatty acids are of two kinds: naturally-occurring and artificial. Naturally occurring trans fatty acids are formed in the gut of some animals and foods (such as milk and meat products). Artificial trans fatty acids are created during industrial processes that add hydrogen using trans bonds to solidify liquid vegetable oils. Trans fatty acids were used in the U.S. because they were easy to use, inexpensive, and long lasting. However, trans fatty acids raise LDL ("bad") cholesterol and lower HLD ("good") cholesterol and increase the risks of developing cardiovascular disease, type 2 diabetes, and stroke. In 2015, the U.S. Food and Drug Administration required that synthetic trans fatty acids be phased out of all foods within three years.

Triglycerides are the main form of lipids that are found in the body and in foods and beverages. Triglycerides are composed of a backbone molecule of glycerol (a sugar alcohol) and three fatty acids that can be saturated, unsaturated, or both. High serum triglycerides are associated with increased risks of cardiovascular disease and strokes and conditions such as hypothyroidism, kidney or liver ailments, metabolic syndrome, obesity, and uncontrolled type 2 diabetes may also be associated with elevated serum triglycerides. By eliminating alcohol, limiting dietary cholesterol and some saturated fats, losing weight, reducing simple carbohydrates, and restricting trans fatty acid intake, the serum triglyceride level may decrease.

Unsaturated fatty acids have one or more of their bonds that are unsaturated, which means that they are not filled. This is generally a good feature since the body can break down and metabolize unsaturated fatty acids more easily. Almonds, avocadoes, flaxseeds, hazelnuts, macadamia nuts, peanut butter, salmon, sardines, seeds, vegetable oils, and walnuts contain unsaturated fatty acids.

How Coconuts Compare

The cardiovascular benefits of coconuts are revealed when each of these fats and oils are compared to the types of fats in coconuts. A comparison of raw coconuts, coconut oil, and coconut water follow:

Cholesterol (high-density or HDL, low-density or LDL, and very-low density or VLDL)

• Since coconuts are from the plant kingdom, raw coconut, coconut oil, and coconut water do not contain any form of cholesterol.

Fats

• One cup of raw coconut contains 26.8 grams of total fat that are mostly saturated (23.8 grams compared to 26.8 grams total).

• One cup of coconut oil contains 218 grams of total fat that are mostly saturated (189 grams compared to 218 grams total).

• One cup of coconut water contains virtually no total fat (0.5 grams per one cup) or saturated fat (0.4 grams per one cup).

Hydrogenation

• Since hydrogenation is a process of converting unsaturated fatty acids into more saturated fatty acids, coconuts in their raw state do not contain hydrogenated fatty acids.

• Hydrogenated coconut oil

- A small portion of the unsaturated fatty acids in coconut oil may be hydrogenated in order to keep the coconut oil solid at higher temperature. Outside of the U.S., hydrogenated and partially hydrogenated coconut oils may be used in the confection industry in baked goods or candies in tropical climates.

Lecithin

• Lecithin may be combined with coconut as an emulsifier; however, coconut oil with its higher concentration of saturated fatty acids is already semi- to fully solidified.

Lipids

• Because lipids are fats and oils, the fats that are found in coconuts are considered lipids.

• Since there is virtually not any total fat or saturated fat in one cup of coconut water, it does not significantly contain any lipids.

Oils

• Coconut oil can be extracted from raw coconut meat. The extraction rate may be as much as 75 percent.

• Coconut oil is in a semi-solid state at room temperature.

Essential fatty acids

• Omega-3 fatty acids

- There are no omega-3 fatty acids in one cup of raw, shredded coconut, one cup of coconut oil, or one cup of coconut water.

• Omega 6 fatty acids

- There are 293 milligrams of omega-6 fatty acids in one cup of raw, shredded coconut.

- There are 3,923 milligrams of omega-6 fatty acids in one cup of coconut oil.

- There are 4.8 milligrams of omega-6 fatty acids in one cup of coconut water.

Phospholipids

• Phospholipids may be present in coconut endosperm and coconut oil.

Sterols

• Phytosterols

- There are 37.6 milligrams of phytosterols in one cup of raw, shredded coconut.

- There are 187 milligrams of phytosterols in one cup of coconut oil.

- There are virtually no phytosterols in one cup of coconut water.

Saturated fatty acids

• The saturated fatty acids in coconuts are lauric (C12), myristic (C14), and stearic (C17).

- There are 23.8 grams of saturated fatty acids in one cup of raw, shredded coconut.

- There are 189 grams of saturated fatty acids in one cup of coconut oil.

- There are virtually no saturated fatty acids (0.4 grams) in one cup of coconut water.

Trans fats

- There are no trans fatty acids in raw coconut, coconut oil, or coconut water.

Trigylcerides

• The saturated fatty acids in coconuts are medium-chain triglycerides that are extracted from coconut meat into coconut oil.

Unsaturated fatty acids

• Monounsaturated fatty acids

- There are 1.1 grams of monounsaturated fatty acids in one cup of raw, shredded coconut.

- There are 12.6 grams of monounsaturated fatty acids in one cup of coconut oil.

- There are virtually zero grams of monounsaturated fatty acids in one cup of coconut water.

• Polyunsaturated fatty acids

- There are 0.3 grams of polyunsaturated fatty acids in one cup of raw, shredded coconut.

- There are 3.9 grams of polyunsaturated fatty acids in one cup of coconut oil.

- There are virtually zero grams of polyunsaturated fatty acids in one cup of coconut water.

Greek Roast Chicken

1 whole roasting chicken (4 to 5 pounds)

3 tablespoons refined coconut oil, divided

2 tablespoons chopped fresh rosemary, plus 2 sprigs

2 cloves garlic, minced

1 small lemon

1¼ teaspoons salt, divided

½ teaspoon black pepper, divided

1 can (about 14 ounces) chicken broth, divided

2 large sweet potatoes, peeled and cut into thick wedges

1 medium red onion, cut into ¼-inch wedges

1 pound fresh asparagus spears, trimmed

> Greek Roast Chicken uses coconut oil for basting whole chicken, with garlic and herbs, red onions, and sweet potatoes for a flavorsome and wholesome roasted entrée that's equally delicious cold.

1. Preheat oven to 425°F. Place chicken, breast side up, in shallow roasting pan. Combine 2 tablespoons oil, chopped rosemary, and garlic in small bowl; brush over chicken.

2. Grate 1 teaspoon peel from lemon; set aside. Cut lemon into quarters; squeeze juice over chicken and place rinds and rosemary sprigs in chicken cavity. Sprinkle ¾ teaspoon salt and ¼ teaspoon pepper over chicken. Pour 1 cup broth into bottom of roasting pan; roast 30 minutes.

3. Reduce oven temperature to 375°F. Arrange sweet potatoes and onion wedges around chicken. Drizzle remaining broth and 1 tablespoon oil over vegetables; roast 15 minutes.

4. Arrange asparagus spears in roasting pan. Sprinkle remaining ½ teaspoon salt and ¼ teaspoon pepper over vegetables. Roast 10 minutes or until chicken is cooked through (165°F) and vegetables are tender. Transfer chicken to cutting board. Tent with foil; let stand 10 to 15 minutes.

5. Sprinkle reserved lemon peel over chicken. Carve chicken and serve with vegetables and pan juices.

Makes 8 servings

Fat to Fight Fat?

Coconut, even with its high total fat and saturated fat content, has actually been shown to help aid weight loss. In this chapter the various ways that the coconut may contribute to the fight against body fat are discussed in depth.

For example, the medium-chain triglycerides (MCTs) in coconut oil may actually help to *burn* body fat and boost metabolism. Coconut has been thought to help metabolize abdominal fat. This is especially encouraging since excess abdominal fat is a known risk for heart disease and diabetes among other health conditions.

While the fat in coconut may help weight loss, it is important to recognize that it has the same number of calories per gram (9 calories/gram) as any other dietary fat, so coconut still should be consumed in moderation. Yet there are still smart ways to incorporate coconuts into healthy diets without being too excessive.

Using coconut oil for cooking instead of canola or olive oil may result in a *thermogenic effect* within the body, which means that it may help increase metabolism and in turn, increase energy. While this amount of energy may be low, it still adds up. Even more, eating coconut can lead to feelings of satiety and reduced appetite. This may result in fewer calories consumed overall.

This chapter also touches on some of the properties of coconut water. Unlike coconut oil, coconut water is virtually fat-free; it's also low in calories and contains nutrients such as vitamin C and potassium. Coconut water can be used for hydration, especially in place of sugary sports drinks or soft drinks, which is very helpful when people try to lose weight healthfully.

Energy

Energy is the ability to do work. It is measured in *calories*. A *calorie* is a unit of energy that often refers to the calorie content of foods and beverages. A calorie produces heat—in fact, a calorie is defined as the amount of heat that is required to raise the temperature of one kilogram of water one degree Centigrade. In the human body, the process of burning calories to produce energy (and heat) increases one's metabolism.

Metabolism is the sum of all of the chemical and physical processes by which energy is created and made available for life. There are many factors that are involved in metabolism and whether a person metabolizes or burns food and beverages quickly or slowly.

Factors that lower metabolism include age, fasting, hormones, sleep, and starvation. As a person ages their metabolism slows down, as it does with severe dieting. Hormones produced by the thyroid gland may either increase or decrease metabolism. And too much sleep means that the body is less active; thus, metabolism may be slower while a person is sleeping.

Factors that raise metabolism include caffeine, fever, gender (male), growth, height, lean body mass, nicotine, and stress. When a person is young, their metabolism is generally high. Gender-wise, taller and more muscular men tend to have a higher metabolism than shorter, rounder women.

Energy-producing nutrients (carbohydrates, lipids, and proteins) also affect metabolism; their effect depends on whether or not they are consumed and in what forms and combinations. As a type of lipid with very distinctive properties, coconut oil and its metabolism into energy can actually contribute to fat loss if used properly. However, do keep in mind that consuming any nutrient in excess may lead to weight gain.

Calories from Nutrients

The energy-producing nutrients each provide a distinct number of calories per gram when they are metabolized. Carbohydrates (sugars and starches) and proteins each yield about four calories per gram (4 calories/gram) while fats and oils each yield about nine calories per gram (9 calories/gram)—about twice as much as carbohydrates or proteins. This is why fats and oils are considered to be so caloric and "fattening."

Weight Loss Strategies

In order to lose weight, a person needs to eat and drink less, exercise more, or some combination of both of these approaches. There must be a caloric deficit for weight loss. Conversely, if more calories are consumed rather than expended, weight will probably be gained.

There are many dietary strategies to accomplish weight loss including gluten-free, high-carbohydrate, high-fiber, high-protein, low-calorie, low-carbohydrate, and countless other approaches, programs, products, and potions. The use of coconut oil with its medium-chain triglycerides may have advantages. To understand how the medium-chain triglycerides that are found in coconuts contribute to weight loss, one must first understand more about fat digestion and metabolism.

Fat Digestion and Metabolism

The digestion of *lipids* (fats and oils) first begins in the mouth, where it is mostly physical. The teeth tear apart fat from other foods and the mouth begins to melt some of the fats. Then the residue passes through the esophagus into the stomach where it is mixed with stomach acid and water and some fat is broken down by the acid.

The process of breaking down lipids into its components of *triglycerides* with their fatty acids and *glycerol* is slow. Since lipids have so many calories per gram, they tend to stay around the stomach longer and may lead to satiety or fullness.

Once the triglyceride remnants pass into the small intestine, the smallest fatty acids (or short-chain fatty acids) and glycerol are able to pass through the intestinal wall into the bloodstream where they are transported to the liver, stored, or converted into other substances.

Longer-chain triglycerides (LCTs) are broken down by bile in the small intestine. *Bile* is an emulsifier that is made in the liver and stored in the gallbladder. It mixes with lipids along with watery digestive secretions and readies the lipids for additional breakdown by intestinal enzymes.

Medium-chain triglycerides (MCTs) have a different fate. For one, they are more easily metabolized than longer-chain triglycerides and may help to burn calories and support weight loss. Medium-chain triglycerides passively diffuse from the gastrointestinal (GI) tract through the portal system to the liver without needing to be broken down, nor the necessity for bile salts for their digestion.

Alcohol, while not a nutrient, contains seven calories per gram (7 calories/gram) and is metabolized as a fat, which is why regular alcohol consumption may also contribute to weight gain.

Medium-chain triglycerides either do not affect total cholesterol nor raise HDL cholesterol and they may also improve the ratio of LDL to HDL-cholesterol (LDL:HDL). Medium-chain triglycerides are also thought to promote quick fat oxidation. This is why some endurance athletes and bodybuilders seem to favor MCTs. However, claims and conclusive results about their effectiveness seem to be mixed.

Besides all of these applications, medium-chain triglycerides may also have the potential to promote weight loss by increasing the metabolism. To fully comprehend why, an understanding of ketosis, particularly for weight loss, is essential.

Ketosis for Weight Loss

Ketogenic diets have been used for fast (and in some cases continued) weight loss for centuries. Ketogenic diets are also said to show promising results for epilepsy and neurodegenerative disorders, such as Alzheimer's and Parkinson's diseases, as discussed in chapter 6.

First of all, let's answer a basic question: what is ketosis? Normally the human body uses glucose for energy. *Glucose* is a simple sugar that is the building block of carbohydrates (sugars and starches). When the human body metabolizes carbohydrates, they break down into glucose that can be used for energy or stored for future energy needs. Consuming too many carbohydrates may lead to excess calories and this may progress to obesity.

When glucose is not available for energy, the human body turns to an "intermediary" state for its energy needs. This is called *ketosis* when the human body produces *ketones*, by-products that form when the body burns stored fat for energy.

Some higher-protein and fat and lower-carbohydrate diets rely upon ketosis for fat loss and decreased body weight. Long term and uncontrolled, ketosis may develop into a state called *acidosis* that may lead to coma or even death. Ketosis may also occur during prolonged starvation.

To comprehend why ketogenic diets work and how medium-chain triglycerides interplay, one must first understand the process of *lipolysis*. Like glycolysis and the breakdown of carbohydrates to produce energy, lipolysis is the breakdown of lipids to produce energy.

When the body needs energy and it calls upon its stored carbohydrates, it may also call upon its lipid stores within its cells—particularly when carbohydrates "run out" as in prolonged starvation or long-term exercise. Enzymes break down stored lipids; then fatty acids and glycerol (from triglycerides) are released into the blood stream. When these fatty acids reach the muscle cells they enter *mitochondria* of the cell, or the cell's powerhouse and energy is released.

As mentioned, lipids have the capacity of supplying twice the amount of energy than carbohydrates or protein (9 calories/gram compared to 4 calories/gram respectively). This is the reason why fats and oils are so calorie dense and also why ketogenic diets may lead to faster weight loss than simple calorie reduction or some other carbohydrate-based diets.

Coconut Shrimp with Pear Chutney

½   **cup shredded unsweetened coconut**

¾   **teaspoon curry powder**

½   **teaspoon salt**

3   **tablespoons coconut oil or melted unsalted butter**

1   **pound large raw shrimp, peeled and deveined**

    Pear Chutney (recipe follows)

1. Prepare Pear Chutney; set aside. Preheat oven to 425°F. Spray baking sheet with non-stick cooking spray.

2. Combine coconut, curry powder, and salt in shallow dish. Toss shrimp with oil or melted butter to coat. Dip shrimp in coconut mixture, pressing lightly to adhere. Place on prepared baking sheet.

3. Bake 4 minutes. Turn over; bake 2 minutes or until shrimp are pink and opaque. Serve with Pear Chutney (recipe in next column).

Makes 4 servings

1   **tablespoon coconut oil**

1   **jalapeño pepper*, seeded and minced**

1   **small shallot, minced**

1   **teaspoon grated fresh ginger**

1   **medium unpeeled ripe pear, cored and cut into ½-inch pieces**

2   **teaspoons cider vinegar**

1   **teaspoon packed brown sugar**

⅛   **teaspoon salt**

1   **tablespoon water, plus more if necessary**

1   **tablespoon chopped green onion**

*Jalapeño peppers can sting and irritate the skin, so wear rubber gloves when handling peppers and do not touch your eyes.

1. Heat oil in medium saucepan over low heat. Add jalapeño, shallot, and ginger; cook and stir 3 minutes or until shallot is tender.

2. Add pear, vinegar, brown sugar, and salt. Stir in water. Cover and cook over low heat 15 minutes or until pear is tender, adding additional 1 tablespoon water if mixture becomes dry. Stir in green onion; cook 1 minute. Cool completely.

Makes 2 cups

Medium-Chain Triglycerides and Weight Loss

The saturated fatty acids that are found in coconut oil with their medium-chain triglycerides are shorter in length than longer-chain triglycerides and they are more water-soluble than some other oils. The body processes these medium-chain triglycerides differently than longer-chain triglycerides. Longer-chain triglycerides must be mixed with a substance called *bile* that is produced by the gallbladder and then assaulted by pancreatic enzymes. Medium-chain triglycerides do not require bile or pancreatic enzymes, so once they reach the small intestine they diffuse through its membrane into the bloodstream where they are more directly routed to the liver, converted into ketones, and metabolized as fuel.

The liver also releases ketones back into the blood stream where they are carried throughout the body. In this manner, ketones may be used for energy by the brain. This is significant since the brain has a protective barrier called the "*blood-brain barrier*" that these ketones can cross.

As a result, ketones have fewer tendencies to be deposited in fat stores and more opportunities to be metabolized by the body for various purposes. Additionally, medium-chain triglycerides provide antioxidant, anti-inflammatory, and even anti-microbial functions inside the gut where they fight potentially harmful bacteria, fungi, parasites, and viruses.

Medium-Chain Triglyceride Structures

Medium-chain triglycerides are distinguished by their carbon lengths:

• Caproic acid (C6) – 6 carbons

• Caprylic acid (C8) – 8 carbons

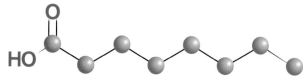

• Capric acid (C10) – 10 carbons

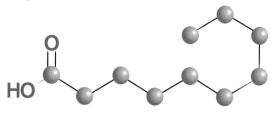

• Lauric acid (C12) – 12 carbons

In general, the fewer number of carbon molecules, the shorter the chain and the easier and more efficiently that medium-chain triglycerides will be converted into ketones for energy with less reactive oxygen that may be damaging to the body.

Coconut oil has a mixture of medium-chain fatty acids, with about 40 percent of it as *lauric acid*.

Some studies suggest that coconut oil with its medium-chain triglycerides and particularly lauric acid may help to reduce one's midsection, but that it may not contribute to improved body mass index (BMI) or significant weight loss.

The ketones also help to control the hormone *ghrelin*, the "hunger" hormone that is produced in the gastrointestinal tract. Ghrelin functions within the central nervous system to increase appetite. *Leptin*, the appetite "suppressor" hormone, controls ketone utilization in the neurons of the *hypothalamus* (the hunger control center of the brain) that helps to decreases one's appetite.

> The body mass index (BMI) is a ratio of weight-to-height that is used to indicate obesity and underweight.

Medium-Chain Triglycerides and Weight

It is known that medium-chain triglycerides may boost *thermogenesis* (heat production) and fat oxidation for energy and that both of these processes may suppress the accumulation of body fat. Another way that medium-chain triglycerides may help with weight loss efforts is by helping with appetite reduction.

Consuming foods and beverages with fat may turn off a desire to eat more calories because fats provide such concentrated calories. Even a little bit of fat that is consumed at meals has staying power.

There is also some speculation that medium-chain triglycerides act on other hormones that may include cholecystokinin, gastric inhibitory peptide, neurotensin, pancreatic polypeptide, and/or peptide YY. The exact modes of operation are unknown. However, it is speculated that these actions may help to decrease appetite and increase satiety.

Coconut Oil and Calories

One tablespoon of coconut oil contains approximately 121 calories. Coconut oil is pretty similar in calories when compared to other oils. In comparison, one tablespoon of the following oils contain:

Type of oil	Calories per 1 Tablespoon
Almond oil	119
Avocado oil	124
Canola oil	124
Corn oil	124
Cottonseed oil	119
Extra-virgin olive oil	120
Flaxseed oil	119
Grapeseed oil	119
Hazelnut oil	119
Hemp seed oil	130
Macadamia oil	120
Olive oil	119
Palm oil	119
Palm kernel oil	116
Peanut oil	119
Safflower oil	119
Sesame oil	119
Soybean oil	119
Sunflower oil	119
Vegetable oil	120
Walnut oil	119
Wheat germ oil	119

It is important to keep in mind that one table-spoon of coconut oil contains about 13.47 grams of total fat (almost all fat). So coconut oil is very calorie-dense, even in smaller quantities. While the medium-chain triglycerides in coconut oil do pass through the digestion, absorption, and metabolism quicker than other oils and fats, consuming too much coconut oil or other oil may lead to extra calories.

Use of Medium-Chain Triglycerides by Endurance Athletes

Coconut oil has been valued for its relationship to weight and energy expenditure among endurance athletes. Coconut oil supplies energy; it has the capability to support fitness since it may boost energy, enhance performance, and support endurance. Also, coconut oil may improve the digestion and absorption of nutrients—especially those that require a little fat for their digestion and assimilation. And coconut oil is thought to assist in blood sugar utilization and insulin secretion. Suggested dosages vary.

Since medium-chain triglycerides are digested easier than longer triglycerides, the thought is that they may help to increase energy metabolism during both medium and high-intensity exercise. Medium-chain triglycerides helped to reduce the body's reliance on carbohydrates as a fuel for exercise and decrease the amount of *lactate* that is produced during exercise that may lead to increased endurance.

High lactate levels increase the acidity of the muscle cells and disrupt other metabolites. Metabolic pathways perform poorly within this type of acidic environment. This is a natural defense mechanism of the body to help prevent permanent damage during extreme exertion by slowing down key systems to help maintain muscle contraction. Then oxygen becomes more available and metabolism can continue for energy and recovery from strenuous exercise. Medium-chain triglycerides may help to prevent or reduce these processes from occurring.

Disadvantages of Medium-Chain Triglycerides

Medium-chain triglycerides may induce *ketogenesis* (the release of ketones by the body when fats are broken down for energy) and *metabolic acidosis* (a condition that occurs when the body produces too much acid or when the kidneys are not removing enough acid from the body). Under certain conditions, ketogenesis may be desirable. However, metabolic acidosis may lead to shock or death.

If medium-chain triglycerides are consumed in high quantities they may provoke gastrointestinal side effects including loose stools.

Coconut Water, Weight, and Sports Performance

Coconut water is virtually fat-free and low in calories with some nutrients including vitamin C and potassium. It can be used for hydration to replace sugary sports drinks or soft drinks, which is important for people who try to lose weight and for athletes to remain healthy while they train and compete.

A comparison of water, coconut water, sports drinks, and soft drinks shows the advantages and disadvantages of these fluids.

Water is a fluid of choice for everyday consumption and for everyday exercise. For exercise that is greater in duration or intensity, or for exercisers who heavily perspire, some fluids may be better for hydration. Some brands of sports drinks and coconut water with potassium may be effective for muscle cramps.

Coconut water is also a natural way to add potassium, hydrate, and reduce sodium in everyday diets that rely upon sports drinks as regular beverages. This is because coconut water has fewer calories and less sodium than some sports drinks. Also, many Americans do not obtain enough potassium in their daily diets from dairy products or fresh fruits and vegetables, so coconut water may help to provide some needed nutrients.

Some athletes may choose to drink coconut water the evening before an intense workout or event—especially during difficult heat conditions.

When a person exercises strenuously in excess of three hours (as the time expended in a marathon) and they sweat heavily, they will probably need easily absorbable carbo-hydrates for energy (such as the sugar that is found in sports drinks), as well as electro-lytes such as potassium and sodium. This is why unsweetened coconut water may be limiting in its use for hydration and sports drinks may be more satisfying and hydrating under extreme conditions.

An option during hot weather events or practice might be to mix coconut water with a little salt. Coconut water with added sodium may be better tolerated than some sports drinks post-exercise and may not cause as much fullness, stomach upset, or nausea as some report.

One concern about the use of coconut water for exercise is whether or not the amount of coconut water consumed replenishes what the body loses during exercise. A simple test is the color of urine that should be clear. It is important to note that taste matters when it comes to replacing body fluids. So if athletes enjoy the taste of coconut water and are able to consume coconut water in adequate amounts, then it might be more efficient for hydration than water.

Coconut water may be combined with protein powder to help the muscles recover after an event or heavy workout. In either case, the use of coconut water before, during, or after heavy exercise or under extreme conditions should first be tested during practice. Athletic trainers and coaches may also provide advice.

Comparison of Calories

A comparison of calories, carbohydrates, fat, and protein in water, coconut water, sports drinks, fruit juice, and cola follow:

- **Tap and non-mineralized water (per 1 fluid ounce)**

    - Zero calories, zero carbohydrates, zero fat, zero protein

- **Unflavored coconut water (per 1 fluid ounce)**

    - 5.45 calories, 1.3 grams sugar, 61 milligrams (mg) potassium, 5.45 milligrams (mg) sodium

- **Sports drinks (per 1 fluid ounce)**

    - 6.25 calories, 1.75 grams sugar, 3.75 milligrams (mg) potassium, 13.75 milligrams (mg) sodium

- **Fruit juice (per 1 fluid ounce)**

    - 3.9 calories, 2.6 grams sugar, 62 milligrams (mg) potassium, 0.3 milligrams (mg) sodium

- **Cola (per 1 fluid ounce)**

    - 11.3 calories, 2.7 grams sugar, 0.6 milligrams (mg) potassium, 1.2 milligrams (mg) sodium

Coconut Water for Weight Management

Consuming a liquid before a meal may cause one to eat less. This is the theory behind a "slow-up liquid." A slow-up liquid can be sipped before a meal, with or without ice and a flavorful herb or fruit slice to boost the flavor.

Try coconut water with a sprig of basil, mint, or parsley or a spear of cucumber, jicama, or fennel. The calories are fairly negligible. It may seem and look like a cocktail, refresh, and help to mitigate the ravishing feeling some may feel right before a meal.

To add the flavor of coconut water to beverages without packing on calories, try freezing coconut water in an ice cube tray, then adding a few cubes to perk up the flavor of ordinary water. The taste will be appealing without overwhelming and may be enjoyed by those who do not enjoy a stronger coconut taste.

For those people who can afford more calories, but prefer to avoid commercial sports drinks, mixing one-half coconut water with one-half fruit juice provides a fuller fruit taste with half of the calories than a full glass of fruit juice. Plus, there is more potassium along with varying amounts of choline, folate, vitamins A, C, calcium, magnesium, and phosphorus depending upon the type of coconut water that is used.

Coconut water also has many applications in cooking and baking. It can be used in some recipes in place of a few teaspoons of water, but keep in mind its sweet taste. In some recipes, coconut water will enhance the sweetness. In other recipes, it may quash the bitterness. And in other recipes, the sweet taste might be tamed by a touch of salt, which may even taste tropical.

Speaking of the tropics, coconut water may be an excellent addition to some Asian or Caribbean recipes because of its natural affinity to the tropical fruits and vegetables in these recipes, but it may also lend a sweet and tasty touch to marinades, sauces, or even soups. It contributes the coconutty taste without the heaviness of coconut oil. In addition, coconut water can be used in some recipes along with coconut oil and even grated coconut.

Coconut Melon Water Smoothie

6   **ounces frozen coconut water (about 6 ice cubes made from coconut water)***

1   **cup cubed melon (cantaloupe, honeydew, or watermelon)**

1   **tablespoon citrus zest (lemon, lime, or orange)**

Mint leaf, to garnish

*Coconut water can be frozen in an ice cube tray. This recipe requires about six coconut water ice cubes; however size and number may vary depending upon the ice cube tray.

1. Combine the first three ingredients into a blender.

2. Blend until smooth, frothy consistency.

3. Garnish with mint, if desired. If a minty flavor preferred, mint leaf can be blended with other ingredients.

Makes about 1⅔ cups, depending upon the size of the ice cubes

> A little bit of natural fruit or vegetable juice can be added to coconut water for additional color, taste, natural sugar, and some vitamins and minerals.

Use Your Brain

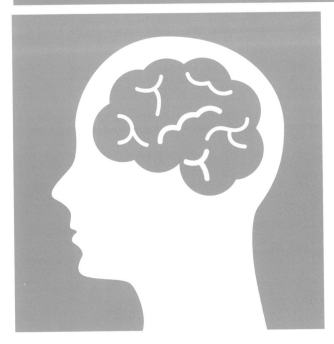

Some of the more interesting research that surrounds the healing power of coconut involves the possible links between coconut oil and decreased dementia and epilepsy. Much of this research surrounds the ketogenic diet: a diet that higher in fat and lower in carbohydrates than is generally recommended, which forces the body to burn fat for fuel.

This chapter describes the ketogenic diet in detail, how coconuts may fit into ketogenic diets, and why ketogenic diets may be beneficial for certain disorders. For example, the ketogenic diet has been shown to be effective at reducing seizures in children with epilepsy. This discovery has led scientists to theorize that coconut oil may be useful for people with Alzheimer's disease and dementia.

This chapter also describes methods by which the coconut may prevent general aging in the brain and help improve memory.

Ketogenic Diets

The *ketogenic diet* has been used for a variety of disorders since the 1920s when it was designed by Dr. Russell Wilder at the Mayo Clinic in Rochester, Minnesota, as a treatment for epilepsy. After anti-seizure medications came to the forefront in the 1940s, the ketogenic diet somewhat lost its appeal. While low-carbohydrate, ketogenic-like diets have a long history, they became popularized in the U.S. in the late 1960s to early 1970s when the Stillman and Atkins diets first became popular. Their premise is pretty much the same: the process of ketosis could effectively be employed for weight loss.

The premise of ketogenic diets is that with higher-fat, adequate protein, and low carbohydrates the body is forced into "burning" its stored body fats for energy rather than carbohydrates, the preferred energy source.

Under "normal" conditions, the human body digests and metabolizes the carbohydrates that are contained in foods and beverages and converts them into glucose for energy. Glucose is then transported to many various body cells and also fuels the brain.

When there are few carbohydrates available, then the liver is capable of converting fat into fatty acids and *ketone bodies*, molecules that can also be oxidized for energy. These ketones bodies can then pass through the *brain barrier* (a highly selective semipermeable membrane that protects the brain) and replace glucose as a source of energy. When ketones are elevated in the blood it may result in a state of ketosis that has both advantages and disadvantages.

The advantages of ketosis are that it can be used as a medical intervention for diabetes or epilepsy, endurance exercise, or significant weight loss. Ketogenic diets may reduce hunger and lower overall food intake that may be particularly effective in treating the severely obese.

The disadvantages of ketosis are that it may alter blood lipid levels (both positively and negatively), lead to fatigue, stress the kidneys, trigger micronutrient deficiencies, and instigate ketoacidosis, which could be fatal at extremes for diabetics.

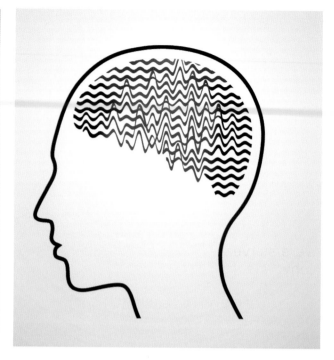

Epilepsy

Fasting to treat disease has been a topic of discourse since ancient Greek and Indian physicians utilized it in their practices. An early treatise in the Hippocratic Corpus "On the Sacred Disease" (supposedly written in 400 BC) describes how dietary alterations may affect epilepsy management—particularly in the abstinence of food and drink.

The first study that examined fasting as an epileptic treatment occurred in France in 1911. Patients were placed on a low-calorie vegetarian diet instead of receiving the treatment of the time, potassium bromide. While potassium bromide curbed the epileptic seizures it also reportedly lowered the mental capacity of the study subjects. The diet plus fasting led to improved mental capabilities.

Three main ketone bodies were at the forefront of diabetes research in the 1920s. When otherwise healthy people were starved or consumed a very low-carbohydrate, high-fat diet, then a higher level of these ketone bodies were produced. This higher level of serum (blood) ketones is referred to as *ketonemia*.

Subsequently, anticonvulsant treatments were used to treat epilepsy. Still, epileptic control was not fully achieved. The ketogenic diet was later reintroduced as a therapy to treat children with epilepsy. After an 18 to 25 day fast some children became seizure free; others showed some improvement, while still other children demonstrated the most success on what was referred to as a "water diet." The idea of fasting subsequently became a conventional treatment for epilepsy along with abiding by dietary carbohydrate restriction.

> Because of the potential dangers of it, any use of ketogenic diets, particularly for children, should first be reviewed with a health care practitioner.

Weight Loss

The use of ketone bodies has also been used for dieting nearly as long as they have been used to treat epilepsy.

In the 1920s, an endocrinologist detected that ketone bodies, produced by the liver as a side effect of fasting or a diet that was high in fat and low in carbohydrates, were effective for weight loss. This type of dietary approach became known as the low-carbohydrate/ketogenic diet. It has had many guises throughout the years. Some of the books that recommended it included the 1958 book *Eat Fat and Grow Slim* by Dr. Richard Mackarness; the 1967 book *The Doctor's Quick Weight Loss Diet* by Dr. Irwin Stillman; and the 1972 book *Dr. Atkins Diet Revolution*.

Ketogenic diets may contain 70 percent or more daily calories from fat; five to 10 percent of total daily calories from carbohydrates (about 20 to 50 grams daily); and the remaining calories from proteins. Some more conservative dietary approaches are higher in carbohydrates (45 to 65 percent of total calories), lower in fat (20 to 35 percent of total calories), and moderate in protein (10 to 35 percent of total calories). Since 1980 and every five years thereafter, the U.S. Dietary Guidelines for Americans were published with renditions of these dietary approaches, which are now less specific in nature.

In order to adhere to a ketogenic diet with these nutritional parameters, one needs to greatly reduce or eliminate carbohydrate-containing foods such as dairy products, fruit, grains, legumes, and starchy vegetables. High protein foods such as eggs, fish, shellfish, meats, and poultry are the mainstays with very-low calorie vegetables as fillers. Fats as butter and oils are also featured. Alcohol is not included.

Some studies show that weight loss may be greater on a ketogenic diet than on a diet that is simply reduced in calories. Other studies indicate that the average weight loss after one year on a ketogenic diet may be greater than a low-fat diet and that serum triglycerides and blood pressure may decrease while high-density lipoproteins (HDL or "good" cholesterol) may increase. Even if weight loss stabilizes, after a few years high-density lipoproteins may continue to improve on a ketogenic diet. Like many diets, weight loss slows as a result of the body acclimating to its dietary parameters.

The later Zone, Paleo, and Dukan diets base their diet strategies and successes on the fundamentals of ketosis.

Blackberry Lime Smoothie

½	cup unsweetened coconut milk
1	cup fresh blackberries
2	ice cubes
1	tablespoon fresh lime juice
2	teaspoons honey
½	teaspoon grated lime peel

Combine coconut milk, blackberries, ice, lime juice, honey, and lime peel in blender; blend until smooth. Serve immediately.

Blackberry Lime Smoothie is a super purple blend of coconut milk, blackberries, ice cubes, fresh lime juice, honey, and grated lime peel. Blackberries are good sources of vitamins A, C, and K, the antioxidants lutein and zeaxanthin, minerals that include copper, folic acid, magnesium, manganese, niacin, potassium, pantothenic acid, pyridoxine, riboflavin, and insoluble and soluble fibers. And the coconut milk and lime create a refreshing and nutritious tropical snack treat.

Positive Aspects of Ketogenic Diets

Meat has been a significant foundation of the U.S. diet, especially post World War II when it has been associated with prosperity. Aside from economics, meat is very satisfying with its fat content and robust taste. It has a very primeval appeal since its protein content is essential for life. Both prehistoric and modern people have sought meat for its amino acids—the staff of life. The ketogenic diet, with its high reliance on meat, is no exception.

In terms of the high fat content of ketogenic diets, fat is a concentrated source of energy with nine calories per gram. Prehistoric people were forced to eat when food was abundant and few parts of animals were left behind. Fat provided the staying power for days at end until the next capture or catch. In modern times fat still is very satisfying for hours on end—sometimes up to nine hours. Satiety from fat may prevent people from scrounging around for sugar- and calorie-filled foods and beverages.

Calorie counting (and often portion control) is not required in some ketogenic diets. This aspect may be very appealing to people who do not have the time nor the interest in doing it.

Perhaps one of the most important features of ketogenic diets is the lack of hunger. This is because ketone bodies tend to lower the level of *ghrelin* in the body. Ghrelin is a hormone that decreases hunger and promotes satiety. This is especially important between meals to help to manage appetite control.

The weight loss on a ketogenic diet may be more rapid than in a reduced-calorie or reduced-fat diet. This phenomenon may be very appealing to dieters because initial weight loss may be very motivational to continue dieting. When carbohydrates are limited as they are on a ketogenic diet, the body turns to its carbohydrates stores in the muscles and to liver glycogen. The initial weight loss on a ketogenic diet tends to be mostly water weight because when stored carbohydrates are broken down for

> Per person, U.S. residents consume more meat than in any other country worldwide.

energy, water is also released (glycogen is stored with water). After about two to three weeks of dieting, this water loss diminishes and fat loss increases, particularly when the diet is accompanied by exercise.

Protein, too, can be used for energy, but this is not the preferred fuel. The muscles, including the heart, are made of protein and these stores must be preserved. This is another benefit of ketogenic diets: most provide more than enough protein to help to "spare" the body's protein stores from use.

Another advantage of a ketogenic diet is its capability of improving serum triglyceride and high-density lipoproteins and potentially lowering the risk of cardiovascular disease. Diets of this nature are also capable of lowering the tendencies for elevated blood sugar, *C-reactive protein* (which is a sign of inflammation and a marker for certain degenerative diseases), insulin, and waist circumference.

Problems with Ketogenic Diets

Eating the same high fat and high protein foods and beverages day in and day out over time may become boring (like so many other diets), which may cause backsliding over time. Other criticisms of the ketogenic diet are that it narrows food choices, compromises nutrient intake, makes it difficult to eat out or socialize since alcohol and many desserts are prohibited, and may even lead to digestive issues.

Since the ketogenic diet is limited or void of carbohydrates with fibers (even fruits, vegetables, and whole grains), normal digestion and elimination might be compromised and a natural fiber supplement may be warranted.

Caution: Higher protein stores may tax the kidneys and the liver that are involved in processing and excreting the by-products of protein breakdown: urea, uric acid, ammonia.

Nutrient deficiencies may also be a concern on a ketogenic diet. Nutrients such as vitamins A, C, D, and thiamine, and minerals such as calcium, magnesium, and selenium may be lacking and might require supplementation. A health professional should be consulted before trying any diet—particularly one long term. Children, pregnant and nursing mothers, and the elderly should take special care and caution.

Coconuts and Ketogenic Diets

Research on ketogenic diets from the 1960s demonstrated that more ketones are produced by medium-chain triglycerides (MCTs) per unit of energy than other sources of energy. This is because medium-chain triglycerides are quickly transported to the liver via the hepatic portal vein as opposed to through the lymphatic system.

It is important to keep the gastrointestinal tract and especially the colon healthy to protect against certain GI diseases and particularly against colon cancer.

It follows that if a diet that is rich in medium-chain triglycerides but reduced in carbohydrates, then it might be effective in treating epilepsy and in weight control management. In fact, a diet with 60 percent medium-chain triglycerides with protein and some carbohydrates has been shown to provide more meal options for children with epilepsy. Dieters may also be able to tolerate fewer carbohydrates without boredom if a little variety is provided.

Coconut to the rescue! The range and depth of recipes and meals with coconut in all of its forms are mind boggling, but for ketogenic diets, coconut oil with its high medium-chain triglycerides are key. Some recommendations suggest taking one to three tablespoons of coconut oil or MCT oil that is made from coconut oil daily. But this practice should support a ketonic diet, not replace it.

The Aging Brain

The brain ages like all bodily systems, organs, muscles, nerves, and cells. Specific changes in the brain due to aging include changes in blood vessels, free radicals, inflammation, neurons and neurotransmitters, plaques, and tangles and shrinkage.

Blood vessels in the brain may be compromised because arteries narrow with aging and there is less growth of new capillaries that occur. This may result in less blood being able to circulate and nourish the brain.

Free radical damage from cigarette smoke, herbicides, pollution, radiation, and a host of other environmental factors may accumulate with age. Free radicals are normally made in the mitochondria inside cells. They help the body's immune system to fight bacteria and viruses. However, free radicals may also damage the cell membranes of neurons or their DNA. This may instigate a chain reaction that releases more free radicals and cause further neurological damage.

Cells and compounds that are known to be involved in inflammation have been located in Alzheimer's disease plaques, so it is thought that inflammation may have a role in the disease. Inflammation increases when the body responds to abnormal situations, disease, injuries, or even stress.

Other changes in the brain are the result of changes in the neurons and neurotransmitters that are responsible for communications among neurons. If and when the white matter of the brain is reduced, then communication among neurons may be compromised.

> Keep in mind that each tablespoon of coconut oil contains about 117 calories and MCT oil about 100 calories, and while calories do not necessarily need to be counted on a ketogenic diet, they may add up substantially.

Structures referred to as *amyloid plaques* and *neurofibrillary tangles* develop both inside and outside of the neurons. *Amyloid plaques* contain largely insoluble deposits of seemingly toxic protein fragments. It is not conclusive whether these plaques cause Alzheimer's disease or whether they are by-products of the disease.

Neurofibrillary tangles are abnormal collections of twisted protein threads within the nerve cells that contain phosphate molecules. These threads may become so enmeshed that they may become tangled within the cells, disrupt the healthy neuron transport network, and damage neuron communication.

Decreased brain glucose metabolism has been identified before the onset of clinically measurable cognitive decline and may contribute to further cascading decline. The process of aging appears to increase the risks of deteriorating glucose utilization in some regions of the brain.

Different parts of the brain actually shrink during aging, particularly the prefrontal cortex at the front of the frontal lobe and the hippocampus. Both are vital to complex mental activities including learning, memory, and planning.

Alzheimer's Disease

Alzheimer's disease (AD) is a progressive neurodegenerative disorder that primarily affects the elderly, but can impact earlier in life. There are two types of Alzheimer's disease: *early* and *late-onset*. Early onset Alzheimer's disease may strike a person as early as their 30s, while late onset Alzheimer's disease may strike a person in their 70s or 80s and is the leading cause of dementia in people over 65 years of age. At the onset, people might experience memory loss and disorientation. As the disease progresses, additional cognitive functions may become impaired.

While there are theories that try to describe the course of the events that lead to Alzheimer's disease, the complete picture remain unknown. There are no totally effective prevention methods or treatments for Alzheimer's disease; however, there are some drugs that act as acetylcholinesterase inhibitors. *Acetylcholinesterase* is an enzyme that serves to terminate synaptic nerve transmission. These drugs enhance the effectiveness of nerve cells that are still functional but do not address the underlying pathology of Alzheimer's disease.

Dementia

Dementia covers a wide range of symptoms that are associated with a decline in memory and/or other skills that are involved in everyday activities. Alzheimer's disease is one form of dementia; it is estimated to account for about 60 to 80 percent of the instances of dementia. Another prominent type of dementia, *vascular dementia*, may occur after a stroke. Other conditions that may contribute to dementia are thyroid problems and vitamin deficiencies.

Signs of dementia may include the decreased ability to focus and pay attention; changes in memory, judgment, and reasoning; communication and language issues; and visual perception alterations. However, other environmental and physical factors may contribute to these signs of dementia.

Memory

Many cells in the body are formed and decline over a person's lifetime. Neurons develop throughout a person's life, but the brain reaches its maximum potential of neurons during a person's early 20s. They then slowly begin to decline in volume. Blood flow to the brain also decreases over time. However, the brain is capable of regrowth and learning and retaining new facts and skills. The more active that a person is, the more frequently their brain is stimulated. The better nourished that a person is, the better the odds that their brain will function well throughout their senior years.

Both episodic and long-term memory decline over time, as well as information processing and learning new information, doing more than one task at a time, and shifting focus to new tasks.

Coconuts in Ketogenic Diets and Brain Health

Coconuts with their medium-chain triglycerides have been associated with improved cognition and a number of enhanced brain functions. Studies have not definitively shown that medium-chain triglycerides can prevent dementia, but people with dementia might discover some short-term benefits by incorporating the medium-chain triglycerides like those that are found in coconuts into their diets.

Small clinical trials in aging individuals that had age-related cognitive decline and diabetic patients have shown that an MCT supplement can preserve cognitive function or lead to cognitive improvement. Medium-chain triglyceride supplementation appeared to help the diabetic patients but not the aging group.

Insulin, the hormone that regulates blood sugar, has been linked to changes in the brain that have been associated with Alzheimer's disease. This is the reason why this study was conducted with diabetic patients. It is not exactly clear what role insulin has in Alzheimer's disease. Furthermore, changes in the brain that are associated with dementia may be unconnected to glucose metabolism.

Medium-chain triglyceride supplements also have been shown to improve cognitive function in people with mild cognitive impairment and Alzheimer's disease. A few studies suggest some cognition improvement and prevention of amyloid plaque formation in animals, but human studies have not been confirmed.

A recent study suggested that although the effects of coconut oil may be temporary, that both Alzheimer's and dementia patients had some short-term benefits from supplementation. Another study that examined the effects of a mild ketogenic diet during exercise, both with and without ketosis, demonstrated that endurance and cognitive function were both increased.

There is strong evidence that exists that the use of medium-chain triglycerides by healthy adults is considered to be low risk. Foods and beverages, such as coconut oil, that are high in medium-chain triglycerides have been widely used with few reported adverse reactions.

The medium-chain triglycerides with lauric acid in organic, cold-pressed, non-hydrogenated virgin coconut oil, which make up nearly 60 percent of the total fat content of coconut oil are preferable. For comparison: one tablespoon of coconut oil contains about 7.4 grams of MCTs; butter contains about 1 gram of MCTs; and palm kernel oil contains about 7.9 grams of MCTs.

In some clinical studies, 10 to 40 grams (0.4 to 1.4 ounces) of medium-chain triglycerides are ingested daily, although some reports indicate that a daily dose up to about 70 grams of medium-chain triglycerides may produce demonstrable results. Mild gastrointestinal side effects may be common in some individuals who consume medium-chain triglycerides. These side effects may be offset by consuming medium-chain triglycerides with food and by slowly incorporating MCTs into one's diet. Like other supplements or medications, it is important to discuss the usage of MCT's with a health care provider before executing.

Primary Considerations

A ketogenic diet must be followed very strictly because the body prefers glucose for metabolism. The simple addition of coconut oil to the diet may not necessarily provide the neurons in the brain with an alternative source for energy. The most optimal use of coconut oil for brain health may be its incorporation into a finely devised ketogenic diet. In this context, the rich concentration of medium-chain triglycerides in coconut oil will probably comprise a prescribed amount of the total daily fat intake and should be in the correct proportion to the amount of carbohydrates and proteins. An experienced dietitian/nutritionist or health care provider may be able to devise and monitor such a diet.

Memory problems may be exacerbated by factors such as anxiety, dehydration, depression, infection, medications, nutrition, stress, substance abuse, or thyroid imbalance.

Butternut Squash Oven Fries

½ **teaspoon garlic powder**

¼ **teaspoon salt**

¼ **teaspoon ground red pepper**

1 **butternut squash (about 2½ pounds), peeled, seeded and cut into thin 2-inch-long sticks**

1 **tablespoon coconut oil**

1. Preheat oven to 425°F. Combine garlic powder, salt, and red pepper in small bowl.

2. Place squash on baking sheet. Drizzle with oil and sprinkle with seasoning mix; gently toss to coat. Arrange in single layer.

3. Bake 20 to 25 minutes or until squash just begins to brown, stirring frequently.

4. Preheat broiler. Broil 3 to 5 minutes or until fries are browned and crisp. Spread on paper towels to cool slightly before serving.

Butternut Squash Oven Fries are a take off on popular sweet potato fries. Butternut squash is rich in vitamin A, beta-carotene (a vitamin A precursor) and folate, niacin, potassium, riboflavin, pantothenic acid, thiamin, vitamin B6, and fiber. Plus, the combination of butternut squash with coconut oil is so richly and sweetly satisfying that one hardly needs dessert!

Things That Go Bump

Not only are coconuts valued for culinary uses, but their medicinal values are also impressive. Coconuts provide the natural substances that are used for the development of many medicinals. Coconuts have a long list of antibacterial, antifungal, antiviral, antiparasitic, antidermatophytic, antioxidant, hypoglycemic, hepatoprotective, and immunostimulant properties. That long list means that coconuts fight bacteria, funguses, viruses, and parasites! They also protect the cells, skin, liver, and immune system, among other bodily parts and functions.

This chapter explores the many ways that coconuts can be used for minor bumps and bruises. The antimicrobial properties of coconuts are described, plus how coconuts can be beneficial for a host of minor ailments. For instance, coconut oil may be used to soothe bee stings, bug bites, and minor scrapes and scratches. Coconut oil may be applied as an insect repellent and reportedly may be used to prevent or treat a lice infestation. When coconut oil is ingested, its antibacterial and antiviral properties may protect against common colds and even strengthen the immune system.

Medicinal Effects

The medicinal effects of coconuts are many and varied, due in great part to their concentration of medium-chain triglycerides and lauric acid that were discussed previously.

> Coconuts contain microminerals and other nutrients that are essential to human health and are used as preventatives and curatives worldwide, mainly in the tropics.

Of late, coconuts have been touted for their antiatherosclerotic, antibacterial, anticancer, anticarie, anticholecystic, antidermatophytic, antidote, antidiabetic, antifungal, antioxidant, antiprotozoal, antithrombic, antiviral, cardioprotective, electrolyte, hepatroprotective, hormone-like, hypolipidemic, and immunostimulatory effects. The following conditions have been recounted, though many have not been thoroughly supported by extensive scientific research.

• **Antiatherosclerotic**: A coconut oil-based diet that is high in saturated fatty acids, particularly lauric acid and monolaurin acid, may lower antigen concentrations and may favorably affect lipoproteins, considered heart-healthy. This is in comparison to diets that are higher in mono- or polyunsaturated fatty acids.

• **Antibacterial**: Around the world, virgin coconut water is used to treat *cholera* (an infectious and sometimes fatal disease of the small intestine), diarrhea, and urinary tract infections, due to its saline and albumen content. The medium-chain triglyceride lauric acid in coconuts may also be effective at destroying lipid-coated bacteria that may lead to dental cavities, food poisoning, sinusitis, stomach ulcers, and urinary tract infections.

• **Anticancer**: Coconut husk fibers may be a source of drugs that work to overcome cancer resistance and promote tumor cell death.

• **Anticarie**: A coconut-based mouthwash that is made with coconut tree roots may be used as a gargle and mouthwash. Coconut extract may have potential in the prevention and treatment of oral disease. Coconut flour with its antimicrobial properties from lauric acid has been used for some oral infections that include mouth sores. And the compound sucrose monolaurate in coconuts may have anticaries benefits by helping to prevent dental plaque. There is more about coconuts and oral health in chapter 9.

- **Anticholecystic**: Coconuts may act as an urinary antiseptic and be effective in the treatment of kidney and urethral stones. They may be 50 to 75 percent effective in dissolving gallstones, due to the compound monoctanoin from the caprylic acid that is one of the three fatty acids that are contained within coconuts.

- **Antidermatophytic**: Coconut oil is used worldwide for its antiseptic effect and as a skin moisturizer. It may selectively combat bacteria and proactively treat atopic dermatitis.

POISON

- **Antidote**: Virgin coconut water is reported to eliminate poisons (as in the case of mineral poisoning) and improve drug-induced toxicity from over dosage.

- **Antidiabetic**: The coconut kernel may help to reverse the levels of glycogen in the body, the activities of carbohydrate metabolizing enzymes and pancreatic damage.

- **Antifungal**: Monolaurin and lauric acid in coconut oil may have an antifungal effect against spore germination and radical growth and may help to combat yeast overgrowth, such as candida and thrush.

- **Antioxidants**: The amino acid L-arginine and vitamin C in virgin coconut water may help to reduce damaging free radicals and lipid peroxidation.

- **Antiprotozoal**: Polyphenolic-rich coconuts may inhibit the growth of *protozoa* (microscopic organisms that flourish in moist environments and human parasites that cause diseases such as amoebic dysentery or malaria).

- **Antithromic**: Virgin coconut oil may lower antigen concentrations and may favorably affect the fibrinolytic system that is closely linked to control of inflammation and associated disease states.

- **Antiviral**: Coconut oil may be effective against lipid-coated viruses that include Epstein-Barr, influenza, pneumono, hepatitis C, and CMV. The medium-chain triglycerides and in particular lauric acid in coconut oil may help to disrupt the viruses' membranes and interfere with their development.

- **Cardio-protective**: Coconut contains the fatty acids caprylic, lauric, myristic, palmitic, stearic, oleic, and linoleic and medium-chain triglycerides, which permits these fatty acids to be directly absorbed by the intestine and routed straight to the liver for speedy metabolism and energy production. The medium-chain triglycerides in coconut oil do not biosynthesize and transport cholesterol. Also, coconut water contains potassium, which has beneficial cardio-protective effects.

- **Electrolytes**: Coconuts are rich in the electrolytes calcium, magnesium, phosphorus, and potassium, which are said to help lower blood pressure and relax the blood vessels.

- **Hypolipidemic**: Virgin coconut oil may inhibit lipid peroxidation due to its high content of coconut protein and polyphenols. These serve to inhibit low-density lipoprotein oxidation, reverse cholesterol transport, and reduce intestinal absorption of cholesterol.

- **Hepatroprotective**: Coconut oil may protect the liver from fatty infiltration or *necrosis*.

- **Hormone-like effects**: Young coconut water is thought to contain phytoestrogen and other sex hormones that may be used in hormone replacement therapy, to help prevent dementia, and in wound healing. Products may vary.

- **Immunostimulatory**: Virgin coconut oil that is enriched with zinc may increase cellular immune function. Coconut protein may increase various levels of immune markers. Both observations may indicate significant immune activity.

> Virgin coconut oil is reported to lower total cholesterol, phospholipids, triglycerides, low-density lipoproteins, and very-low-density lipoproteins and increase high-density lipoprotein cholesterol—all cardio-protective measures.

Red Bell Pepper Soup

2   **tablespoons coconut oil (refined)**

8   **large red bell peppers, stemmed, seeded, and quartered**

1   **large onion, thinly sliced**

3   **cloves garlic, minced**

1   **teaspoon black pepper**

1   **teaspoon dried oregano**

2   **tablespoons balsamic vinegar**

1½ **tablespoons fresh thyme, divided**

1. Coat 6-quart or larger slow cooker with oil. Add bell peppers, onion, garlic, black pepper, and oregano; stir gently to combine. Cover and cook on HIGH 4 hours, or until bell peppers are very tender; stirring halfway through cooking.

2. Purée soup in slow cooker using immersion blender or transfer in batches to blender or food processor and blend until smooth. Stir in balsamic vinegar. Ladle soup into bowls; garnish with thyme.

Makes 4 to 6 servings

This slow cooker recipe, Red Bell Pepper Soup, is a beautiful red-orange color, made with coconut oil, red bell peppers, onion, garlic, oregano, balsamic vinegar, and fresh thyme. Red bell peppers are rich in antioxidant vitamins A and C and of course coconut oil lends some additional antioxidants and lusciousness. The balsamic vinegar adds piquancy.

Antibacterial and Antiviral Properties

These are how some of these theoretical medicinal effects of coconuts translate into practical usages. As always, check with a health care practitioner before starting any of these practices.

Acne

Coconut oil with its antibacterial properties from lauric acid may be applied to skin that is broken out or has acne. Use a clean cotton ball that is soaked with warm coconut oil and apply it first to a small area of the face or body to observe if there are any reactions. Then another clean cotton ball filled with warmed coconut oil can be swabbed over the face and body. The lauric acid may inhibit bacterial growth and reduce inflammation. A naturally scented essential oil, such as lemon or rosemary, may be added, if desired. This application should be repeated as needed. It may eventually reduce blotches, redness and/or irritation.

Simple cuts, burns, or other skin injuries may also benefit by this application. The healing properties are again due, in part, to the lauric acid in coconut oil.

> To keep the scalp and hair smelling fresh and clean, a few drops of an essential oil of your choice may be added to the warmed coconut oil before application.

Dandruff Remedy

Dandruff may be more than dry skin on the scalp. Dandruff may be produced by an overly oily scalp that causes skin cells to clump together and resemble white flakes; skin conditions that include eczema, psoriasis, or *seborrheic dermatitis* (a red, itchy rash that is common in children); or by a fungus that similar to the fungus that causes yeast infections.

Coconut oil may have antifungal properties. When it is rubbed into the scalp it may help old skin cells to slough away. A simple head massage with warmed coconut oil may help to loosen the oily cells that built up, promote healthier oil production and distribution, and improve circulation, which are all good measures to reduce dandruff.

Use the fingertips instead of fingernails to avoid damaging the scalp and increasing the infection. Allow the warmed coconut oil to remain some time on the scalp to revitalize it. Covering the scalp and hair with a cap or wrap will enhance the process.

Deodorant

Coconut oil is moisturizing and may help to keep the armpits virtually free from bumps, chafing, flakes, or itching while smelling pleasant. The lauric acid in coconut oil may also be antibacterial and antifungal when coconut oil is used as a deodorant.

A small scoop of coconut oil may be used right from the container and applied to the underarms, face, or legs as needed. Any excess should be wiped with a clean, dry cloth. The thin coconut layer should be left to dry before dressing as to avoid any stains on garments.

Coconut Deodorant

¼ **cup baking soda**

½ **cup arrowroot or cornstarch**

Essential oil (such as lavender, lemon, rosemary, or thyme), if desired

6 **tablespoons coconut oil**

Sterilized, dry glass jar with lid

1. Blend baking soda and arrowroot or cornstarch in medium-sized bowl.

2. Add a few drops of essential oil, if desired.

3. Add coconut oil; blend with back of spoon until well blended.

4. Store in sterilized glass jar in cool location.

A simpler method is to mix about one tablespoon of arrowroot powder into three to four tablespoons of coconut oil and blend well. A little beeswax can be used to help to solidify the mixture.

Coconut deodorant can be easily made with baking soda and cornstarch, scented or unscented. Coconut oil may help to decrease the bacteria that cause body odor.

Disinfectant

Coconut soap has been shown to be effective as a disinfecting agent when it is used to brush dentures. Lautericide, a disinfectant that contains coconut acid, has bacterial and fungicidal properties.

Sore Throat

When you have a cold, a swish of coconut oil with its inherent lauric acid may be soothing for sore throats and may decrease the length of time of discomfort, improve immunity, and prevent additional sore throats.

A teaspoon of apple cider vinegar, warm water, and coconut oil may be especially soothing and restorative for sore throats.

Immunological Properties

Let's look at some specific conditions and remedies!

Allergens

Allergy sufferers are plagued with a host of allergic symptoms, sometimes yearlong. These may include coughing, headaches, itchy eyes, sinusitis, sneezing, or respiratory infections. Due to the reported antibacterial, antimicrobial, and antiviral properties of coconut oil, it has been said to help decrease sensitivities to allergens in the environment and allergic conditions, including respiratory discomfort, sinus pressure, and sneezing.

One to three tablespoons daily of coconut oil in food or on its own may help to protect the body against common allergic ailments and/or diminish their severity. A little coconut oil that is lightly swabbed at the base of the nostrils may also be effective. Thanks to the lauric acid in coconut oil, the body may then be able to build up its defense.

Some preventative measures may also help those with allergies such as showering after periods of being outdoors during high allergy seasons; driving with the car windows shut; and/or consuming local honey to build immunity against the local allergens.

Bumps and Bruises

A few tablespoons of coconut oil with its anti-inflammatory properties taken daily reportedly may help the body to efficiently and quickly repair, rebuild, and restore.

Bruising occurs when there is trauma to the skin and broken blood vessels manifest in colors that range from green to blackish-purple. The lauric acid and medium-chain triglycerides in coconut oil are anti-inflammatory and preventative against future injuries to the body.

After a minor bruise, ice the injured area first. Ice compresses and alleviates the swelling and pain. Ice may also help decrease the enlargement of the bruise, while it speeds up the healing process. Ice should be placed on the bruised region for about 15 to 20 minutes and repeated as needed.

Then the bruised area should be elevated to help prevent the accumulation of blood, discoloration, and swelling. Gently massaging the bruised area helps to break down the injured blood cells and improves circulation and the lymphatic process that removes toxins, waste, and other unwanted body materials.

One to three tablespoons of coconut oil can then be applied to the injured area with a clean, dry cotton ball. Then a gentle massage with clean fingertips may help to distribute the remnants of the broken blood vessels so that they may dissipate and be internally removed.

Older adults tend to bruise more easily than when they were younger because the skin becomes less flexible, thinner, and has less fat for cushioning. Women tend to bruise more easily than men. The tendency to bruise easily may be genetic.

Coconut Oil Salve

2 to 3   cups coconut oil

8 to 10 ounces dried herbs (such as calendula, comfrey, rosemary, or yarrow)

1   ounce beeswax per 8 ounces herbal oil

Essential oil (such as lavender, lemon, Roman chamomile, or tea tree)

1. Add coconut oil to upper pot of a double boiler.

2. Sprinkle dried herbs over coconut oil.

3. Add water to bottom pot of double boiler; heat to just before simmer.

4. Place pot of coconut oil/herb mixture over pot of heated water; heat until mixture melts, is unified in color, and the herbs are no longer dry.

5. Remove from heat and cool.

6. Drain coconut oil from herbs by slowly pouring through a cheesecloth-lined strainer into medium bowl.

7. Repeat with any remaining oil and herbs, if needed.

8. Carefully wring contents of cooled cheesecloth and herbs into bowl until no longer residue.

9. Dispose of any remaining dried herbs and cheesecloth.

10. Add one-ounce beeswax per 8-ounces herb-infused oil back into upper pot of double boiler. Reheat water in lower pot of double boiler just before simmer.

11. Upon melting, add a few drops of essential oils to mixture*. Mix well; set aside to fully cool.

12. Once cooled, pour the herbal mixture into clean, sanitized containers.

As a component of salve, coconut oil may nourish the skin and transfer essential oils and herbs, depending upon the salve's composition. With its antibacterial and antioxidant properties, the coconut oil within the salve may also help to protect and heal the body. Add dried herbs to coconut oil, and blend in beeswax and essential oils of choice for a soothing, pleasantly smelling salve for relaxation, rough skin, or sore muscles.

NOTE: The herbal coconut oil salve in this recipe will semi-harden as coconut oil does. To prevent rancidity, store in refrigerator and remove only enough to use as needed. Warm a tablespoon or more in the palm of the hands as desired.

*Depending on the essential oil used in this recipe and its freshness, this might require about 10 or more drops of essential oil per one cup of herbal oil in step 11. The essential oil can be used on its own or mixed with a complementary type.

Fungal Infections

Another reported immunological use of coconut oil is in the prevention of fungal infections. With its antifungal and probiotic attributes, coconut oil may help to rid the body of yeast infections that are caused by the yeast *candida* and its overgrowth. When a cell's mucosal barriers is impeded or the immune system is compromised then candida may invade and trigger infection.

The lauric acid in coconuts may help to reduce the pain and itching that are associated with yeast infections, minimize the spread of yeast infections, and ease the inflammation. A few tablespoons of coconut oil that are ingested daily might be preventative. It is best to check with a health care practitioner before using coconut oil topically.

Insect Repellent

The use of *dodecanoic acid* (DDA) against ticks has been validated and DDA is patented. The active ingredient DDA is a naturally occurring *carboxylic acid*, which is the broader classification of the acids that are found in coconut oil. Coconut oil has also been shown to exhibit some repellency against mosquitoes.

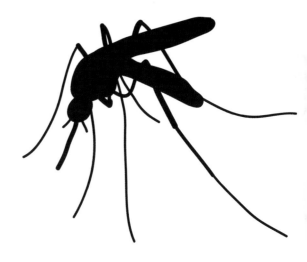

Lice Prevention and Treatment

Lice are wingless insects that live externally on warm-blooded hosts. In number, lice are called *louse* and their eggs are called *nits* that hatch into *nymphs*.

Lice favor clean hair and scalp so that they can freely move throughout the hair and their nits can create strong bonds to the hair strands. Lice are contagious, irritating, and are often difficult to remove; however, lice generally do not spread disease. If the scalp is scratched and then inflamed, infection may develop.

Lice can only live off of the human scalp a short amount of time since their only food source is human blood. They cannot live on any other species but they can reside on bed linens, carpets, and furniture—that's why it is important to do a thorough cleaning after lice infestation.

> Dogs and other animals have a form of lice that is uniquely theirs. This form cannot survive on humans.

Over-the-counter (OTC) products with highly concentrated pesticides may be absorbed through the skin. Also, head lice may build up resistance to them and these OTC products may become ineffective at killing nits.

Instead, different types of oils have been used around the world for centuries to treat lice. While coconut oil may not kill lice, it may temporarily immobilize and suffocate them. The viscous consistency of coconut oil is sometimes effective in killing adult lice, but it may be ineffective in killing nits or baby louse. In order for the nits to die they must be manually removed from the strands of hair where they have infiltrated.

A natural treatment for lice infestation is as follows:

• Rinse the scalp with apple cider vinegar.

• Let the apple cider vinegar remain on the hair to dry.

• Carefully comb the hair while removing as many nits as possible.

• Mix a combination of one cup of coconut oil and 1 to 3 tablespoons of essential oils (such as anise or ylang-ylang with their antibacterial, antifungal, and insecticidal properties).

• Apply this mixture to the hair and scalp.

• Cover the hair and scalp with a thin shower cap or wrap and allow it to set for 12 or more hours, if possible.

• The hair should then be shampooed, rinsed, and combed with a special lice comb that has small, closely spaced teeth to remove as many nits and eggs as are visible.

• This process can be repeated until the lice are eliminated.

Massage Oil

The type of massage oil that one chooses may either enliven or soothe the body, depending upon its consistency and aroma. Coconut oil provides lubrication and moisturizing for kneading, rubbing, and relaxing the body.

Simply blend one cup of coconut oil with a few drops of essential oils of choice, such as sweet and fragrant orange, geranium, rose, vanilla, or ylang-ylang, or spicy and invigorating bergamot, cypress, fennel, frankincense, helichrysum, lavender, myrrh, lemon grass, or rosemary. The sweeter essential oils may promote relaxation while the spicier oils may be uplifting. Essential oils are concentrated and work best when they are blended into a nourishing medium, such as coconut oil with its wonderful skin-friendly and protective capric and lauric acids.

Nosebleed Prevention

Coconut oil may be used to prevent nosebleeds that are attributed to dry nostrils from air pollutants, allergies, or extremes in temperature or humidity. These conditions often result in inflammation or cracks in the mucus membranes and subsequent bleeding.

A little coconut oil that is dabbed onto the base of the nostrils may help to soften them and prevent cracking or drying. Make sure that the hands are clean, especially under the fingernails. Coconut oil taken by mouth may also help to keep these tissues pliable from the inside by protecting and strengthening the capillaries of the nasal passages. Make sure that your antioxidant intake (especially vitamins A and C) is also sufficient.

Soothes Bee Stings, Bug Bites, Minimal Scrapes and Scratches

The three ways that coconut oil affects simple wound healing are:

1. It has the ability to accelerate *re-epithelialization* (the process of covering a wound's surface).

2. It improves antioxidant enzyme activity.

3. It stimulates higher collagen cross-linking within the tissue being repaired to form a barrier between the skin and the environment.

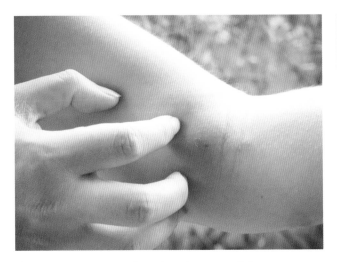

Bugs can transmit microbes and foster disease and illness, especially when the skin is infected. Coconut oil with capric and lauric acids combined with tea tree oil (a natural derivative of the *melaleuca* plant) is an easy, effective, and reportedly safe solution for bites.

Simply add about 10 drops of tea tree oil to about one-half cup of warmed coconut oil and blend well. This mixture can be applied with a clean cotton ball to the skin, or poured into a clean spray bottle so that a thin layer can be sprayed over the affected areas. This mixture may help to soothe the skin, safeguard the skin against future insect bites, and moisturize the skin in the process.

> Coconut oil may help heal small nicks from shaving on the face, as well as on the under-arms and legs.

Sun Protection

Consuming coconuts and applying coconut oil to the skin may help to protect the skin from the sun both from the inside and outside of the body. Damaging UVA and UVB rays may lead to skin cancer or other skin disorders besides drying and weathering the skin, which exacerbates aging skin. UVA rays may penetrate deep within the thickest layer of the skin, or the dermis. UVB rays may often burn the superficial layers of the skin and may play a key role in skin cancer.

Coconut oil alone or blended with equal amounts of cocoa butter may help to soften dehydrated, sun-dried skin, and retard peeling from sunburn. It may not be effective against the harsh effects of the sun since it has a Sun Protection Factor (SPF) of 4 or less depending upon laboratory testing, especially if homemade.

Replacements of Fluid and Electrolytes

Coconut water is low in calories (about 5.45 calories per ounce or abut 65.4 calories per 12-ounces depending upon the brand) and naturally fat- and cholesterol free. Coconut water contains more potassium than one medium banana (862 milligrams per 12-ounces of coconut water versus 422 milligrams in one medium banana). Benefits like these are why coconut water is often called "Mother Nature's Sports Drink."

Coconut water is naturally refreshing with its sweet and nutty taste. Its natural sugar content is easily digestible and it contains some electrolytes that are needed for rehydration, specifically potassium and sodium. Coconut water also contains calcium and minor amounts of magnesium, phosphorus, and zinc.

Ounce for ounce, when typical coconut water is compared to common sports drinks it can be seen that coconut water is slightly less caloric per ounce, with slightly less sugar, more potassium, and less sodium. The reason why some sports drinks are so effective for rehydration is that their composition of nutrients closely resembles that of perspiration. This feature may increase their effectiveness and appeal.

Coconut water contains less sugar than some sodas and fruit juices, but its sugars may add up if coconut water is consumed in excess.

Coconut Water	Sports Drinks
5.45 calories/ounce	6.25 calories/ounce
1.3 grams sugar	1.75 grams sugar
61 milligrams potassium	3.75 milligrams potassium
5.45 milligrams sodium	13.75 milligrams sodium

Still, some athletes feel that coconut water is very hydrating because it is not overly sweet and coconut water is so drinkable. A study of professional athletes has shown that coconut water (especially when it was enhanced with sodium) replenishes body fluids similarly to sports drinks and water as long as it is flavored and athletes tolerate significant amounts to keep hydrated. For rehydration, coconut water has been shown to be as good as sports drinks and causes less fullness, nausea, and stomach upset when it is consumed in large amounts that are required for rehydration.

Since hydration is critical for everyone, but particularly for recreational and professional athletes, if the taste and hydrating abilities of coconut water encourage people to consume more fluids, then coconut water may be considered an effective hydrating beverage.

Since people need to be hydrated daily, the natural hydrating capacity of coconut water with its potassium supply is beneficial. Keep in mind that fruits, vegetables, and dairy products are also ample in potassium and should be part of a well-rounded diet.

If people lose weight after heavy exercise and/or perspire heavily, then neither coconut water nor sports drinks may provide enough replacement carbohydrates or sodium. Their diet may need extra calorie and sodium supplementation post exercise. A handful of pretzels or raisins will supply some simple and complex carbohydrates for immediate and longer energy and the sodium in the pretzels will to help to replenish this electrolyte.

Making Your Own

In this hectic world in which we live, it might be overwhelming to considering making some of these homemade products and potential remedies compared to the ease of purchasing their commercial varieties.

This may be true; however, coconut-based products may be more economical, environmental friendly, and in some cases, work as effectively if not better than their commercial counterparts.

It might be fun to try an easy mixture and notice any results. The coconut just may find its place as a go-to ingredient for many surprising invaders that cause harm.

Green Coconut Water Smoothie

- ½ cup frozen banana, cut into chunks
- ¼ cup frozen mango, cut into chunks
- 2 cups fresh greens (kale, spinach, watercress, or mixed greens)*
- 1 cup coconut water (plus more to thin)
- 1 teaspoon ground walnuts or pistachios, to garnish (optional)

1. Combine the first four ingredients into a blender.

2. Blend until smooth, frothy consistency.

3. Thin with additional coconut water, if desired.

4. Garnish with ground walnuts or pistachios, if desired.

Makes about 3 to 3¾ cups, depending upon how greens are packed into cup measure.

Coconut the Beautiful

Not only can people consume the goodness of the coconut, people can wear coconuts, too—on their face and body, that is! Coconuts have been extolled for their radiant properties in beauty and personal care. Coconut oil may be one of the best skin creams, hydrating serums, and moisturizing lotions available. That said, some of the magic-like qualities of coconuts are valid while others maybe more folklore. Let's explore!

The unique properties of coconuts make them extremely versatile and useful for a myriad of beauty and hygienic habits. This chapter will sort out the rights and wrongs for using coconuts for beautification purposes.

Skin Care

The cell membranes in the skin are made up of three fat-containing substances: *glycolipids* (lipids with a carbohydrate component that helps to identify cells), *phospholipids* (lipids with a phosphate component that provide structure and function to cells), and cholesterol (the waxy, fat-like substance that is found in all cells of the body).

Phospholipids, made of saturated and unsaturated fatty acids, are the largest component of cell membranes. The balance of these three fatty acids is important for proper cell function and it is critical to human and animal health. The fatty acids in coconuts contribute to a healthy balance of these fatty acids in the cell membranes of the skin.

Aging, heat and cold, medications, skin treatments, and the sun can affect the hydration of the skin in a multitude of ways. Replacing this hydration can be done both externally and internally.

Coconut Lip Balm

2 **ounces coconut oil**

2 **ounce clean, sterilized, dry container**

Microwavable bowl

Clean spoon for mixing

Additional flavored or non-flavored oil, if desired (argan, avocado, jojoba, or olive)

Lipstick, if desired

1. Place coconut oil and a few drops of additional flavored or non-flavored oil (if desired) into microwavable bowl.

2. Mix well with spoon until smooth consistency.

3. Add a few shavings from lipstick tube, if desired.

4. Microwave about 10 to 30 seconds depending upon microwave setting until mixture melts.

5. Remove from microwave; blend again with spoon.

6. When cool, place in refrigerator to harden.

7. Keep cool; warm with fingertip to apply.

Proper hydration is essential for the skin's cell membranes. The surface skin cells do not dry out as fast or as much and the dead skin cells are reduced or are easily eliminated. As a result, the skin's pores do not get as clogged with dirt and impurities and excess oils do not accumulate, which also reduces the possibility of acne and infections. Firmness and natural elasticity are generally retained and stretch marks and wrinkling also may be reduced in appearance.

Coconut oil provides hydration and essential fatty acids for healthy skin along with proper skin care. Coconut oil helps to protect the skin from free radicals and their aging effects and may help to improve the skin's appearance with its anti-aging benefits. Coconut oil acts as an antioxidant since it is stable, resists oxidation, and contributes some vitamin E, an antioxidant vitamin.

Homemade coconut lip balm can be made clear or colored, almost fragrant-free, or scented.

When coconut oil is absorbed into the skin and connective tissues, it may help to reduce the appearance of fine lines and wrinkles. It accomplishes this by supporting the strength and suppleness of connective tissues. It also aids in the exfoliation of the outer layer of dead skin cells, which makes the skin look smoother. Plus, it has a delightful aroma that bathes the skin to the enjoyment of the wearer and those in the immediate vicinity, so no other cologne or perfume may be necessary.

Skin-enhancing Qualities of Coconut Oil

Several of the skin-enhancing qualities of coconut oil and coconut products include:

Acne relief:
Coconut oil helps to keep skin hydrated and the pores open to reduce impurities and acne-related skin conditions.

Age spot minimizer:
Coconut oil may diminish the look of age spots when used on a regular basis. It may accomplish this by keeping the area of the age spots and also the skin around the age spots supple.

Anti-aging defense: By smoothing the look of wrinkled skin, coconut oil may help to make skin appear younger. Younger skin does have more moisture that may dissipate over the years.

Baby lotion/massage oil: Warmed coconut oil with essential oil such as lavender, mint, rosemary, or vanilla help to provide a relaxing, rejuvenating massage.

Bath/body moisturizer: Scented (or unscented) coconut massage oil can be applied to the skin both in and out of the bath or shower.

Body balm: Coconut-oil-based body balm is dense, hydrates, and repairs. It is similar to a lotion with light consistency that moistures but does not repair and a cream that is usually thicker, but is formulated for the face.

Body scrub: Coconut oil and coarse salt or sugar acts as an exfoliator for dry skin. Either fragrant (such a eucalyptus or lavender) or non-fragrant essential oils may be added.

Coconut Body Scrub acts as an all-in-one body wash, exfoliator, and moisturizer. It can be made with granulated sugar, salt, or a combination of these two ingredients and with or without essential oil.

Coconut Body Scrub

¼ to ½ **cup granulated sugar or coarse salt**

½ **cup coconut oil**

Essential oil (citrus or herbal, such as lemon or rosemary), optional

1. Combine granulated sugar, coarse salt, or combination of sugar and salt with coconut oil. Do not heat to melt the coconut oil.

2. Add a few drops of essential oil, if desired; blend ingredients well.

3. Place into sanitized, dry container.

Bruise reducer: Coconut oil may not directly reduce the appearance of bruises, but similar to its effects on scars, sores, and stretch marks, it may promote the healing of the surrounding skin over time.

Cold sore reliever: Cold sores, often due to viruses, may benefit from coconut oil's antiviral properties due to its composition of lauric and stearic fatty acids, know for their curative properties.

Deodorant: Coconut oil mixed with arrowroot powder, baking soda, cornstarch, and scented or unscented essential oils can be used as a natural deodorant.

Diaper rash relief: Unless there is a known sensitivity to coconuts, a thin layer of coconut oil may provide some relief for chafed skin.

Dry feet remedy: Apply coconut oil to cracked skin and dry spots to smooth dry feet, especially in winter or after hot, dry summer sun.

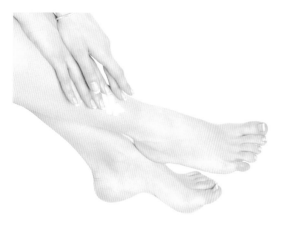

Emollient: An emollient is a cream or an ointment that acts like a moisturizer. It is designed to help make the *epidermis* (outer layer of the skin) softer and suppler. Versatile coconut oil can be used as a base for homemade bath or body emollients or moisturizers.

Facial mask: The antioxidants and fatty acids in coconut oil help to lubricate, smooth, and soften the skin when it is mixed with baking soda, lemon, turmeric, or yogurt as a facial mask.

Lip balm: Coconut oil is a remedy for chapped lips since it is semisolid at room temperature and can easily be spread by fingertips. Coconut balm is particularly soothing for the lips. A touch of natural extract, such as vanilla, gives coconut lip balm a tropical flavor.

Makeup remover: Apply coconut oil directly to the face to cleanse it, or let it remain on the skin to rehydrate. Be particularly careful around the eyes so as not to over-oil them.

Night cream: Apply coconut oil at night for its maximum moisturizing benefits, particularly around fine lines or wrinkles. A little left on the pillow at night will also moisturize the hair.

Nursing mothers' aid/nipple soother: Use coconut oil delicately around sore or cracked nipples to rehydrate, soften, and heal. This practice can be checked with an obstetrician or nurse midwife first before trying.

Shave cream: Coconut oil helps to provide a smoother, closer shave that leaves the arms, face, and legs evenly soft and moisturized.

Skin protection (dishpan hands, eczema, psoriasis): Coconut oil and coconut balm offers relief from allergic and chronic skin conditions that can be heightened by over-exposure to chemicals, sun, water, and other skin-damaging factors. Check with an allergist first before applying to very sensitive skin.

Stretch mark/scar reducer: Pregnant women and people with minor scrapes and scratches can use coconut oil as a topical treatment for marks and scars. Coconut oil probably will not directly cause fading, but it may help to prevent dark spots and/or blisters from forming. Coconut oil may also help the surrounding skin retain its moisture and healthy glow.

Sun block/soother: Coconut oil is soothing and has a natural sunscreen of SPF 4. It is still sensible to stay out of direct exposure of the sun. Sunscreens with a higher SPF should offer more protection from the sun's harmful ultraviolet (UV) radiation.

Under eye cream: Applied under the eyes and around fine lines, coconut oil combats a dried-out appearance and it is light and delicate for most skin types.

To make a simple, soothing shave cream, use a combination of ⅔ cup coconut oil, ⅔ cup shea nut oil or shea butter, and ¼ cup olive oil or grapeseed oil, blended with the following optional ingredients: a few drops of essential oils, 2 tablespoons of baking soda, and the contents of two vitamin E capsules, beaten until frosting consistency.

Hair and Nails

Like healthy skin, healthy hair and nails are formed, in great part, by a healthy diet that includes proper hydration. An unhealthy diet can lead to hair that is brittle, dull, or lifeless; a scalp that is flaky; nails that break and chip easily; and ragged cuticles. Coconut oil plays a role in radiant hair, smooth nails, and neat cuticles due to its fat content and along with coconut milk and coconut water helps hydration.

Coconut oil can be applied directly to the scalp, hair, nails, and nail beds. While excess coconut oil can be removed, the residue can remain for a healthy glow and moisturizing. Or, coconut oil can be mixed with some warm water, gently applied to the scalp, then allowed to soak into the scalp and hair before washing with shampoo and conditioner—coconut-based, of course! Plus, when coconuts are consumed they help to nourish the hair and nails from the inside out!

These are some of the uses of coconut products to enrich the hair and nails:

Adds shine and conditions hair: Coconut oil hydrates hair over time since it replaces the natural oils that shampoos tend to strip away. As a leave-in conditioner, coconut oil may condition the hair immediately and then benefit the hair over time. Some people think that application to wet hair is more desirable for sealing in moisture than on dry hair, but water and oil do not mix (consider vinegar and oil salad dressing), so it is best to experiment.

Dandruff control: Dandruff along with dry scalp may be chronic problems. The daily use of coconut oil literally confronts the root of the problem. A light head massage with warm coconut oil may also be invigorating.

Defrizzes hair and reduces split ends: Frizzy hair is often the result of dry conditions: too many chemicals in shampoos and conditioners, coloring, perms, or general over-processing. Coconut oil helps to calm frizzy hair and restore its luster. While regular trims are best for split ends, coconut oil may tame their unruliness in the short-term before the haircut.

Enhances eyebrows and eyelashes: Coconut oil may penetrate the hair follicles in the eyebrows and eyelashes and prevent a scaly look so that they appear to be soft and shiny.

Provides protection from ultraviolet (UV) radiation: Sunlight helps to create a pre-cursor of vitamin D on the skin's surface that is necessary for healthy bones and teeth, the heart, and immune function. But too much UV radiation may damage the skin and lead to some cancers. Coconut oil and its richness provide some measures of protection. But the wisest advice is to stay out of dangerous noon-day or tropical sun.

Reduces fungal infections: Coconut oil with its antimicrobial properties may help to prevent fungal infections of the nails (particularly toenails) and scalp. Coconut oil is even said to reduce *candida*, a systemic fungal infection. Make sure to check with a health care practitioner for specific advice.

Softens cuticles: Coconut balm or coconut oil soothes rough and ragged cuticles before they get out of hand. When either of these nurturing coconut products is applied to the nail base, they may enhance the nails and hands.

Stimulates nail growth: Nails need a moisturized environment in which to thrive. Coconut oil helps to prevent the nails from becoming overly brittle and split that may hinder their growth. Ample protein, biotin, B-complex vitamins, calcium, iron, magnesium, omega-3 fatty acids, and zinc are some of the nutrients that are needed for healthy nails.

Coconut Beard Oil

½ **ounce fractionated coconut oil (about 1 tablespoon)**

½ **ounce jojoba oil (about 1 tablespoon)**

½ **ounce sweet almond oil (about 1 tablespoon)**

3 to 4 **drops cedarwood oil**

3 to 4 **drops sandalwood oil**

Small bottle with cap or eyedropper

Fractionated coconut oil is made from regular coconut oil and mainly consists of 2 medium-chain fatty acids. Fractionated coconut oil is primarily used for personal care products.

1. Add jojoba oil to clean, sanitized bottle.

2. Add sweet almond oil and fractionated coconut oil to bottle.

3. Add 3 to 4 drops of cedarwood oil and 3 to 4 drops of sandalwood oil into bottle.

4. Return cap/lid to the bottle and close tightly. Shake well.

5. Apply a few drops and gently massage oil into beard. For best results, brush beard to finish.

Makes 2 to 3 ounces

Supports natural chemical balances in hair and nails: The body is a maze of natural chemicals and reactions that maintain its many functions. On low-fat diets, sometimes there is not enough fat or even protein for normal operations. Coconuts and their products may help support the body's quest for equilibrium of nutrient intake to keep it working smoothly.

Treats hair and scalp: Warmed coconut oil can be applied to the hair and scalp to treat dry hair before using shampoo and conditioner. The longer that it is left on the hair and scalp, the greater its moisturizing benefits. Stronger hair may be spared from dry ends that break or split up the hair and into the hair shaft.

Wards off infection: If used regularly, coconut oil may form a protective barrier on the skin around the nails to impede some common infections. Dry, cracked skin is more vulnerable. Make sure manicures are both safe and sanitary.

> You can use coconut oil as a cleanser for your hairbrush and comb! Remove any tangled hair from the hairbrushes and combs. Rub warmed coconut oil completely throughout the hairbrushes and combs and let set a few hours. Wash the hairbrushes and combs well and dry with a clean, dry cloth. A little residue may be desirable to revitalize the bristles and teeth, plus it might transfer to the hair the next time they are used.

Muscles

Proper muscle tone requires a muscle-building and maintenance program. One needs muscle-building exercises, a regular exercise routine, and healthy muscle cells and surrounding tissues that support all of this muscular work. Of course, a good diet with protein and muscle-building nutrients such as B-vitamins, calcium, magnesium, and vitamins C, D, and E are vital.

The right kinds of fatty acids in sufficient quantity are essential to build and maintain healthy cellular membranes within muscle cells. Coconuts and coconut oil with their saturated fats supply some of this raw material. The size of muscles depends on genetic predisposition and on a dedicated muscle-building program, but a balanced diet supports these factors.

Cellulite, or subcutaneous fat within fibrous connective tissue, makes the skin look dimpled and nodular. Cellulite is common in the pelvic region, including the abdomen, buttocks and lower limbs. Its causes may be genetic, hormonal, or lifestyle-related.

Effective treatments for cellulite are varied and debated. The use of coconut oil to reduce the look and texture of cellulite is one of these deliberations. The theory is that the human body requires certain substances to help to metabolize or break down its fat stores into energy.

The medium-chain triglycerides and lauric acid in coconut oil help to reduce inflammation, boost metabolism, and break down fatty accumulations. They work in conjunction with specific enzymes that break down fats into fatty acids and glycerol that are further broken down in the liver or used for energy. The enzymes are activated by the hormones epinephrine, glucagon, and growth hormone.

In the process of using these medium-chain triglycerides and lauric acid, the skin may become more elastic, silkier, and smoother in appearance and the bumpy, holey look of cellulite may be diminished.

Spider veins are small and twisted blood vessels that may be visible through the skin. They may look more pronounced when the skin is dry or saggy in appearance. Coconut oil can be gently massaged into the areas where spider veins appear on the face or legs. They may help to restore the surrounding cells and detract from the redness.

Teeth and Gums

The fat-soluble vitamins A, D, E, and K require fat for proper absorption and assimilation. In particular, vitamins A and D are essential for strong bones and teeth. By remineralizing tooth enamel, these vitamins help to build up the protective qualities of the teeth and help to guard against cavities. The anti-inflammatory, analgesic, and antipyretic (fever-reducing) properties of coconut oil may help to defend the teeth against decay. Healthy teeth and gums are one of the body's first lines against infection.

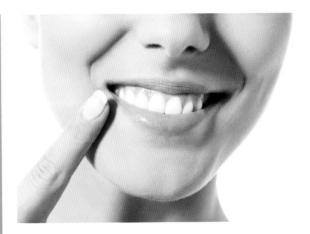

In particular, coconut oil:

- **Helps prevent periodontal disease and tooth decay**: Due to coconut oil's anti-inflammatory abilities, it may help to keep the mouth and gums healthy and even fight infection.

- **Improves calcium and magnesium absorption and supports the development of strong bones and teeth**: Coconut oil with its medium-chain triglycerides may have the capacity to increase calcium and magnesium absorption, which in turn may help to promote strong bones and teeth. Many other dietary factors are still in play, such as calcium, phosphorus, potassium, and vitamin A, C, D, and K intake.

- **Whitens teeth and acts as a mouthwash**: With its antifungal and antibacterial properties, coconut oil that is mixed with a little baking soda makes a natural whitening and protective paste. A few drops of an essential oil, such as anise with its licorice taste or mint or may be added.

- Gargling with a spoonful of coconut oil may help to reduce oral bacteria and contribute to fresher breath and healthier gums. You can learn more about this practice of "oil-pulling" in chapter 9.

Sun Damage and Aging

Sun damage is due to sun exposure throughout the years from everyday activities to conscious sun bathing. The changes in the earth's ozone layer are also responsible for undesirable ultraviolet (UV) radiation. Fair-skinned and darker-skinned individuals are both prone to sun damage; however, fairer-skinned individuals are more at risk.

In some parts of the world where there is intense and nonstop sun exposure, residents do not seem to have the same type of sun damage than they do in other locations. It may be that their local diets are more abundant in antioxidant-rich foods and vegetables that feed and protect the skin from the inside out.

Cellular degeneration may be caused by *free radicals* in the environment. Free radicals may be formed as the result of exposure to sunlight and air pollutants, but they may also be due to alcohol consumption, diet, drugs, exercise, inflammation, smoking, and one's diet.

One method to delay or prevent cellular degeneration from free radicals is with a diet that is rich in antioxidants (substances that help to halt oxidation which causes cellular destruction). Coconut oil has some antioxidants, but it is more valuable for its saturated fatty acids.

A diet that is high in polyunsaturated fatty acids may lead to cellular membrane instability and make one more prone to cellular damage by the sun and environmental factors. Saturated fats are more protective.

Kiwi Green Dream

- ¾ **cup coconut water**
- 2 **kiwis, peeled and quartered**
- ½ **cup frozen pineapple chunks**
- ½ **avocado, pitted and peeled**
- 1 **tablespoon chia seeds**

Combine water, kiwis, pineapple, and avocado in blender; blend until smooth. Add chia seeds; blend until smooth. Serve immediately.

Makes 2 servings

Kiwi Green Dream is a smoothie made with coconut water, kiwis, frozen pineapple, avocado, and chia seeds. Its vibrant green color that is speckled with kiwi seeds is inviting and its coconut-pineapple flavor is refreshing and reminiscent of lazy, indulgent beach days.

Coconut oil, when liberally applied to the skin, also helps to retain the skin's moisture and shiny appearance in hot, dry conditions and promotes all-over tanning, if desirable.

Aging affects the skin since it loses hydration and flexibility and the healing process takes longer than in younger skin. When coupled with the constant exposure to ultraviolet radiation and increased damage by free radicals, aging skin may look dry, old, saggy, and wrinkly.

Coconut oil to the rescue! Coconut oil may be used to treat weathered skin or even to help guard against the grim ravages of ultraviolet radiation. However, coconut oil may not be a cure-all for advanced skin problems. Before using, check with a specialist for prescribed care.

Traditional Beauty Rituals

Many diverse cultures worldwide have valued coconuts and specifically coconut oil for centuries for various beauty rituals. This is in addition to their culinary uses and traditional medicinal remedies that may include abscesses, asthma, baldness, bronchitis, bruises, burns, colds, constipation, cough, dropsy, dysentery, earache, fever, flu, gingivitis, gonorrhea, irregular or painful menstruation, jaundice, kidney stones, lice, malnutrition, nausea, rash, scabies, scurvy, skin infections, sore throat, swelling, syphilis, toothache, tuberculosis, tumors, typhoid, ulcers, upset stomach, weakness, wounds, and many more. The use of coconuts and coconut oil for these treatments varies from culture to culture and many of the miraculous claims may have other causations and cures.

Coconuts and coconut products have also been respected for thousands of years for their esteemed importance in local folklore. This reverence for the coconut and its oil helps explain its variety of usages in the following settings:

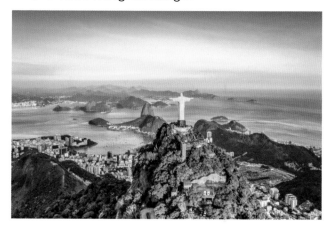

Central and South America

In the coastal jungles of Central and South America, coconuts and coconut oil are used both as food and as medicine by traditional healers who attempt to nourish and treat the ill back to health, including minor maladies such as skin ailments.

Ethiopia, Nigeria, and Somalia

Palm kernel oil, which is an oil that is very similar in scope to coconut oil, is a very popular treatment for a host of illnesses and conditions in these parts of Africa.

India

Coconut oil is an important component of *Ayurvedic medicine*, a type of alternative or complementary form of traditional medicine that was established more than 3,000 years ago in India. Ayurvedic medicine is based on the belief that health and wellness depend on a delicate balance between the mind, body, and spirit.

In addition to coconut oil's medicinal applications, Indian women are said to have favored coconut oil to give their hair luster and volume.

Indonesia

In Indonesia women historically applied coconut oil on their hair and body to keep their hair and skin healthy, as well as using it for culinary purposes. Coconut oil is still important for these reasons and for the Indonesian economy today.

Jamaica

Coconut oil was the "go-to" elixir for common illnesses and it was reportedly used as a health tonic since it was considered to be heart-healthy. Today, coconut oil is used to bind the natural protein structure of hair, seal the hair after moisturizing, tame frizz, and as a pre-shampoo treatment and scalp massage.

Panama

Panamanians have been known to drink a glass of coconut oil as a preventative against illness and to speed recovery. Today, Panamanian coconut oil is found throughout its Pacific beaches, where it is used for healthy skin, hair care, massage oil, make-up removal, weight loss, and for cooking.

Kitava

Kitava is one of the tiny Trobriand Islands of Papua New Guinea. The Kitavan population consumes a significant amount of coconuts and while their lifespan may be shorter than others worldwide, they are healthy and fit—much attributed to their coconut-rich diet. Kitavans are said to possess healthy skin without acne.

Papua New Guinea

The native residents of Papua New Guinea have been using virgin coconut oil for centuries for cooking, treating cuts and bruises, hair treatments, and as a skin moisturizer. Papua New Guinea coconut oil is considered to be one of the best coconut oils in the world due to its pristine and unspoiled remote growing regions. The native residents of Papua New Guinea have used this type of coconut oil on their hair as a convenient and natural hair conditioner and to tame its coarseness.

Philippines

In the Philippines, coconut oil that is rubbed throughout the hair is said to maintain color, shininess, and thickness throughout old age. It is also allegedly used for healing bruises, burns, cuts, and even broken bones. When coconut oil is massaged into aching joints and muscles, it offers relief and comfort according to these islanders.

Samoa

The native healers of Samoa used coconut oil as a natural remedy for different types of illness and injuries. Samoan mothers were reported to have used coconut oil to massage their children's bodies so that they would have healthy skin without blemishes or infections and strong bones. The soft spot on infants' heads was gently massaged with coconut oil as a safeguard and teething babies were massaged with coconut oil to reduce any pain they might feel.

Sri Lanka and Thailand

Coconut oil was the mainstay of Sri Lankan and Thai people for cooking, cosmetics, and medicine. The majority of their diets were composed of coconut "cream" and coconut "milk" and coconuts are still staples today. Virgin coconut oil is a much sought after ingredient in beauty and personal care products today.

Butternut Squash in Coconut Milk

⅓ cup sweetened flaked coconut

2 teaspoons coconut oil

½ small onion, finely chopped

2 cloves garlic, minced

1 cup unsweetened coconut milk

¼ cup packed brown sugar

1 tablespoon fish sauce

⅛ to ¼ teaspoon red pepper flakes

1 butternut squash (about 2 pounds), peeled and cut into large cubes

1 tablespoon chopped fresh cilantro

1. Preheat oven to 350°F. Spread coconut in baking pan. Cook 5 to 7 minutes, stirring occasionally, until golden brown. Set aside to cool and crisp.

2. Heat oil in large saucepan over medium-high heat. Add onion and garlic; cook and stir 3 minutes or until tender. Add coconut milk, brown sugar, fish sauce, and red pepper flakes; stir until sugar is dissolved.

3. Bring mixture to a boil; add squash. Reduce heat to medium. Cover and simmer 30 minutes or until squash is tender. Transfer squash to serving bowl with slotted spoon.

4. Increase heat to high; boil remaining liquid until thickened, stirring constantly. Pour liquid over squash in bowl. Sprinkle with toasted coconut and chopped cilantro. Garnish, if desired.

Makes 4 to 6 servings

Butternut Squash in Coconut Milk combines flaked coconut, coconut oil, onions, garlic, coconut milk, brown sugar, fish sauce, butternut squash, red pepper flakes, and cilantro for a nutritious and delicious combination of tastes that are utterly indulgent.

Tokel

In Tokel in the South Pacific, Tokelauans consume over 60 percent of their calories from coconuts. They are one of the largest consumers of saturated fat in the world and yet they are in relatively good health with no evidence of heart disease.

Zanzibar

Along with beauty, cooking, and health practices, coconut oil was used for candle making, diesel fuel, and as a fuel for lighting.

It is remarkable that the coconut can be so good for you and so beautifying, too. For hundreds of years, people from around the world have captured and utilized this secret for their appearance, health, and well-being—not to mention their taste and culinary satisfaction!

Oil-Pulling: Yea or Nay?

This chapter focuses on the ritual of "oil-pulling," which has been used for thousands of years in some parts of the world, but has recently become more popularized in Western countries, including the U.S. Oil-pulling practitioners swish coconut oil in their mouths for several minutes or up to 20 minutes to kill bacteria, improve gum health, prevent cavities, and strengthen teeth.

The American Dental Association (ADA) has cautioned against this practice because it states that oil-pulling has not been studied in depth. Plus, some oil-pulling practitioners report that they have noticed no improvement in their overall mouth health.

Still, some oil-pulling advocates believe that the possible pros for oil-pulling seem to outweigh the potential cons. To fully understand the logic behind oil-pulling, read on.

Overview of Oil-Pulling

Oil-pulling is an ancient Indian therapy that involves swishing about one tablespoon of oil inside of the mouth, permitting it to move about the gums, teeth, and tongue, and then spitting the oil out of the mouth. Supposedly the oil "pulls" bacteria, impurities, and other germs from the oral cavity and rids the body of infection. A variety of oils have been used for oil-pulling throughout its use in history.

The use of coconut oil for oil-pulling has increased in popularity. This is probably due to the potential germ-fighting properties of coconut oil due to the lauric acid in coconut oil that attacks "bad" bacteria while it promotes "good" bacteria.

Traditional Uses

To fully understand the process of oil-pulling, one needs to examine its venerated history. Oil-pulling as a type of oral therapy has been practiced in Ayurvedic medicine, one of the oldest systems of medicine in the world, for 3,000 years. Today, many practitioners of Ayurvedic medicine reside in India or Southeast Asia. Ayurvedic medicine may be used singularly as the primary medical approach or in combination with different therapies of conventional Western medicine.

Ayurvedic Medicine

Ayurvedic medicine is a traditional eastern Indian approach to life science that emphasizes balance, harmony, and interconnectedness. According to Ayurvedic medicine, good health is a balance among body, mind, the senses, and the soul—not the absence of illness.

In fact, the term "Ayurveda" blends the Sanskrit words *ayur* (life) and *veda* (knowledge or science). The key concepts of Ayurvedic medicine are the body's constitution, life forces, and universal connectedness. These concepts blend *prakriti* (the body's constitution) with people, their health, and the universe (interconnectedness) with *dosha* (life forces) in a not-so dissimilar way to the Greek Biological Humors System of ancient times.

Ayurvedic Medicine and Individualized Health

Ayurvedic medicine does not promote generalized treatments; rather, its premise is individualized, based upon the dominant dosha, or life force of the body and nature. Ayurvedic physicians promote balance. Individualized prescribed treatments may include some combination of diet, exercise, lifestyle recommendations, and unique blends of herbs and of other proprietary ingredients.

In the ancient Greek Biological Humors System the four "humors" are the metabolic agents of the four elements of the human body. These four humors include blood that represents air, phlegm that represents water, yellow bile that represents fire, and black bile that represents Earth. According to this system, to maintain health it is essential to have the right balance of these humors and to ensure their purity. It is natural that organic extra-virgin olive oil-pulling is common today—perhaps a nod to olive oil's Mediterranean roots.

These proprietary Ayurvedic products may either be all herbal or made from a combination of herbs, metals, minerals, and other ingredients. The process in which this composition is created is called *rasa shastra*.

Rasa shastra combines metals such as copper, gold, iron, lead, silver, tin, or zinc and other substances that may include coral, feathers, salts, and/or seashells in a purification process that is then combined with herbs to treat various illnesses. A criticism of rasa shastra is that some of these ingredients, such as the heavy metals, may be harmful with improper use or without adequate instruction by a trained Ayurvedic practitioner.

Aside from rasa shastra, another practice in traditional Ayurvedic medicine is the process of gargling to treat different bodily imbalances among the doshas, or life forces. These treatments, called *gandusha* or *kavala graha*, are considered as remedies. They are used to help "cure" such conditions as asthma, diabetes, migraines, and sinusitis as well as for dental and oral care. In *gandusha* one's mouth is filled completely with oil and it is held for about three to five minutes. In *kavala graha* a smaller amount of oil is used, then swished between the teeth and even gargled at the back of the throat.

Ayurvedic Medicine and Oil-Pulling

Historically, in Ayurvedic text, the use of sesame oil is recommended as a preventative to reduce *vata dosha*, or the dryness of the mouth along with burning sensation and inflammation. Coconut oil, herbal oils, and sunflower oil are also recommended, especially after specific ailments are diagnosed. The concept is that by extracting bacteria, fungi, and toxins from the oral cavity before they move into the body and integrated with the body systems, oil-pulling will both restore and maintain the body's natural balance.

The Physiology of the Mouth and Oil-Pulling

The mouth is a receptacle of both bad and good bacteria. The process of swishing fluids around the oral cavity may dislodge bits and pieces of food and coat the teeth and gums. Oil-pulling may not necessarily "pull" out impurities; rather, it may help to extricate them. Also, oil-pulling should not replace everyday oral hygiene, but it may be an adjunct to daily brushing and flossing. In developing countries where there is not access to modern dental care, oil-pulling may be one of the only alternatives.

Oil-Pulling Benefits

Oil-pulling is said to help fight gingivitis, plaque, and microorganisms that contribute to bad breath. The idea is that the oral microorganisms are encased within a lipid or fatty membrane that adheres to other fats. When oils are swished around the mouth, they stick to the undesirable microorganisms within the oral cavity and are spit out after a few minutes of swishing.

Oil-Pulling Practices

The practice of oil-pulling with coconut oil is said to benefit from its lauric acid content with its antimicrobial benefits.

Merely five minutes daily of gentle pushing, sucking, and swishing of coconut oil around the mouth and through the teeth is said to be effective. Smaller amounts are advised (maybe one to two teaspoons to start). As much as twenty minutes daily may be difficult on the jaws. Extended periods of time swishing may pose a risk of *lipoid pneumonia* from accidentally breathing in small amounts of oil.

As the oil mixes with saliva it might become thicker and milkier in appearance. Swallowing is not recommended. A bowl or pot close by for removal is preferred to the sink or toilet. After spitting, it is advised that one rinses well with water. Some people add a little salt to the rinse water. Then brushing and flossing are generally advised afterward.

Oil-Pulling Support

Some small pilot studies have suggested that daily oil swishing may indeed affect oral bacteria. In a 2008 study by Asokan *et al.* that was published in the *Journal of Indian Society of Pedodontics and Preventive Dentistry* it was determined that there was a reduction in *Streptococcus mutans* in the saliva and plaque of adolescents who used oil-pulling with *chlorhexidine* mouthwash. *Streptococcus mutans* are bacterium that are commonly found in the human oral cavity and significantly contribute to tooth decay. Chlorhexidine mouthwash has antibacterial properties that may control and kill oral bacteria and help to prevent tooth decay. This study concluded that oil-pulling may be used as an effective preventative treatment for the maintenance and improvement of oral health.

Another study in 2011 by Asokan *et al.* that was published in the same journal evaluated the effect of oil-pulling with sesame oil on halitosis and the contributing microorganisms, also compared with chlorhexidine mouthwash. Halitosis, considered as "bad breath," may be caused by bacteria that are present below the gum line and the back of the tongue. Disorders of the esophagus, lungs, nasal cavities, stomach, and/or throat may also be contributory.

This study also used adolescents as the study subjects. The researchers concluded that oil-pulling therapy was equally effective to chlorhexidine mouthwash for treating halitosis and the microorganisms that are associated with halitosis.

Asokan postulated that *saponification* (the process by which a vegetable oil or animal fat is mixed with a strong alkali) and *emulsification* (the breakdown of fat globules into tiny droplets) with their mechanical cleansing actions might be indicative of how oil-pulling works. It seems that rinsing with oil leaves an oil residue for these reasons and that swishing or pulling with oil may have a mechanical cleaning action.

In another small pilot study reported by Huributt in 2014 that involved healthy young adults with high levels of oral bacteria, it was concluded that those who used sesame oil to oil-pull experienced a five-fold decrease in oral bacteria compared to a water-only group. Those who used coconut oil to oil-pull experienced a two-fold decrease. When oil-pulling was stopped, the bacteria levels increased. Furthermore, Huributt recommended if people wanted to add oil-pulling to their dental hygiene practice that they should be cautious of allergies or hypersensitivities, use organic, edible oil, and not swallow it.

Oil-Pulling Concern

As stated, the American Dental Association has cautioned again the practice of oil-pulling since it is not studied in depth. Furthermore, the studies previously reported were conducted with eastern Indian subject participants in small sample sizes, and there have not been repeated studies with wider applications.

While the kidneys and the liver serve to remove toxins from the body, the oral cavity is only thought to do so through the practice of Aryuvedic medicine. With more supportable research, exact recommendations for usage, and cautions for any possible side effects, oil-pulling (especially with coconut oil and its antimicrobial lauric acid) may finally see its day.

Oral Health Uses of Coconut Oil

The antibacterial and antifungal properties of coconut oil might be useful to clean dentures, invisible braces, mouth guards, or retainers. Simply rub a little coconut oil on a clean cotton ball and on to the mouth device after rinsing it at night. The lauric acid in the coconut oil may help to keep it clean and reduce bacteria overnight until its next use. Plus, the pleasing smell and taste of coconut oil may be soothing when these mouth devices are used again.

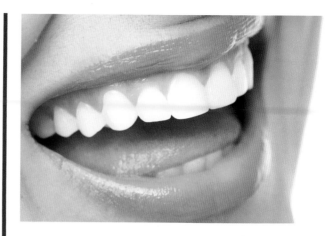

Vitamin E oil with its antioxidant properties may also be used in this manner. Any residue may be absorbed and support healthy gum tissue. Vitamin E oil may be mixed with coconut oil for combined benefits.

As with any therapeutic use of coconut oil, vitamin E oil, or any oil for that matter, it is best to check with a dental professional before their use in these and other capacities.

Nutrients for Oral Health

B vitamins (for epithelial cell turnover): Since there are many B-vitamins, each with specific sources, by consuming a wide-range of food and beverages many of the B-vitamin daily requirements should be met.

Glazed Parsnips and Carrots

1 **pound parsnips (2 large or 3 medium), quartered lengthwise and cut into sticks**

1 **package (8 ounces) baby carrots**

2 **tablespoons coconut oil (divided)**

    Salt and black pepper

¼ **cup orange juice**

1 **tablespoon honey**

⅛ **teaspoon ground ginger**

1. Preheat oven to 425°F.

2. Spread vegetables in shallow roasting pan. Drizzle with 1 tablespoon oil and season with salt and pepper; toss to coat. Bake 30 to 35 minutes or until fork-tender.

3. Combine orange juice, remaining oil, honey, and ginger in large skillet. Add vegetables; cook and stir over high heat 1 to 2 minutes or until glazed.

Makes 6 servings

Parsnips, carrots, and orange juice (with antioxidant vitamins A and C), coconut oil, honey, and butter combine to make a slightly thickened sweet-tart glazed vegetable side dish that is colorful, crispy, and earthy in its deliciousness.

Folate (for healthy mucosal/connective tissue development and immune function and protection against periodontal disease): Food sources of folate include asparagus, chickpeas, broccoli, Brussels sprouts, fortified breakfast cereals, liver, peas, and spinach. Raw, shredded coconut meat contains about 20.8 micrograms of folate per cup.

Calcium-rich foods (for protection and reconstruction of tooth enamel for healthy tooth structure and enhanced enamel mineralization): Food and beverage sources of calcium include almonds, canned salmon, dairy products, dark leafy green vegetables, and fortified soy foods and beverages (including tofu). Raw, shredded coconut meat contains about 11.2 milligrams of calcium per cup.

Iron (for healthy mucosal/connective tissues and immune function): Food sources of iron include dark green leafy vegetables such as kale and spinach, iron-fortified breads and breakfast cereals, dried fruit as apricots and raisins, legumes, peas, pork, poultry, red meat, and seafood. Raw, shredded coconut meat contains about 1.9 milligrams of iron per cup.

Omega-3 fatty acids (for healthy mucosal/ connective tissues and immune function and inflammatory response modulation): Food sources of omega-3 fatty acids include chia seeds, fatty fish, fish oil, fish roe, seafood, spinach, soybeans, and walnuts.

Proteins (for healthy tooth structure, musosal/connective tissue development and immune function): Food sources of proteins include both animal and vegetable foods and beverages such as meats, dairy products, grains, legumes, and vegetables.

Vitamin A (for healthy mucosal/connective tissue development and immune function): Food sources of vitamin A include bell peppers, cantaloupe, carrots, dark leafy green vegetables, dried apricots, fish, liver, mango, papaya, sweet potatoes, and winter squash.

Phosphorus (for protection and reconstruction of tooth enamel for healthy tooth structure): Food and beverages sources of phosphorus include dairy products, eggs, fish, and lean meats. Raw, shredded coconut meat contains about 90.4 milligrams of phosphorus per cup.

Vitamin C (for healthy gums and quick would healing): Food sources of vitamin C include broccoli, citrus fruits, peppers, potatoes, spinach, and tomatoes. Raw, shredded coconut meat contains about 2.6 milligrams of vitamin C per cup.

Vitamin D (for healthy mucosal/connective tissue development and immune function and enhanced enamel remineralization): Food and beverage sources of vitamin D include beef liver, cheese, egg yolks, fatty fish such as herring, mackerel, salmon, sardines, and tuna and fortified dairy products.

Zinc (for healthy musosal/connective tissue development and immune function): Food sources of zinc include beef, dairy products, fortified breakfast cereals, legumes, nuts, oysters, seafood (particularly crab and lobster), and whole grains. Raw, shredded coconut meat contains about 0.9 milligrams of zinc per cup.

Last Look

While the philosophy behind oil-pulling is centuries old, the considerations for oil-pulling are ever ongoing. Contemplate the advantages and disadvantages of oil-pulling and individual body and health stipulations. Choose wisely, practice (if you do) oil-pulling smartly and as always, check with dental and health care professionals before attempting any new routine.

Salmon and Wild Rice Chowder

1	teaspoon coconut oil
1	red onion, chopped
1	red bell pepper, chopped
1	cup green beans, cut into 1-inch pieces
1½	teaspoons minced fresh dill weed
1	teaspoon salt
⅛	teaspoon black pepper
3	cups vegetable broth
1	cup cooked wild rice
12	ounces skinless salmon fillet, cut into 1-inch pieces
½	cup milk
2	teaspoons all-purpose flour

1. Melt coconut oil in large saucepan over high heat. Add onion, bell pepper, and green beans; cook and stir 5 minutes. Stir in dill, salt, and black pepper. Pour in broth; bring to a simmer.

2. Add wild rice and salmon to saucepan. Reduce heat to low; cover and simmer 6 to 8 minutes or until salmon flakes easily when tested with fork.

3. Whisk milk into flour in small bowl until smooth. Stir into saucepan. Cook until heated through.

Makes 8 servings

Red onion and red bell pepper (with vitamins A and C), sautéed in delectable coconut oil, with green beans and fresh dill mixed with skinless salmon (with calcium, protein, and vitamin D), milk (with vitamins A and D and protein) and wild rice (with B-vitamins) make a hearty one-dish meal that is great for the teeth, bones, and appetite!

A Natural Alternative

While coconuts are delicious and versatile and their meat, oil, and water do amazing things for our appearance and health, there are some other surprising and lesser-known ways that the coconut can support a natural, healthful lifestyle.

Coconut products can act as household cleansers, lubricants, and conditioners; shine jewelry, leather goods, and shoes; remove rust; and are the basis for useful homemade items. They can even provide raw materials for various building and household goods.

Household Cleanser, Lubricant, and Conditioner

One of the concerns about household cleansers is that their chemicals are emitted into our homes and we are exposed to their ingredients. Instead, a growing number of people are interested in "green" cleaners, or products that are produced with biodegradable, natural, and nontoxic ingredients. Coconut and its by-products can claim all three attributes.

As a household cleanser, coconut oil can remove simple dirty marks from surfaces that can handle commercial cleansers. Of course, it is always sensible to try a test area first before wider application.

Coconut oil may grease hinges and small appliances as it gently removes rust and it may remove simple stains and condition wooden floors and moldings. Once applied, make sure to dry and buff the treated areas with a soft cloth and be sure to walk on these parts carefully.

Cleanses and Conditions Household Items

Coconut oil can be used as a handy, inexpensive, and natural household cleanser to clean brushes and remove chewing gum, crayon marks, and ink spills on clothing, furniture, or floors. This may take a few applications, drying and fluffing or buffing with a soft, dry cloth.

Coconut oil can be lightly melted, then applied with a clean, dry, and soft cloth to clean and add shine and protection to a host of natural household surfaces instead of using synthetic cleaners and conditioners. Follow with another dry buffing cloth. A little residue can be left behind for extra shine and conditioning. If anything adheres to the coconut oil residue, then a simple rinse may be needed before using.

Cleanses and Smoothens Brushes

After paintbrushes are used and cleaned, they may become hardened—even if water-based paints are used. Coconut oil will keep paintbrushes supple and ready for use. Make sure that they are impeccably cleaned before applying so the paint is not activated.

Makeup Brush Cleaner:
Rub warmed coconut oil on makeup brushes and let set a few hours. Wash thoroughly and dry well with a clean, dry cloth. A little residue may be desirable to revitalize the brush hairs and for makeup application.

Removes Chewing Gum from Hair or Furniture

When coconut oil is applied to hardened chewing gum it may ease the adherence and make it easier to dislodge, without leaving behind any residual colors or stains.

Liberal amounts of coconut oil may be applied onto the chewing gum and left to remain for about two to five minutes. Then a soft, dry cloth can be used to dislodge the chewing gum and remove the residue. Depending upon the fabric and care directions, a mild soap may be used to remove any excess coconut oil. A clean, dry cloth can then be used to blot any extra coconut oil.

Coconut oil can also be used to remove labels or other sticky residue in a similar manner. Try it with labels that adhere to glass, plastic, wood, or other hard surfaces, but be sure to check the care instructions first.

Cleans Metal Items

Assorted metal items may benefit from a thin layer of coconut oil. These metal items include cars, cast iron equipment, decorative objects, hinges, kitchen appliances, lawn mowers, snow shovels, zippers, bike chains, and much more.

Cleans Crayon Marks, Ink Spills, and Spots

Crayon marks, ink smears, smudges, and skid marks may be removed with coconut oil by using a clean cloth or soft brush. Once the coconut oil sets for a few minutes, it can then be removed with another dry, clean cloth.

Maintains and Details Cars

Coconut oil adds a lustrous sheen to the dashboard or to leather car seats. Since materials differ, test a little area first with a clean cloth and buff it dry with another clean, dry cloth. Remember that the coconut oil residue may be slightly slippery when passengers use the seats. Coconut oil can also be used to buff out little exterior scratches with a dry, clean cloth or to remove bugs or sap off of a car's exterior. First let it coat the exterior for a few moments before wiping clean and dry.

Lubricates Small Motors and Kitchen Appliances

A small amount of coconut oil can be used to lubricate small motors, such as those in blenders, food processors, hand mixers, or juicers—much like it can be used to oil hinges. Make sure that there is little-to-no residue that can solidify and prevent normal operation of these small household items.

A thin layer carefully rubbed over the blades of kitchen appliances helps keep them running smoothly. Be extra cautious to unplug the appliances first before application and to carefully wipe in one direction and away to help prevent any accidents.

Prevents Kitchen Items from Sticking:

• Apply coconut oil in measuring cups or spoons before filling with sticky ingredients, such as honey or maple syrup.

• Rub the inside of plastic storage containers with a little coconut oil to prevent deeply-colored stains from gravies, soy sauce, tomato sauce, or other highly-pigmented items.

• "Grease" the inside of cake pans or muffin tins with coconut oil before the batter is added to help easily remove baked goods. It is important to use a clean, dry cloth and apply a thin layer, then wipe off any extra coconut oil with another clean, dry cloth since any residue may smoke in the oven. Also, be careful as the items might be slippery.

Seasons Cast Iron Cooking Equipment

Cast iron cooking equipment is prized for its ability to conduct heat and transfer from the stovetop to the oven then to the table. The process of seasoning cast iron cooking equipment involves coating it with a layer for protection and to act as a nonstick surface. Coconut oil is excellent for both of these purposes and can be used like other vegetable oils.

A generous amount of coconut oil can be applied to the inside of cast iron cooking equipment. It can then be placed in a 250 to 350 degree Fahrenheit oven for about an hour.

If the coconut oil smells or starts smoking, remove the cooking equipment and turn down the heat. When the oven cools, put the items back into the oven. A cookie sheet can also be placed under the items to prevent any coconut oil from spilling.

Once the cooking equipment is removed from the oven, any excess coconut oil can be wiped off with a clean, dry cloth and discarded. This process should be repeated a few times until the surfaces are functionally nonstick.

Maintains Lawn Mower Blades and Knives

A thin layer of coconut oil that is rubbed over clean lawn mower blades helps to prevent clumps of grass from sticking and jamming the lawn mower. Likewise, stained, dulled knives may be refreshed with a thin layer of coconut oil. As with the small appliances blades, stroke away and in one direction.

Slicks Snow Shovels

Sometimes snow and ice cling to shovels and other winter removal equipment. Once a thin layer of coconut oil is applied to this equipment, the snow or ice should be able to be removed more easily. This process may need to be repeated with ongoing snow, ice, and other weather issues.

Reduces Squeaky or Sticky Hinges

A little coconut oil may be all that is needed to reduce the stickiness or squeakiness in cabinet or door hinges.

Unzips Zippers and Greases Bike Chains

A thin layer of coconut oil can be applied to jammed bike chains or heavy-duty zippers. Coconut oil functions as a natural lubricant for bike chains and to keep zippers operating smoothly.

Just a little coconut oil that is applied to a jammed clothing zipper should help it to move more easily or get back on track. Make sure that it is rubbed into both sides of the zipper before moving it and that any excess is removed so as not to damage garments or leather goods.

Reduces and Removes Rust

Rust is caused by the reaction of iron and oxygen in the presence of air or water. To remove rust, apply a thin layer of coconut oil over a rusty area. First rub a little coconut oil on metal objects, such as car accessories, outdoor metal furniture, silverware, or other metal items that are disposed to rusting to test the results. Then, apply just a thin layer of coconut oil with a soft, dry cloth and let it remain on the metal object for a few hours. The coconut oil can then be wiped or washed off with warm water, depending upon the surface of the object and if there are any care instructions that advise otherwise. The object can be cleaned of any rusty residue and dried with a clean, dry cloth. Repeat the process if necessary. The improvement should be fairly immediate and provide longer-range protection.

Eliminates Soap Scum

Apply a thin layer of coconut oil to soap scum in the bathtub or shower and let it remain about 10 to 20 minutes. Soap is alkaline and coconut oil (as are other oils) is acidic, so the coconut oil works to break down soap scum. Vinegar can be added to the coconut oil to increase its acidity, or coconut oil can be mixed with baking soda into a paste. Dry the area with a clean, dry cloth and be careful to avoid slipping.

Polishes Metals

Coconut oil that is rubbed over clean metal with a soft cloth, left for a few moments, then buffed to a shine helps restore the polished look of metal surfaces. Coconut oil is particularly useful for polishing bronze items.

Cleans and Polishes Granite Surfaces

Apply coconut oil onto granite countertops, tables, or other stone surfaces to clean and remove dust, cover minor scratches, and add shine. Like other applications, it is best to try a small area first.

While some granite is intended to shine, other granite surfaces are meant to be duller in appearance. The sheen may be able to be adjusted.

Many creams and polishes form a layer of synthetic chemicals to create sheen and coat granite surfaces. Coconut oil is absorbed into any cracks or crevices and may last longer. Plus, coconut oil lends a pleasant smell throughout the kitchen and the rest of the house.

Conditions Cutting Boards

Kitchen cutting boards should first be cleaned with a damp towel. Then they should be dried well before coconut oil is applied. A different soft cloth should be used to rub some coconut oil into the surface of the cutting board. After the cutting board absorbs the coconut oil for about 10 to 15 minutes, then another fresh, dry cloth should be used for buffing.

A little lemon essential oil or lemon juice can be added to the coconut oil first to remove any odors and to provide a pleasant lemon scent.

Conditions Leather Chairs and Sofas

Rub a small amount of coconut oil into real leather chairs or sofas to soften and condition them. While a little residue can remain, too much may residue may transfer to clothing or cause slippage.

Shines Plant Leaves

Just a dab of coconut oil applied with a clean, dry cloth and gently rubbed across the surface of broad plant leaves helps them to look shiny and keeps them relatively dust-free. Repeat this process as needed. Some plant leaves do not thrive with a coating of any kind, so it is best to check with a nursery or plant care guide before any application.

Shines Jewelry

Some types of jewelry can be polished with coconut oil, but it is best to check the care instructions first and try a little dab on the underside of the jewelry before possibly damaging the item. Bronze items may particularly benefit.

A dab of doconut oil is even handy for removing rings when they become too tight and get stuck on the fingers.

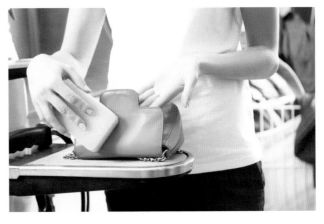

Shines and Revitalizes Leather and Patent Leather Items

Rubbing coconut oil on leather or patent leather boots, shoes, and other items helps them to shine and revitalizes their overall appearance, including any buff or scratch marks. This process may need to be repeated over time. As with other leather goods, it is best to try a test area first before full application.

Deters Pests and Soothes Bites

As an insect repellent, coconut oil has many applications. Coconut oil can be mixed with essential oils such as citronella, peppermint, rosemary, or tea tree oil, or herbs such as catnip, mint, or rosemary to make a natural insect repellent to repel bees, flies, or gnats. Apply liberally. This mixture provides a safer alternative to some insect repellents and can usually be applied all over the body. If bitten, coconut oil dabbed directly onto a cleansed and sanitized bug bite might offer some relief.

Creates Useful Homemade Items

Items as simple as candles, laundry detergent, and play dough can be made with coconut oil. It is generally easy to use, inexpensive, natural, and perfumes the house, clothing, and hands with its attractive tropical coconut smell.

Turning a hard coconut shell into a bowl or makeshift musical instrument is also a creative use of the coconut.

Play Dough

Play dough is a popular childhood product that can be made with melted coconut oil, salt, flour, water, cream of tartar, and natural food coloring with this recipe:

1	**tablespoon coconut oil**
½	**cup salt**
1	**cup flour**
1	**cup water**
2	**teaspoon cream of tartar**
	Natural food coloring

1. In a large, heavy pot, melt 1 tablespoon coconut oil over low heat.

2. Gradually mix the next four ingredients into the melted coconut oil.

3. Stir until the mixture forms a ball.

4. Add the natural food coloring and mix well.

5. Remove from heat and cool before using.

6. Store in an airtight container.

Laundry Detergent

Melt pure soap, then mix with coconut oil and essential oils and add a little water. Pour this mixture into a container or mold to harden. It makes a nontoxic liquid or solid, depending upon the amount of water that can be used as a laundry detergent to clean clothes. This combination should not be irritating or affect fabrics, but is it best to try a little on a small patch of skin and item of clothing before using. People who are prone to allergies and/or have sensitive skin may benefit from this use.

Musical Instruments

Empty coconut shells can be turned on their cut ends and played as percussion instruments—much like they have been used around the world for centuries for musical entertainment. Even children can use coconut shells for simple drums that can be first decorated.

Serving Utensils

The hard, outside shells of coconuts can be cleaned well, dried, and prepped with coconut oil, then used as serving bowls for dried foods, such as chips or crackers. Make sure to clean these containers well after each use and prep with coconut oil again as needed.

Scents

Mix coconut oil and essential oil in an oil diffuser to create economical, natural, and inviting scents without artificial ingredients.

Aromatherapy

Add a few drops of comforting essential oil to warmed coconut oil. Dab on the back of the neck, the tip of the nose, on the chest, or on the temples. Try eucalyptus or peppermint essential oil for congestion or stress reduction, or for an upset stomach, try a citrus-based essential oil, such as lemon, lime, or orange.

Protecting Your Pet

The coconut's healing and protective properties don't just apply to you—they can help your pet as well! Coconut oil can be used to clean dog or cats' ears and to moisturize dry, cracked paw pads or noses. It can even be used to make homemade, natural treats for some pets. And coconut oil helps prevent cat litter from sticking to the bottom of a litter box when the box is rubbed with a thin layer of coconut oil.

Grooms Pets

Just like coconut oil is beneficial for human skin and hair, coconut oil contributes to the silky coats of dogs and cats. It can be added to pet shampoo or warmed by human hands and lightly massaged into a pet's coat.

Relieves Dry, Injured, or Sensitive Skin

Besides being delicious, nutritious, and soothing for pets, a small amount of coconut oil may be nurturing when it is applied to a pet's sensitive or injured skin. Coconut oil may help nourish dry, inflamed, or irritated skin that results from allergens, chemicals, insect bites, among other causes.

Some examples follow:

• One-half teaspoon of coconut oil that is applied to cat's paws may smooth dryness. A similar amount that is applied to a cat's furry exterior may promote a shiny coat and reduce hairballs.

• A similar amount of coconut oil that is rubbed into a dog's paws may prevent or reduce cracked paw pads. Dog paws tend to be calloused, rough, tough, and/or thickened to handle the dog's daily walks.

Both dogs and cats might enjoy the taste of coconut oil and lick their paws clean. This might lead to increased licking and soreness, so it is best to monitor the process. It is also wise to apply the coconut oil to a dog's paws outside and away from delicate carpets or floors.

• Some warm coconut oil may be rubbed onto a cat or dog's nose that is chronically dry or cracked. Be aware that the tastiness of coconut oil may promote constant licking and may defeat the original purpose of lubricating the cracked skin. Keep trying, as the newness of this application may eventually dissipate.

• A little warm coconut oil may be used to clean a pet's ears. First, any dirt should be gently removed with a cotton ball or soft cloth. Then, a little warm coconut oil may be gently rubbed into the underside of the ears with another clean cotton ball or soft cloth. Make sure to remove any residue beyond a thin layer. While a dog's ear canal is in an L-shape, it is still advised not to insert anything too far inside of a dog's ears. The coconut oil may help to keep the skin's interior supple and reduce itching. It is best to check first with a veterinarian before application— especially for smaller dogs.

• Coconut oil may also be used for dental hygiene. Add a few drops of coconut oil on a soft toothbrush to keep a dog's teeth clean, its gums healthy, and its breath smelling pleasantly. While coconut oil is edible and there is little health risk if pets lick it off, there may be exceptions. As with other usages of coconut oil for animals, exercise caution.

Nourishes Pets and Supports Pet Health

Similar to humans, dogs and cats may benefit from coconut oil added to their diet. The pet maladies that seem to benefit the best from coconut oil enhanced pet food are skin allergies, irritations or wounds, and digestive upsets.

A veterinarian should be first consulted. Dogs weighing over 40 pounds may benefit from one-half to one tablespoon of coconut oil; dogs weighing under 30 pounds may benefit with half this amount or less to help to improve their dry skin and promote a healthy coat.

It is best to start with a few drops to about one-half teaspoon of warmed coconut oil added to food daily; watch for any reactions. If there is unusual stomach upset or other contraindications, then cut back and contact a veterinarian if any ill effects continue.

The saturated fatty acids in coconut oil, particularly the medium-chain triglycerides, provide energy for pets as they do for humans. There is some debate about the use of medium-chain triglycerides in the diet of cats, so it is best to talk to a veterinarian before using it.

Coconut water can be frozen in ice cube trays and the coconut water ice cubes can be given to pets on hot days as a cool and tasty refresher.

Coconut oil and peanut butter can be blended with a little coconut water to thin the mixture, poured into ice cube trays, and frozen. These coconut pet treats are cold, nutritious, and tasty—especially during hot, dry summers.

Coconut Oil Dog Treats

½   **cup coconut flour**

½   **cup fruit puree**
     (applesauce, apricot, or pear)

1   **tablespoon honey**

2   **tablespoons coconut oil**

3   **tablespoons water, plus more if**
     necessary

1. Preheat oven to 350°F.

2. Line cookie sheet with parchment paper.

3. Combine all ingredients; mix well until smooth consistency. Add more water if needed.

4. Pinch small pieces of dough with fingers; roll into ½ to 1-inch balls.

5. Place uniformly on parchment paper, leaving room between each ball.

6. Bake for five minutes; turn once, then bake an additional five minutes. Cool on rack.

7. Store in refrigerator or freeze.

Putting It All Together

In the previous chapters, we've discussed the many ways that you can put the coconut to work for you, the ways it may benefit your heart and brain health, its cosmetic applications, and the ways it may be used in a natural lifestyle. No one food or material can be a miracle cure—but the coconut has many versatile applications.

So now that you know, where do you go from here?

Cooking with Coconut

All of the additional recipes in the next chapter were specifically designed with the coconut in mind. But with some ingenuity, the coconut can be incorporated in a number of other tasty and inspiring recipes. Simply start by substituting a cooking oil with coconut oil in equal amounts and notice how the recipe changes. It will likely perk up the flavor and lend a rich-tasting texture. Remember the subtle sweetness of coconut oil when it is added to savory foods. It could temper the taste or create a new flavor of its own. The other ingredients may have to be adjusted to compensate. When adding coconut oil to sweet ingredients it will likely increase the sweetness.

Make sure that the recipe is compatible for this change. The other ingredients may need adjustment.

Fresh coconut, coconut water, and coconut milk have a wide range of culinary applications.

Coconuts provide the backbone flavor in many tropical recipes with southern Indian, Southeast Asian, African, and South American roots. Unless they are toasted or kept very dry, coconuts tend to have a lasting flavor and chewy texture.

Flaked or grated coconut or coconut milk can be used in puddings, pies, and cakes for taste, moisture, and texture. Coconut can be sprinkled over fruit or compotes and added to cookies, candies, and confections. It can be blended into curries and sambals (curry accompaniments) and mixed into sides, soups, stews, and stir-fries to elevate simple proteins, starches, and vegetables to create distinctive aromatic and appetizing dishes. Some of these dishes have appeared in this book, and we've included a few more here!

Banana Berry Coconut Milk Smoothie

1	cup unsweetened coconut milk
1	medium banana, peeled
1	cup berries (blueberries, raspberries, and/or strawberries)
4 to 5	whole ice cubes
1	tablespoon coconut oil (optional)
	Nutmeg (optional)

1. Place the first four ingredients into a blender.

2. Blend at low speed until smooth.

3. Dribble with coconut oil, if desired*.

4. Blend at medium speed until well blended.

5. Top with sprinkle of nutmeg, if desired.

*The coconut oil should be added slowly while the blender is running after the main ingredients are blended. This will ensure that it is evenly distributed. If the coconut oil is added sooner, it might harden into little beads and prevent a smooth consistency.

Makes 2 cups

Coconut Selection

Before you cook, you'll have to shop for your coconut or coconut by-products. Here are some tips:

• The hard, green coconut shells are generally removed before coconuts are marketed. What remains are the smaller, rounded brown shell that are usually covered with brown, hairy fibers. The best seasons for purchasing coconuts are fall and winter.

• Select heavy coconuts that are filled with liquid which can be heard when a coconut is shaken. Whole coconuts are easier to crack open and remove the coconut meat if they are heated first since the coconut becomes brittle. Whole coconuts last about 6 months at room temperature, depending upon their degree of ripeness, and about one month once refrigerated.

• It is best to avoid coconuts that are cracked, moldy, or weep from the eye end. Once the coconut is cracked open, if the coconut is yellowed it is best to discard it since it is likely spoiled.

• Coconuts are also available processed in flaked, grated, and shredded forms, unsweetened and sweetened, and dry and moistened.

• Shredded coconut is found in cans and packages; coconut in cans is usually moister.

• Canned or dried coconut lasts about 18 months unopened and one month once opened and refrigerated.

Coconut Conversions

• One medium coconut yields about three to four cups of grated coconut meat.

• One 7-ounce bag of shredded coconut is about 2½ cups of shredded coconut.

• One 3½-ounce can of shredded coconut is about 1¼ cups of shredded coconut.

Cracking Coconut

To crack a coconut, follow these steps:

1. Drive a long, thin spike though one of the coconut's three "eyes," which are located at one end of the coconut.

2. Drain the liquid and strain. It can be consumed or refrigerated.

3. Crack the nut with a hammer or other strong implement. You may want to cover the nut with a kitchen towel to prevent any flying pieces.

4. Continue to break the nut with the hammer or other strong implement until it splits into smaller pieces.

5. Carefully cut the white coconut "meat" away from the shell with a sharp knife. A kitchen towel may help to stabilize the larger pieces as they are cut.

6. If the coconut meat is covered with coconut debris, then gently rinse and pat dry with a clean, dry cloth.

7. Chop or grate the coconut meat with a sharp knife, box, or rotary grater or a food processor.

8. Bag and refrigerate the chopped or grated coconut for up to five days.

Toasting Coconut

Spread a thin layer of flaked, grated, or shredded coconut evenly on a nonstick baking sheet. Bake in preheated 350°F oven for about 5 to 10 minutes or until light golden brown. Stir the coconut frequently as it browns very rapidly. Remove the baking sheet from the oven and allow to cool. Refrigerate or wrap the coconut in freezer paper; leave some "head space" and freeze.

Personal Care

Because coconut oil is so economical and versatile, the use of coconut oil in personal care recipes holds a wealth of possibilities. Look for old apothecary-type recipes and substitute coconut oil (and maybe a little coconut water) for the fats in the recipes. Or add a little smidgeon of coconut oil to recipes for its richness and moisturizing properties. Make sure to use sterilized equipment, clean hands, and sanitized and dry cloths to ensure safety. And do refrigerate the finished products for safekeeping.

The coconut nourished, cleaned, protected, and outfitted people around the world for centuries and still functions in these varied capacities today. Explore the vast range of practices that are outlined in this book and see what it may do for you!

Additional Recipes
Smoothies & Shakes

Banana Chai Smoothie

- ¾ **cup water**
- ¼ **cup unsweetened coconut milk**
- 2 **frozen bananas**
- 1 **teaspoon honey**
- ¼ **teaspoon ground ginger**
- ¼ **teaspoon ground cinnamon**
- ¼ **teaspoon vanilla**
- **Pinch ground cloves (optional)**

1. Combine water, coconut milk, bananas, honey, ginger, cinnamon, vanilla, and cloves, if desired, in blender.

2. Blend until smooth.

Makes 2 servings

Coconut Milkshake

- 1 **tablespoon honey, divided**
- 3 **tablespoons flaked coconut, divided**
- 1 **cup coconut sorbet**
- ½ **cup unsweetened canned coconut milk**
- ¼ **cup crushed ice**

1. Dip rim of glass into ½ tablespoon honey; dip into 1 tablespoon flaked coconut.

2. Combine sorbet, coconut milk, ice, remaining 2 tablespoons flaked coconut, and ½ tablespoon honey in blender.

3. Blend until smooth. Pour into prepared glass; serve immediately.

Makes 1 serving

Smoothies & Shakes

Kiwi Pineapple Cream

- ¾ **cup unsweetened coconut milk**
- 1½ **cups fresh pineapple chunks**
- 2 **kiwis, peeled and quartered**
- **Grated peel and juice of 1 lime**

1. Combine coconut milk, pineapple, kiwis, lime peel, and lime juice in blender.

2. Blend until smooth.

To make a Kiwi Chai Smoothie, add ¼ teaspoon vanilla, ⅛ teaspoon ground cardamom, ⅛ teaspoon ground cinnamon, ⅛ teaspoon ground ginger, and a pinch of ground cloves to the mixture before blending.

Makes 2 servings

Refreshing Green Smoothie

- ¾ **cup unsweetened coconut milk**
- 1 **cup baby spinach**
- ¾ **cup frozen pineapple chunks**
- ½ **teaspoon grated lemon peel**

1. Combine coconut milk, spinach, pineapple, and lemon peel in blender.

2. Blend until smooth.

Makes 1 serving

Smoothies & Shakes

Tropical Breeze Smoothie

- ½   **cup unsweetened coconut milk**
- 1   **cup frozen mango chunks**
- 1   **cup frozen pineapple chunks**
- 1   **tablespoon honey**

1. Combine coconut milk, mango, pineapple, and honey in blender.

2. Blend until smooth.

Makes 2 servings

Carrot Cake Smoothie

- ½   **cup coconut water**
- 3   **carrots, peeled and cut into chunks**
- ½   **banana**
- ½   **cup frozen pineapple chunks**
- 1   **teaspoon honey**
- ⅛   **teaspoon ground cinnamon**
- ⅛   **teaspoon ground ginger**

1. Combine coconut water, carrots, banana, pineapple, honey, cinnamon, and ginger in blender.

2. Blend until smooth.

Makes 1 serving

Smoothies & Shakes

Kiwi Strawberry Smoothie

- 1½ cups unsweetened coconut milk
- 3 kiwis, peeled and quartered
- 1½ cups sliced fresh strawberries
- ¾ cup ice cubes
- 1½ tablespoons honey

1. Combine coconut milk, kiwis, strawberries, ice, and honey in blender.

2. Blend until smooth.

Makes 3 servings

Piña Colada Milkshake

- 2 cups (1 pint) coconut sorbet
- 2 cups (1 pint) vanilla frozen yogurt or ice cream
- ¾ cup pineapple juice
- ¼ cup dark rum or ½ teaspoon rum extract

1. Combine sorbet, frozen yogurt, pineapple juice, and rum in blender.

2. Blend until smooth.

3. Pour into four glasses; serve immediately.

Makes 4 servings

Cuban Batido

- ¾ cup unsweetened coconut milk
- ½ cup orange juice
- 1½ cups fresh pineapple chunks
- 1 cup ice cubes
- 1 tablespoon lime juice

1. Combine coconut milk, orange juice, pineapple, ice, and lime juice in blender.

2. Blend until smooth.

A batido is a popular Latin American drink made with water, milk, fruit, and ice. It is similar in texture to a smoothie and literally means "beaten" in Portuguese.

Makes 3 servings

Green Power Smoothie

- ½ cup coconut water
- 2 cups packed spinach
- 1 cup fresh pineapple chunks
- 1 cup frozen mango chunks
- ½ frozen banana

1. Combine coconut water, spinach, pineapple, mango, and banana in blender.

2. Blend until smooth.

Makes 3 servings

Breakfast & Breads

Blueberry Coconut Flour Muffins

  6   **eggs**

  ½   **cup sugar**

  ¼   **cup (½ stick) butter, melted**

  ¼   **cup whole milk**

  ½   **cup plus 2 teaspoons coconut flour,* divided**

  2   **teaspoons grated lemon peel**

  ½   **teaspoon salt**

  ½   **teaspoon baking powder**

  ½   **teaspoon xanthan gum**

  1   **cup fresh blueberries**

*Coconut flour is a gluten-free, high fiber flour available in the specialty flour section of many supermarkets. It can also be ordered online.

1. Preheat oven to 375°F. Line 12 standard (2½-inch) muffin cups with paper baking cups.

2. Whisk eggs, sugar, butter, and milk in medium bowl until well combined.

3. Mix ½ cup coconut flour, lemon peel, salt, baking powder, and xanthan gum in medium bowl. Sift flour mixture into egg mixture. Whisk until batter is smooth.

4. Combine blueberries with remaining 2 teaspoons coconut flour in small bowl. Stir gently into batter. Pour evenly into prepared muffin cups.

5. Bake 12 to 15 minutes or until toothpick inserted into centers comes out clean. Cool in pan on wire rack 5 minutes. Remove from pan; serve warm.

Makes 12 muffins

Breakfast & Breads

Pumpkin Granola

3	cups old-fashioned oats
¾	cup coarsely chopped almonds
¾	cup raw pumpkin seeds (pepitas)
½	cup canned pumpkin
½	cup maple syrup
⅓	cup coconut oil, melted
1	teaspoon vanilla
1	teaspoon ground cinnamon
½	teaspoon salt
¼	teaspoon ground ginger
¼	teaspoon ground nutmeg
¾	cup dried cranberries
	Pinch ground cloves

For Pumpkin Chocolate Granola, follow this same recipe but reduce amount of maple syrup to ⅓ cup. Stir in ¾ cup semisweet chocolate chips after baking. You can substitute pecans or walnuts for the almonds, and/or add ¾ cup flaked coconut to the mixture before baking.

1. Preheat oven to 325°F. Line large rimmed baking sheet with parchment paper.

2. Combine oats, almonds, and pumpkin seeds in large bowl. Combine pumpkin, maple syrup, oil, vanilla, cinnamon, salt, ginger, nutmeg, and cloves in medium bowl; stir until well blended. Pour over oat mixture; stir until well blended and all ingredients are completely coated. Spread mixture evenly on prepared baking sheet.

3. Bake 50 to 60 minutes or until granola is golden brown and no longer moist, stirring every 20 minutes. (Granola will become more crisp as it cools.) Stir in cranberries; cool completely.

Makes about 5½ cups

Breakfast & Breads

Loaded Banana Bread

½ cup (1 stick) butter, softened

½ cup granulated sugar

½ cup packed brown sugar

2 eggs

1½ cups mashed bananas
     (about 3 ripe bananas)

¼ cup sour cream

½ teaspoon vanilla

1½ cups all-purpose flour

2½ teaspoons baking powder

¼ teaspoon salt

1 can (8 ounces) crushed
     pineapple, drained

⅓ cup flaked coconut

¼ cup mini semisweet chocolate chips

1. Preheat oven to 350°F. Spray 9x5-inch loaf pan with nonstick cooking spray.

2. Beat butter, granulated sugar, and brown sugar in large bowl with electric mixer at medium speed until light and fluffy. Beat in eggs, one at a time, scraping down bowl after each addition. Add bananas, sour cream, and vanilla. Beat just until combined.

3. Sift flour, baking powder, and salt in small bowl. Gradually beat flour mixture into banana mixture just until combined. Fold in pineapple, coconut, and chocolate chips. Spoon batter into prepared pan.

4. Bake 50 minutes or until toothpick inserted into center comes out almost clean. Cool in pan 1 hour; remove from pan.

Makes 1 loaf (about 12 servings)

Breakfast & Breads

Toasted Coconut Doughnuts

- 2¾ **cups all-purpose flour**
- ¼ **cup cornstarch**
- 1½ **teaspoons baking powder**
- 1 **teaspoon salt**
- ½ **teaspoon ground cinnamon**
- ½ **teaspoon ground nutmeg**
- 1 **cup granulated sugar**
- 2 **eggs**
- ¼ **cup (½ stick) butter, melted**
- ¼ **cup applesauce**
- 1 **teaspoon vanilla**
- ¾ **cup unsweetened canned coconut milk, divided***
- **Vegetable oil for frying**
- 1 **teaspoon dark rum or vanilla**
- 1½ **cups sifted powdered sugar**
- 1 **cup flaked coconut, toasted****

*Shake the can vigorously to blend before opening the can, or pour contents of can into bowl and whisk to combine.

**Spread coconut in large skillet; cook over medium-low heat about 10 minutes or until mostly golden brown, stirring frequently.

1. Whisk flour, cornstarch, baking powder, salt, cinnamon, and nutmeg in large bowl.

2. Beat 1 cup granulated sugar and eggs in large bowl with electric mixer on high speed 3 minutes or until pale and thick. Stir in butter, applesauce, and vanilla. Add flour mixture alternately with ½ cup coconut milk, mixing on low speed after each addition. Press plastic wrap directly onto surface of dough; refrigerate at least 1 hour.

3. Pour about 2 inches of oil into Dutch oven or large heavy saucepan; clip deep-fry or candy thermometer to side of pot. Heat over medium-high heat to 360°F to 370°F.

4. Meanwhile, generously flour work surface. Turn out dough onto work surface and dust top with flour. Roll dough about ¼-inch thick; cut out donuts with floured donut cutter. Gather and reroll scraps. Line large wire rack with paper towels.

5. Working in batches, add donuts to hot oil. Cook 1 minute per side or until golden brown. Do not crowd the pan and adjust heat to maintain temperature during frying. Drain on prepared wire racks.

6. Whisk remaining ¼ cup coconut milk and rum in medium bowl. Whisk in powdered sugar to form smooth, thick glaze. Dip tops of donuts in glaze, letting excess drip back into bowl; immediately dip in coconut. Let stand until glaze is set.

Makes 14 to 16 doughnuts

Breakfast & Breads

Cherry Coconut Cheese Coffeecake

- **2½ cups all-purpose flour**
- **¾ cup sugar**
- **½ teaspoon baking powder**
- **½ teaspoon baking soda**
- **6 ounces cream cheese, softened, divided**
- **¾ cup milk**
- **2 tablespoons coconut or vegetable oil**
- **2 eggs, divided**
- **1 teaspoon vanilla**
- **½ cup flaked coconut**
- **¾ cup cherry preserves**
- **2 tablespoons butter**

1. Preheat oven to 350°F. Grease and flour 9-inch springform pan.

2. Combine flour and sugar in large bowl. Reserve ½ cup flour mixture; set aside. Stir baking powder and baking soda into remaining flour mixture. Cut in half of cream cheese with pastry blender or two knives until mixture resembles coarse crumbs; set aside.

3. Combine milk, oil, and 1 egg in medium bowl. Add to cream cheese mixture; stir just until moistened. Spread batter on bottom and 1 inch up side of prepared pan. Combine remaining cream cheese, egg, and vanilla in small bowl; whisk until smooth. Pour over batter, spreading to within 1 inch of edge. Sprinkle coconut over cream cheese mixture. Spoon preserves evenly over coconut.

4. Cut butter into reserved flour mixture with pastry blender or two knives until mixture resembles coarse crumbs. Sprinkle over preserves.

5. Bake 55 to 60 minutes or until golden brown and toothpick inserted into crust comes out clean. Cool in pan on wire rack 15 minutes. Remove side of pan; serve warm.

Makes 10 servings

Breakfast & Breads

Maple Pecan Granola

- ½ **cup maple syrup**
- ½ **cup packed dark brown sugar**
- 1 **tablespoon vanilla extract**
- 1 **teaspoon ground cinnamon**
- 1 **teaspoon kosher salt**
- ¾ **cup vegetable oil**
- 6 **cups old-fashioned rolled oats**
- ½ **cup ground flaxseeds**
- 1½ **cups flaked coconut**
- 3 **cups pecans, coarsely chopped**

1. Preheat oven to 350°F. Line two baking sheets with parchment paper. Set oven racks to upper third and lower third positions.

2. Whisk maple syrup, brown sugar, vanilla, cinnamon, salt, and oil in large bowl. Stir in oats, flaxseeds, coconut, and pecans until evenly coated.

3. Divide mixture between prepared baking sheets, pressing granola into even layer. Bake 30 minutes or until mixture is golden brown and fragrant, stirring and rotating baking sheets from top to bottom. Let granola cool completely on baking sheets. Spoon evenly into jars, reserving extra for another use.

Makes about 13 cups

Breakfast & Breads

Piña Colada Muffins

2   **cups all-purpose flour**

¾   **cup sugar**

¾   **cup flaked coconut, divided**

2   **teaspoons baking powder**

½   **teaspoon baking soda**

½   **teaspoon salt**

2   **eggs**

1   **cup sour cream**

1   **can (8 ounces) crushed pineapple in juice, undrained**

¼   **cup (½ stick) butter, melted**

⅛   **teaspoon coconut extract**

1. Preheat oven to 400°F. Line 18 standard (2½-inch) muffin cups with paper baking cups or spray with nonstick cooking spray.

2. Combine flour, sugar, ½ cup coconut, baking powder, baking soda, and salt in large bowl; mix well.

3. Beat eggs in medium bowl with electric mixer at medium speed 1 to 2 minutes or until frothy. Beat in sour cream, pineapple with juice, butter, and coconut extract. Stir into flour mixture just until combined. Spoon batter into prepared muffin cups, filling three-fourths full.

4. Bake 15 to 20 minutes or until toothpick inserted into centers comes out clean, sprinkling with remaining ¼ cup coconut after 10 minutes. If desired, sprinkle tops of muffins with additional coconut after first 10 minutes. Cool in pans 2 minutes. Remove to wire racks; cool completely.

Makes 18 muffins

Soups & Sides

Chickpea and Orange Squash Stew

1	teaspoon coconut oil
¾	cup chopped onion
½ to 1	jalapeño pepper, seeded and minced
1	(½-inch) piece fresh ginger, peeled and minced
1	clove garlic, minced
2	teaspoons ground cumin
½	teaspoon ground coriander
1	cup cubed peeled butternut squash, sweet potato, or pumpkin
1	cup canned chickpeas, rinsed and drained
½	cup water
2	teaspoons soy sauce
1	cup unsweetened canned coconut milk
	Juice of 1 lime
¼	cup chopped fresh cilantro
	Spinach leaves (optional)

1. Heat oil in medium saucepan over medium-low heat. Add onion, jalapeño pepper, ginger, and garlic; cook and stir 2 to 3 minutes or until onion is translucent. Add cumin and coriander; cook and stir 1 minute.

2. Add squash, chickpeas, water, and soy sauce to saucepan. Bring to a boil. Reduce heat; simmer 15 minutes or until squash is tender. Add coconut milk; cook and stir 2 to 3 minutes or until heated through. Stir in lime juice and cilantro. Garnish with spinach (optional).

Makes 2 servings

Soups & Sides

Coconut-Lime Sweet Potatoes with Walnuts

- 2½ **pounds sweet potatoes, cut into 1-inch pieces**
- 8 **ounces shredded carrots**
- ¾ **cup flaked coconut, toasted, divided***
- 1 **tablespoon coconut oil or butter, melted**
- 3 **tablespoons sugar**
- ½ **teaspoon salt**
- 3 **tablespoons walnuts, toasted and coarsely chopped****
- 2 **teaspoons grated lime peel**

*To toast coconut, spread in single layer in heavy-bottomed skillet. Cook and stir over medium heat 2 to 3 minutes or until lightly browned. Remove from skillet; cool completely.

**To toast walnuts, spread in single layer in small skillet. Cook and stir over medium heat 1 to 2 minutes or until nuts are lightly browned.

Slow Cooker Directions

1. Combine potatoes, carrots, ½ cup coconut, oil, sugar, and salt in slow cooker. Cover; cook on LOW 5 to 6 hours. Remove to large bowl.

2. Mash potatoes with potato masher. Stir in walnuts and lime peel. Sprinkle with remaining ¼ cup coconut.

Makes 8 servings

Soups & Sides

Caribbean Callaloo Soup

 1 teaspoon coconut oil

 1 large onion, chopped

 4 cloves garlic, minced

 12 ounces boneless skinless chicken breasts, thinly sliced crosswise

 1½ pounds butternut squash, cut into ½-inch cubes

 3 cans (about 14 ounces each) chicken broth

 2 jalapeño peppers, seeded and minced

 2 teaspoons dried thyme

 ½ (10-ounce) package fresh spinach, stemmed and torn

 ¼ cup plus 2 tablespoons flaked coconut, toasted*

*To toast coconut, spread in single layer in heavy-bottomed skillet. Cook and stir over medium heat 2 to 3 minutes or until lightly browned. Remove from skillet; cool completely.

1. Heat oil in large nonstick skillet over medium-low heat. Add onion and garlic; cook and stir 5 minutes or until onion is tender. Add chicken; cover and cook 5 to 7 minutes or until chicken is no longer pink in center.

2. Add squash, broth, jalapeño peppers, and thyme; bring to a boil over medium-high heat. Reduce heat to low. Cover and simmer 15 to 20 minutes or until squash is very tender.

3. Remove from heat; stir in spinach until wilted. Ladle into bowls and sprinkle with toasted coconut.

Makes 6 servings

Soups & Sides

Toasted Coconut-Pecan Sweet Potato Casserole

2   **cans (15 ounces each) sweet potatoes in heavy syrup, drained**

½   **cup (1 stick) butter, softened**

¼   **cup packed brown sugar**

1   **egg**

½   **teaspoon vanilla**

⅛   **teaspoon salt**

½   **cup chopped pecans**

¼   **cup flaked coconut**

2   **tablespoons golden raisins**

1. Preheat oven to 325°F. Spray 8-inch square baking dish with nonstick cooking spray.

2. Combine sweet potatoes, butter, brown sugar, egg, vanilla, and salt in food processor or blender; process until smooth. Spoon into prepared dish. Sprinkle evenly with pecans, coconut, and raisins.

3. Bake 22 to 25 minutes or until heated through and coconut is light golden brown.

Makes 4 servings

Soups & Sides

Asian Sweet Potato and Corn Stew

- 1 tablespoon coconut or vegetable oil
- 1 large onion, chopped
- 2 tablespoons minced peeled fresh ginger
- ½ jalapeño or Serrano pepper, seeded and minced
- 2 cloves garlic, minced
- 1 cup corn
- 2 teaspoons curry powder
- 1 can (about 13 ounces) unsweetened coconut milk
- 1 teaspoon cornstarch
- 1 can (about 14 ounces) vegetable broth
- 1 tablespoon soy sauce
- 4 sweet potatoes, peeled and cut into ¾-inch cubes

  Hot cooked jasmine or other long grain rice

  Chopped dry-roasted peanuts, chopped green onions, and/or chopped fresh cilantro (optional)

Slow Cooker Directions

1. Heat oil in large skillet over medium heat. Add onion, ginger, minced jalapeño pepper, and garlic. Cook about 5 minutes, stirring occasionally, or until onion softens. Remove from heat and stir in corn and curry powder.

2. Whisk coconut milk and cornstarch together in slow cooker. Stir in broth and soy sauce. Add sweet potatoes, then top with corn mixture. Cover; cook on LOW 5 to 6 hours or until sweet potatoes are tender.

3. Stir gently to smooth cooking liquid without breaking up sweet potatoes (coconut milk may look curdled). Adjust seasoning. Spoon over rice in serving bowls; garnish as desired.

Makes 6 servings

Soups & Sides

Ambrosia

1   can (20 ounces) DOLE® Pineapple Chunks, drained

1   can (11 or 15 ounces) DOLE® Mandarin Oranges, drained

1   DOLE® Banana, sliced

1½ cups seedless grapes

½   cup miniature marshmallows

1   cup vanilla low-fat yogurt

¼   cup flaked coconut, toasted

Prep time: 15 minutes

1. Combine pineapple chunks, mandarin oranges, banana, grapes, and marshmallows in medium bowl.

2. Stir yogurt into fruit mixture. Sprinkle with coconut.

Makes 4 servings

Main Dishes

Baked Fish with Thai Pesto

1 to 2	jalapeño peppers, seeded and coarsely chopped
1	lemon
4	green onions, thinly sliced
2	tablespoons chopped fresh ginger
3	cloves garlic, minced
1½	cups lightly packed fresh basil leaves
1	cup lightly packed fresh cilantro leaves
¼	cup lightly packed fresh mint leaves
¼	cup roasted peanuts
¼	cup flaked coconut
½	teaspoon sugar
½	cup peanut oil
2	pounds boneless fish fillets (such as salmon, halibut, cod, or orange roughy)
	Lemon and cucumber slices

1. Place jalapeño peppers in blender or food processor.

2. Grate peel of lemon. Juice lemon to measure 2 tablespoons. Add peel and juice to blender.

3. Add green onions, ginger, garlic, basil, cilantro, mint, peanuts, coconut, and sugar to blender; blend until finely chopped. With motor running, slowly pour in oil; blend until mixed.

4. Preheat oven to 375°F. Rinse fish and pat dry with paper towels. Place fillets on lightly oiled baking sheet. Spread solid thin layer of pesto over each fillet.

5. Bake 10 minutes or until fish begins to flake when tested with fork and is just opaque in center. Transfer fish to serving platter with wide spatula. Garnish with lemon and cucumber slices.

Makes 4 to 6 servings

Main Dishes

Coconut-Macadamia Shrimp

 1   **pound large raw shrimp, peeled and deveined (with tails on)**

1½ **teaspoons salt, divided**

      Ground red pepper

 ½   **cup all-purpose flour**

 ¼   **teaspoon white pepper**

 1   **cup flaked coconut**

 ⅔   **cup panko bread crumbs**

 ½   **cup finely chopped macadamia nuts**

 2   **eggs**

 ¼   **cup wheat beer**

 1   **cup peanut oil**

      Apricot or pineapple preserves

1. Spread shrimp on paper towels and pat dry. Season with ½ teaspoon salt and red pepper.

2. Combine flour, remaining 1 teaspoon salt, and white pepper in shallow dish. Combine coconut, panko, and macadamia nuts in another shallow dish. Whisk eggs and beer in small bowl.

3. Heat oil in deep heavy saucepan over medium-high heat to 350°F.

4. Working in small batches, dredge shrimp in flour mixture. Dip in egg mixture and roll in coconut mixture. Place carefully in oil; fry 2 minutes per side. Drain on paper towels.

5. Serve immediately with preserves for dipping.

Makes 6 to 8 servings

Main Dishes

Balsamic Grilled Pork Chops

2 tablespoons balsamic vinegar

2 tablespoons coconut aminos*

1 teaspoon Dijon mustard

1 teaspoon honey

⅛ teaspoon red pepper flakes

2 boneless pork chops, trimmed (about 4 ounces each)

2 teaspoons olive oil

*Coconut aminos is a dark, salty soy-free sauce containing 17 amino acids. It is made from the sap of the coconut tree, which is dried and blended with sea salt. It does not have a pronounced coconut flavor and is often used as a substitute for soy sauce in paleo diet recipes. Coconut aminos can be found in health food and vitamin stores, some grocery stores, or online.

1. Combine vinegar, coconut aminos, mustard, honey, and red pepper flakes in small bowl; mix well. Reserve 1 tablespoon marinade; refrigerate until ready to serve.

2. Place pork in large resealable food storage bag. Pour remaining marinade over pork. Seal bag; turn to coat. Marinate in refrigerator 2 hours or up to 24 hours.

3. Brush grill pan with oil; heat over medium-high heat. Remove pork from marinade; discard marinade. Cook pork 4 minutes per side or until barely pink in center. Drizzle with reserved 1 tablespoon marinade.

Makes 2 servings

Main Dishes

Pumpkin Curry

1	tablespoon coconut oil
1	package (14 ounces) extra firm tofu, drained and cut into 1-inch cubes
¼	cup Thai red curry paste
2	cloves garlic, minced
1	can (15 ounces) pumpkin puree
1	can (about 13 ounces) unsweetened coconut milk
1	cup water
1½	teaspoons salt
1	teaspoon sriracha sauce
4	cups cut-up vegetables (broccoli, cauliflower, red bell pepper, sweet potato)
½	cup peas
2	cups hot cooked rice
¼	cup shredded fresh basil (optional)

1. Heat oil in wok or large skillet over high heat. Add tofu; stir-fry 2 to 3 minutes or until lightly browned. Add curry paste and garlic; cook and stir 1 minute or until tofu is coated. Add pumpkin, coconut milk, water, salt, and sriracha; bring to a boil. Stir in vegetables.

2. Reduce heat to medium; cover and simmer 20 minutes or until vegetables are tender. Stir in peas; cook 1 minute or until heated through. Serve over rice; top with basil, if desired.

Tip: Don't worry if the coconut milk looks separated. Just add it all to the wok and it will come together as it heats.

Makes 4 servings

Main Dishes

Roasted Pork Tenderloin with Fresh Plum Salsa

Pork Tenderloin

    Fresh Plum Salsa

1   pound pork tenderloin, trimmed

¼   cup coconut aminos

2   tablespoons lime juice

2   teaspoons dark sesame oil

2   cloves garlic, minced

1½   tablespoons honey

Fresh Plum Salsa

2   cups coarsely chopped red plums (about 3)

2   tablespoons chopped green onion

1   tablespoon honey

1   tablespoon chopped fresh cilantro

2   teaspoons lime juice

    Dash ground red pepper

Pork Tenderloin

1. Prepare Fresh Plum Salsa (recipe follows).

2. Place pork in large resealable food storage bag. Combine coconut aminos, lime juice, oil, and garlic in small bowl; mix well. Pour over pork. Seal bag; turn to coat. Marinate in refrigerator 8 hours or overnight, turning occasionally.

3. Preheat oven to 375°F. Remove pork from marinade, reserving 2 tablespoons marinade in small saucepan. Add honey to saucepan; bring to a boil over medium-high heat. Boil 1 minute, stirring once.

4. To ensure even cooking, tuck narrow end of pork under roast to form even thickness. Tie with cotton string. Place pork on rack in shallow roasting pan; brush with honey mixture.

5. Roast 15 minutes; brush with remaining honey mixture. Roast 10 minutes or until 145°F. Transfer pork to cutting board. Tent with foil; let stand 10 minutes.

6. Remove string from pork. Cut into thin slices; serve with salsa.

Makes 4 servings

Fresh Plum Salsa

Combine all ingredients in medium bowl; mix well. Cover and refrigerate at least 2 hours.

Makes 1 cup

Main Dishes

Vegetarian Rice Noodles

- ½ **cup soy sauce**
- ⅓ **cup sugar**
- ¼ **cup lime juice**
- 2 **fresh red Thai chiles or 1 large jalapeño pepper, finely chopped**
- 8 **ounces thin rice noodles (rice vermicelli)**
- ¼ **cup coconut oil**
- 8 **ounces firm tofu, drained and cut into triangles**
- 1 **jicama (8 ounces), peeled and chopped or 1 can (8 ounces) sliced water chestnuts, drained**
- 2 **medium sweet potatoes (1 pound), peeled and cut into ¼-inch-thick slices**
- 2 **large leeks, cut into ¼-inch-thick slices**
- ¼ **cup chopped dry-roasted peanuts**
- 2 **tablespoons chopped fresh mint**
- 2 **tablespoons chopped fresh cilantro**

1. Combine soy sauce, sugar, lime juice, and chiles in small bowl until well blended; set aside.

2. Place rice noodles in medium bowl. Cover with hot water; let stand 15 minutes or until soft. Drain well; cut into 3-inch lengths.

3. Meanwhile, heat oil in large skillet over medium-high heat. Add tofu; stir-fry 4 minutes per side or until golden brown. Remove with slotted spatula to paper towel-lined baking sheet.

4. Add jicama to skillet; stir-fry 5 minutes or until lightly browned. Remove to baking sheet. Stir-fry sweet potatoes in batches until tender and browned; remove to baking sheet. Add leeks; stir-fry 1 minute.

5. Stir soy sauce mixture; add to skillet. Heat until sugar dissolves. Add noodles; toss to coat. Gently stir in tofu, vegetables, peanuts, mint, and cilantro.

Makes 4 servings

Main Dishes

Turkey Lettuce Wraps

- **1**   **teaspoon dark sesame oil**
- **1**   **pound ground turkey**
- **½**   **cup sliced green onions**
- **2**   **tablespoons minced fresh ginger**
- **1**   **can (8 ounces) water chestnuts, chopped**
- **1**   **teaspoon coconut aminos**
- **¼**   **cup chopped fresh cilantro**
- **12** **large lettuce leaves**

    Chopped fresh mint leaves (optional)

1. Heat oil in large skillet over medium-high heat. Add turkey, green onions, and ginger; cook 6 to 8 minutes, stirring to break up meat.

2. Add water chestnuts and coconut aminos to skillet; cook and stir 3 minutes or until turkey is cooked through. Remove from heat; stir in cilantro.

3. Spoon ¼ cup turkey mixture onto each lettuce leaf. Top with mint, if desired. Roll up to enclose filling.

Makes 12 wraps (about 6 servings)

Broiled Hunan Fish Fillets

3   **tablespoons coconut aminos**

1   **tablespoon finely chopped green onion**

2   **teaspoons dark sesame oil**

1   **clove garlic, minced**

1   **teaspoon minced fresh ginger**

¼   **teaspoon red pepper flakes**

4   **red snapper, scrod, or cod fillets (5 to 7 ounces each)**

1. Preheat broiler. Oil rack of broiler pan. Combine coconut aminos, green onion, oil, garlic, ginger, and red pepper flakes in small bowl; mix well.

2. Place snapper on prepared broiler rack; brush with green onion mixture.

3. Broil 4 to 5 inches from heat 10 minutes or until fish begins to flake when tested with fork.

Makes 4 servings

Main Dishes

Tofu Satay with Peanut Sauce

Satay

1	package (14 ounces) firm tofu, drained and pressed*
⅓	cup water
⅓	cup soy sauce
1	tablespoon dark sesame oil
1	teaspoon minced garlic
1	teaspoon minced fresh ginger
24	white button mushrooms, trimmed
1	large red bell pepper, cut into 12 pieces

Peanut Sauce

1	can (about 13 ounces) unsweetened coconut milk
½	cup creamy peanut butter
2	tablespoons packed brown sugar
1	tablespoon rice vinegar
1 to 2	teaspoons red Thai curry paste

*Cut tofu in half horizontally and place it between layers of paper towels. Place a weighted cutting board on top; let stand 15 to 30 minutes.

1. Cut tofu into 24 cubes. Combine water, soy sauce, sesame oil, garlic, and ginger in small bowl. Place tofu, mushrooms, and bell pepper in large resealable food storage bag. Add soy sauce mixture; seal bag and turn gently to coat. Marinate 30 minutes, turning occasionally. Soak eight 8-inch bamboo skewers in water 20 minutes.

2. Preheat oven to 400°F. Spray 13x9-inch glass baking dish with nonstick cooking spray.

3. Drain tofu mixture; discard marinade. Thread tofu, mushrooms, and bell peppers alternately on skewers. Place skewers in prepared dish.

4. Bake 25 minutes or until tofu cubes are lightly browned and vegetables are softened.

5. Meanwhile, whisk coconut milk, peanut butter, brown sugar, vinegar, and curry paste in small saucepan over medium heat. Bring to a boil, stirring constantly. Reduce heat to low; cook about 20 minutes or until creamy and thick, stirring frequently. Serve satay with sauce.

Makes 4 servings

Main Dishes

Coconut Butternut Squash

1 **tablespoon margarine**

½ **cup chopped onion**

1 **pound butternut squash, peeled, seeded, and cut into 1-inch pieces**

1 **pound sweet potatoes, peeled and cut into 1-inch pieces**

1 **can (about 14 ounces) coconut milk***

3 **tablespoons packed brown sugar, divided**

½ **teaspoon salt**

½ **teaspoon ground cinnamon**

¼ **teaspoon ground nutmeg**

¼ **teaspoon ground allspice**

1 **tablespoon grated fresh ginger**

*Shake vigorously before opening to mix thoroughly.

1. Melt margarine in large skillet over medium-high heat. Add onion; cook and stir 4 minutes or until translucent. Add squash, sweet potatoes, coconut milk, 1 tablespoon brown sugar, salt, cinnamon, nutmeg, and allspice; bring to a boil over medium-high heat.

2. Reduce heat to low; cover and simmer 10 minutes. Uncover and cook 5 minutes or until vegetables are tender, stirring frequently. Remove from heat. Stir in ginger.

3. Transfer mixture to blender or food processor; blend until smooth. Spoon into serving bowls; sprinkle with remaining 2 tablespoons brown sugar.

Tip: When selecting a butternut or other winter squash, choose one that is rock solid. Press hard to make sure there are no soft spots, as these would indicate the squash is immature or way past its prime. Make sure the stem is in place and firm—if the stem is missing, bacteria can enter and spoil the flesh. Butternut squash will keep for months if it's in good shape to begin with and stored in a dry place at cool room temperature.

Makes 6 servings

Main Dishes

Shrimp and Veggie Skillet Toss

¼ cup coconut aminos

2 tablespoons lime juice

1 tablespoon dark sesame oil

1 teaspoon grated fresh ginger

⅛ teaspoon red pepper flakes

1 tablespoon olive oil, divided

8 ounces medium raw shrimp, peeled and deveined (with tails on)

2 medium zucchini, cut in half lenthwise and sliced

6 green onions, trimmed and halved lengthwise

12 grape tomatoes

1. Combine coconut aminos, lime juice, sesame oil, ginger, and red pepper flakes in small bowl; mix well.

2. Heat half of olive oil in large nonstick skillet over medium-high heat. Add shrimp; cook and stir 3 minutes or until shrimp are opaque. Remove from skillet.

3. Heat remaining olive oil in same skillet. Add zucchini; cook and stir 4 to 6 minutes or just until crisp-tender. Add green onions and tomatoes; cook and stir 2 minutes. Add shrimp; cook 1 minute or until heated through. Remove to large bowl.

4. Add sauce to skillet; bring to a boil. Remove from heat. Stir in shrimp and vegetables; toss gently to coat.

Makes 4 servings

Main Dishes

Herbed Lamb Chops

⅓   **cup olive oil**

⅓   **cup red wine vinegar**

2   **tablespoons coconut aminos**

1   **tablespoon lemon juice**

3   **cloves garlic, minced**

1   **teaspoon salt**

1   **teaspoon chopped fresh oregano or ¼ teaspoon dried oregano**

1   **teaspoon dried rosemary**

1   **teaspoon ground mustard**

½   **teaspoon white pepper**

8   **lamb loin chops, 1 inch thick (about 4 ounces each)**

1. Combine all ingredients except lamb in large resealable food storage bag. Reserve ½ cup marinade in small bowl. Add lamb to remaining marinade. Seal bag; turn to coat. Marinate in refrigerator at least 1 hour.

2. Prepare grill for direct cooking.

3. Remove lamb from marinade; discard marinade. Grill lamb over medium-high heat 8 minutes or to desired doneness, turning once and basting often with reserved ½ cup marinade. Do not baste during last 5 minutes of cooking. Discard any remaining marinade.

Makes 4 to 6 servings

Desserts

Banana-Coconut Cream Pie

Crust

1	**cup almonds**
1	**tablespoon sugar**
½	**cup flaked coconut**
¼	**cup (½ stick) butter, cut into small pieces**
	Pinch salt

Filling

2	**bananas**
1	**teaspoon lemon juice**
½	**cup sugar**
¼	**cup cornstarch**
¼	**teaspoon salt**
3	**cups whole milk**
2	**egg yolks**
1	**teaspoon vanilla**

Topping

1	**banana**
2	**tablespoons flaked coconut, toasted***
	Whipped cream

*To toast coconut, spread evenly on ungreased cookie sheet. Toast in preheated 350°F oven 5 to 7 minutes, stirring occasionally, until light golden brown.

1. Preheat oven to 350°F. Grease 9-inch pie pan.

2. Place almonds and 1 tablespoon sugar in food processor; process using on/off pulses until almonds are ground. Add ½ cup coconut; pulse to combine. Add butter and pinch of salt; pulse until mixture begins to stick together. Press mixture onto bottom and up side of prepared pan. Bake 10 to 12 minutes or until golden around edge. Cool completely.

3. Slice 2 bananas; sprinkle with lemon juice. Layer on bottom of prepared crust.

4. Combine ½ cup sugar, cornstarch, and ¼ teaspoon salt in medium saucepan. Whisk milk and egg yolks in medium bowl until well blended; slowly stir into sugar mixture. Cook and stir over medium heat until thickened. Bring to a boil; boil 1 minute. Remove from heat; stir in vanilla.

5. Pour mixture over bananas in crust. Cover and refrigerate at least 2 hours or until ready to serve.

6. Slice remaining banana; arrange on top of pie. Sprinkle with 2 tablespoons coconut and top with whipped cream.

Makes 8 servings

Desserts

Chocolate Coconut Almond Macaroons

1⅓ cups flaked coconut

⅔ cup sugar

2 egg whites

½ teaspoon vanilla

¼ teaspoon almond extract

Pinch salt

4 ounces sliced almonds, coarsely crushed

18 whole almonds

Chocolate Ganache (recipe follows)

1. Combine coconut, sugar, egg whites, vanilla, almond extract, and salt in medium bowl; mix well. Fold in sliced almonds. Cover and refrigerate at least 1 hour or overnight.

2. Preheat oven to 350°F. Line cookie sheet with parchment paper.

3. Shape tablespoonfuls of dough into balls. Place 1 inch apart on prepared cookie sheet. Press 1 whole almond on top of each cookie.

4. Bake 15 minutes or until light brown. Cool on cookie sheet 5 minutes. Remove to wire rack; cool completely.

5. Meanwhile, prepare Chocolate Ganache.

6. Dip bottom of each cookie into ganache. Place cookies onto clean parchment or waxed paper-lined cookie sheet. Refrigerate until ganache is set. Store covered in refrigerator.

Chocolate Ganache

Place ½ cup semisweet chocolate chips in shallow bowl. Heat ¼ cup whipping cream in small saucepan until bubbles form around edge. Pour cream over chocolate; let stand 5 minutes. Stir until smooth. Let cool 10 to 15 minutes.

Makes 1½ dozen cookies

Desserts

Dark Chocolate Coconut Cake

1   package (about 15 ounces) devil's food cake mix, plus ingredients to prepare mix

1   cup strong coffee

½   cup evaporated milk

¼   cup (½ stick) butter, divided

3   cups mini marshmallows*

1   package (14 ounces) flaked coconut

1   cup whipping cream

2   cups (12 ounces) semisweet chocolate chips**

*Or substitute 24 large marshmallows.

**For more intense chocolate flavor, use bittersweet or dark chocolate chips.

1. Preheat oven to 350°F. Spray two 8-inch round cake pans with nonstick cooking spray. Prepare cake mix according to package directions, substituting coffee for water. Pour batter evenly into prepared pans. Bake 23 to 25 minutes or until toothpick inserted into centers comes out clean. Cool completely in pans on wire racks.

2. For filling, bring evaporated milk and 2 tablespoons butter to a boil in medium saucepan over medium heat. Add marshmallows; stir until smooth. Remove from heat; stir in coconut. Cool completely.

3. For ganache, heat cream and remaining 2 tablespoons butter in medium saucepan over medium-low heat. (Do not boil.) Remove from heat; add chocolate chips. Let stand 1 minute; stir until smooth.

4. Cut each cake layer in half horizontally. Place one cake layer on serving plate; spread with one third of filling almost to edge. Repeat layers twice. Top with remaining cake layer. Frost top and side of cake with ganache; refrigerate until set. Store leftovers in refrigerator.

Makes 12 to 16 servings

Desserts

Tropical Fruit Cobbler

⅔ pineapple, peeled, cored, and cut into 1-inch pieces (about 4 cups)

2 mangoes, peeled, pitted, and cut into 1-inch pieces (about 4 cups)

2 bananas, halved lengthwise and cut crosswise into 1-inch pieces

½ cup plus 5 tablespoons sugar, divided

2 tablespoons cornstarch

¼ teaspoon ground allspice

1 cup all-purpose flour

¼ cup flaked coconut

1 teaspoon baking powder

¼ teaspoon salt

¼ cup (½ stick) cold butter, cut into small pieces

½ cup plus 2 tablespoons whipping cream, divided

½ teaspoon coconut extract

1. Preheat oven to 375°F. Spray 2-quart oval baking dish with nonstick cooking spray.

2. Combine pineapple, mangoes, bananas, ½ cup sugar, cornstarch, and allspice in large bowl; toss to coat. Spoon into prepared baking dish.

3. Combine flour, coconut, 3 tablespoons sugar, baking powder, and salt in medium bowl; mix well. Cut in butter with pastry blender or two knives until mixture resembles coarse crumbs. Add ½ cup cream and coconut extract; stir until rough dough forms. Knead dough several times in bowl until it holds together.

4. Turn out dough onto lightly floured surface; roll into 8- to 9-inch circle about ¼ inch thick. Cut circle into 1-inch-wide strips; cut each strip on a diagonal to form 2½X1-inch diamond shapes (or cut into squares). Arrange shortbread diamonds over fruit mixture. Brush dough with remaining 2 tablespoons cream; sprinkle generously with remaining 2 tablespoons sugar.

5. Bake 45 to 47 minutes or until filling is thick and bubbly and shortbread is golden brown. Let stand 30 minutes before serving.

Makes 8 servings

Desserts

Chocolate Coconut Toffee Delights

½	cup all-purpose flour
¼	teaspoon baking powder
¼	teaspoon salt
1	package (12 ounces) semisweet chocolate chips, divided
¼	cup (½ stick) butter, cut into small pieces
¾	cup packed brown sugar
2	eggs, beaten
1	teaspoon vanilla
1½	cups flaked coconut
1	cup toffee baking bits
½	cup bittersweet chocolate chips

1. Preheat oven to 350°F. Line cookie sheets with parchment paper. Combine flour, baking powder, and salt in small bowl.

2. Place 1 cup semisweet chocolate chips and butter in large microwavable bowl. Microwave on HIGH 1 minute; stir. Microwave at additional 30-second intervals, stirring after each interval, until mixture is melted and smooth.

3. Beat brown sugar, eggs, and vanilla with electric mixer at medium speed. Beat in chocolate mixture until well blended. Add flour mixture; beat at low speed until blended. Stir in coconut, toffee bits, and remaining 1 cup semisweet chocolate chips. Drop dough by heaping ⅓ cupfuls 3 inches apart onto prepared cookie sheets. Flatten with rubber spatula into 3½-inch circles.

4. Bake 15 to 17 minutes or until edges are firm to the touch. Cool on cookie sheets 2 minutes; slide parchment paper and cookies onto wire racks. Cool completely.

5. For chocolate drizzle, place bittersweet chocolate chips in small microwavable bowl. Microwave on HIGH 30 seconds; stir. Microwave at additional 30-second intervals, stirring after each interval, until melted and smooth. Drizzle over cookies. Let stand until set.

Makes 1 dozen large cookies

Desserts

Coconut Panna Cotta

- **3**   **tablespoons water**
- **1**   **envelope (2½ teaspoons) unflavored gelatin**
- **1**   **can (about 13 ounces) unsweetened coconut milk**
- **½**   **cup sugar**
- **½**   **teaspoon vanilla**
- **4**   **tablespoons toasted flaked coconut**
- **2**   **slices (½ inch thick) fresh pineapple, cut into pieces**

1. Place water in small bowl and sprinkle with gelatin; set aside.

2. Heat coconut milk, sugar, and vanilla in medium saucepan over medium heat. Cook and stir until sugar is dissolved and mixture is smooth. (Do not boil.) Add gelatin mixture; stir until gelatin is completely dissolved.

3. Pour mixture evenly into four 5-ounce custard cups. Refrigerate about 3 hours or until set.

4. To unmold, run knife around outside edges of cups; place cups in hot water about 30 seconds. Place serving plate over cup; invert and shake until panna cotta drops onto plate. Serve with toasted coconut and pineapple. Refrigerate leftovers.

Tip: Panna cotta is best eaten within 2 days.

Makes 4 servings

Desserts

Spicy Coconut-Lime Cupcakes

1¾ cups all-purpose flour

1½ teaspoons baking powder

1   teaspoon salt

½   teaspoon baking soda

½   teaspoon ground red pepper

¾   cup sugar

½   cup (1 stick) butter, softened

¾   cup unsweetened canned coconut milk, well shaken

2   eggs

¼   cup milk

    Grated peel and juice of 2 limes

⅓   cup flaked coconut

    Coconut-Lime Whipped Cream (recipe follows)

⅓   cup flaked coconut, toasted*

    Additional grated lime peel (optional)

*To toast coconut, spread evenly on ungreased cookie sheet. Toast in preheated 350°F oven 5 to 7 minutes, stirring occasionally, until light golden brown.

1. Preheat oven to 350°F. Line 12 standard (2½-inch) muffin cups with paper baking cups.

2. Combine flour, baking powder, salt, baking soda, and ground red pepper in medium bowl. Beat sugar and butter in large bowl with electric mixer at medium speed until creamy. Add coconut milk, eggs, milk, lime peel, and lime juice; beat until blended. Add flour mixture and ⅓ cup coconut; beat at low speed just until blended. Spoon batter evenly into prepared muffin cups.

3. Bake 18 to 20 minutes or until toothpick inserted into centers comes out clean. Cool cupcakes in pan 5 minutes. Remove to wire rack; cool completely.

4. Prepare Coconut-Lime Whipped Cream. Frost cupcakes; top with toasted coconut and additional lime peel, if desired. Store in refrigerator.

Coconut-Lime Whipped Cream

Beat 1 cup whipping cream in large bowl with electric mixer at medium-high speed until soft peaks form. Add 2½ tablespoons well-shaken coconut milk, 1 tablespoon sugar, and grated peel, and juice of 1 lime; beat until stiff peaks form.

Makes 12 cupcakes

Desserts

Cranberry Coconut Bars

Filling

- 1½ cups sweetened dried cranberries or cherries
- ½ cup flaked coconut
- ⅔ cup half-and-half
- 1 teaspoon vanilla

Crust

- 2 cups quick-cooking oats
- 1 cup packed dark brown sugar
- ¾ cup all-purpose flour
- ½ teaspoon baking soda
- ½ teaspoon ground cinnamon
- ½ cup (1 stick) butter, melted

1. For filling, heat cranberries, coconut, and half-and-half in medium saucepan over medium heat. Cook 10 to 12 minutes or until mixture boils and thickens, stirring occasionally. Remove from heat; stir in vanilla. Cool in saucepan.

2. For crust, combine oats, brown sugar, flour, baking soda, and cinnamon in medium bowl; mix well. Add melted butter; stir until moist and crumbly. Firmly press about two thirds of crust mixture into bottom of ungreased 8-inch square baking pan. Refrigerate 30 to 60 minutes or until firm.

3. Preheat oven to 350°F. Spread cooled filling evenly over crust. Sprinkle remaining crust mixture over filling; press gently into filling.

4. Bake 25 to 30 minutes or until topping is crisp and lightly browned. Cool completely in pan on wire rack. Cut into bars.

Tip: You can turn old-fashioned oats into quick-cooking oats by pulsing them in a food processor or blender.

Makes 12 to 16 bars

Desserts

Fruity Coconut Oatmeal Cookies

2	cups old-fashioned oats
1⅓	cups all-purpose flour
¾	teaspoon baking soda
½	teaspoon baking powder
½	teaspoon salt
¼	teaspoon ground cinnamon
1	cup packed brown sugar
¾	cup (1½ sticks) butter, softened
¼	cup granulated sugar
1	egg
1	tablespoon honey
1	teaspoon vanilla
½	cup finely diced dried mangoes
½	cup finely diced dried apples
½	cup finely diced dried cherries
3	cups flaked coconut, divided

1. Preheat oven to 350°F. Line cookie sheets with parchment paper. Combine oats, flour, baking soda, baking powder, salt, and cinnamon in medium bowl.

2. Beat brown sugar, butter, and granulated sugar in large bowl with electric mixer at medium speed until light and fluffy. Add egg, honey, and vanilla; beat until well blended. Gradually add flour mixture; beat just until blended. Stir in mangoes, apples, cherries, and ½ cup coconut.

3. Spread remaining 2½ cups coconut in shallow bowl. Drop dough by rounded tablespoonfuls into coconut and roll to coat; place on prepared cookie sheets.

4. Bake 15 to 17 minutes or until puffed and golden. Cool 5 minutes on cookie sheets. Remove to wire racks; cool completely.

Tip: As a variation, you can substitute 1 package (6 ounces) of tropical medley dried chopped fruit for the mangoes, apples, and cherries.

Makes about 3 dozen cookies

Desserts

Sweet Potato Coconut Bars

30 vanilla wafers, crushed

1½ cups finely chopped walnuts, toasted, divided

1 cup flaked coconut, divided

¼ cup (½ stick) butter, softened

2 cans (15 ounces each) sweet potatoes, well drained and mashed (2 cups)

2 eggs

1 teaspoon ground cinnamon

½ teaspoon ground ginger

¼ to ½ teaspoon ground cloves

¼ teaspoon salt

1 can (14 ounces) sweetened condensed milk

1 cup butterscotch chips

1. Preheat oven to 350°F.

2. For crust, combine vanilla wafers, 1 cup walnuts, ½ cup coconut, and butter in medium bowl until well blended. (Mixture will be dry and crumbly.) Press two thirds of crumb mixture onto bottom of 13x9-inch baking pan to form even layer.

3. For filling, beat mashed sweet potatoes, eggs, cinnamon, ginger, cloves, and salt in large bowl with electric mixer at medium-low speed until well blended. Gradually add sweetened condensed milk; beat until well blended. Spoon filling evenly over crust. Top with remaining crumb mixture, pressing lightly into sweet potato layer.

4. Bake 25 to 30 minutes or until knife inserted into center comes out clean. Sprinkle with butterscotch chips, remaining ½ cup walnuts, and ½ cup coconut. Bake 2 minutes. Cool completely in pan on wire rack. Cover and refrigerate 2 hours before serving.

Makes 2 to 3 dozen bars

Desserts

Amaretto Coconut Cream Pie

- ¼ **cup flaked coconut**
- 1 **container (8 ounces) whipped topping, divided**
- 1 **container (6 ounces) coconut or vanilla yogurt**
- ¼ **cup amaretto liqueur**
- 1 **package (4-serving size) coconut instant pudding and pie filling mix**
- 1 **(6-ounce) graham cracker pie crust**

  Fresh strawberries (optional)

1. Preheat oven to 350°F. Spread coconut in even layer on baking sheet. Bake 5 minutes or until golden brown, stirring frequently. Cool completely.

2. Combine 2 cups whipped topping, yogurt, and amaretto in large bowl; stir until blended. Add pudding mix; whisk 2 minutes or until thickened.

3. Spread mixture evenly in pie crust; spread remaining whipped topping over filling. Sprinkle with toasted coconut. Garnish with strawberries. Refrigerate until ready to serve.

Makes 8 servings

Desserts

Tropic Pops

2	bananas, cut into chunks
1½	cups unsweetened coconut milk
1½	cups pineapple juice
2	tablespoons sugar
½	teaspoon vanilla
⅛	teaspoon ground nutmeg
¼	cup sweetened flaked coconut
8	(5-ounce) plastic or paper cups or pop molds
8	pop sticks

1. Combine bananas, coconut milk, pineapple juice, sugar, vanilla, and nutmeg in blender or food processor; blend until smooth. Stir in flaked coconut.

2. Pour mixture into cups. Cover top of each cup with small piece of foil. Freeze 2 hours.

3. Insert sticks through center of foil. Freeze 6 hours or until firm.

4. To serve, remove foil and gently twist pops out of plastic cups or peel away paper cups.

Tip: For a ridged texture, use plastic cups.

Makes 8 pops

Desserts

No-Bake Coconut Cream Pie

2　tablespoons water

1　packet (¼ ounce) unflavored gelatin

1　can (about 14 ounces) unsweetened coconut milk

1　package (8 ounces) cream cheese, softened

6　tablespoons sugar

2　teaspoons vanilla

1　teaspoon coconut extract

1　(6-ounce) graham cracker pie crust

¼　cup flaked coconut, toasted*

*To toast coconut, spread in single layer in heavy-bottomed skillet. Cook and stir over medium heat 2 to 3 minutes or until lightly browned. Remove from skillet; cool completely.

1. Place water in small microwavable bowl. Sprinkle gelatin over water; let stand 1 minute. Microwave on HIGH 20 seconds or until gelatin is completely dissolved.

2. Combine coconut milk, cream cheese, sugar, vanilla, coconut extract, and gelatin mixture in blender; blend until smooth. Pour mixture into prepared crust; cover and chill about 4 hours or until firm.

3. Before serving, sprinkle toasted coconut over pie.

Makes 12 servings

Desserts

Coconut Raspberry Bars

- 2 cups graham cracker crumbs
- ½ cup (1 stick) butter, melted
- 1⅓ cups flaked coconut
- 1 can (14 ounces) sweetened condensed milk
- 1 cup red raspberry jam or preserves
- ½ cup chopped pecans
- ½ cup semisweet chocolate chips
- ½ cup white chocolate chips

1. Preheat oven to 350°F.

2. Combine graham cracker crumbs and butter in medium bowl. Press evenly onto bottom of ungreased 13x9-inch baking pan. Sprinkle with coconut; pour sweetened condensed milk evenly over coconut.

3. Bake 20 to 25 minutes or until lightly browned; cool completely in pan on wire rack.

4. Spread jam over coconut layer; sprinkle with pecans. Refrigerate for 3 to 4 hours.

5. Place semisweet chocolate chips in small resealable food storage bag; seal bag. Microwave on HIGH 1 minute. Turn bag over; heat on HIGH at 30-second intervals or until chocolate is melted. Knead bag until chocolate is smooth. Cut off very tiny corner of bag; drizzle chocolate onto jam layer. Melt white chocolate chips as directed for chocolate chips. Drizzle over top of chocolate layer; chill until chocolate is set. Cut into bars.

Makes 2 to 3 dozen bars

Desserts

Chocolate Peppermint Macaroons

4   **ounces bittersweet chocolate, chopped (½ cup)**

2   **squares (1 ounce each) unsweetened baking chocolate**

2   **egg whites, at room temperature**

⅛   **teaspoon salt**

½   **cup sugar**

½   **teaspoon peppermint extract**

2¾ cups flaked coconut

½   **cup finely crushed peppermint candies***

*About 18 peppermint candies will yield ½ cup finely crushed peppermints. To crush, place unwrapped candy in a heavy-duty resealable food storage bag. Loosely seal the bag, leaving an opening for air to escape. Crush with a rolling pin, meat mallet, or the bottom of a heavy skillet.

1. Line cookie sheets with parchment paper or lightly grease.

2. Place bittersweet and unsweetened chocolate in medium microwavable bowl. Microwave on HIGH at 30-second intervals, stirring between each interval, until melted and smooth.** Let stand 15 minutes.

3. Preheat oven to 325°F. Beat egg whites and salt in large bowl with electric mixer at high speed until soft peaks form. Gradually add sugar, beating until stiff peaks form. Add chocolate; beat at low speed just until blended. Stir in peppermint extract. Fold in coconut until blended.

4. Shape level tablespoonfuls into 1-inch balls; place 2 inches apart on prepared cookie sheets. Make small indentation in center. Sprinkle crushed candy into indentations. Bake 12 minutes or until outside is crisp and inside is moist and chewy. Remove to wire racks; cool completely.

**Or place chocolate in top of double boiler over simmering water. Stir constantly until melted and smooth. Remove from heat immediately. Avoid getting any water in the chocolate or it will become brittle and hard.

Makes 2 dozen macaroons

Desserts

Gluten-Free Coconut Lemon Bars

Crust

1 cup gluten-free shortbread cookie crumbs

½ cup (1 stick) butter, melted

Filling

1 package (8 ounces) cream cheese, softened

Grated peel and juice of 1 lemon

1 egg

2 tablespoons sugar

1 cup (6 ounces) white chocolate chips

1 cup flaked coconut

½ cup chopped macadamia nuts

1. Preheat oven to 350°F. Spray 13x9-inch baking pan with nonstick cooking spray.

2. Combine cookie crumbs and butter in medium bowl; stir until well combined. Press crumb mixture onto bottom of prepared pan.

3. Beat cream cheese, lemon peel, lemon juice, egg, and sugar in medium bowl with electric mixer at low speed until smooth. Spread evenly over crumb mixture.

4. Layer evenly with white chocolate chips, coconut, and macadamia nuts, pressing down each layer firmly with fork.

5. Bake 25 to 30 minutes or until lightly browned. Cool completely. Cover and refrigerate until ready to serve.

Makes about 32 bars

Desserts

Coconut Cake

1   package (about 15 ounces) white cake mix

1   can (about 13 ounces) unsweetened coconut milk

4   egg whites

1   container (16 ounces) vanilla frosting

2   cups flaked coconut

1. Preheat oven to 350°F. Spray two 8-inch round cake pans with nonstick cooking spray; line bottoms with parchment paper.

2. Beat cake mix, coconut milk, and egg whites in large bowl with electric mixer at low speed 30 seconds. Beat at medium-low speed 2 minutes or until well blended. Divide batter evenly between prepared pans.

3. Bake about 30 minutes or until toothpick inserted into centers comes out clean. Cool in pans 10 minutes. Remove to wire racks; cool completely.

4. Place one cake layer on serving plate; spread with vanilla frosting. Top with remaining layer; frost side and top of cake with remaining frosting.

5. Press coconut into frosting on top and side of cake.

Makes 10 to 12 servings

Desserts

Coconut Cream Pie Bowls

2   cups milk

¼   cup sugar

3   tablespoons cornstarch

⅛   teaspoon salt

1   egg

¾   cup flaked coconut

1   tablespoon butter

1   teaspoon vanilla

1   teaspoon coconut extract

¾   cup whipped cream or whipped topping

1. Combine milk, sugar, cornstarch, and salt in medium saucepan. Whisk until well blended and cornstarch is dissolved. Cook over medium heat until mixture thickens and begins to boil, stirring constantly. Boil 1 minute; remove from heat.

2. Whisk 2 tablespoons milk mixture into egg in small bowl until well blended. Slowly pour mixture back into saucepan, stirring rapidly to avoid lumps. Cook over medium heat 5 minutes until mixture thickens, stirring constantly. Remove from heat.

3. Stir in coconut, butter, vanilla, and coconut extract. Pour into six 6-ounce ramekins; refrigerate until firm. Top with whipped topping before serving.

Makes 6 servings

Desserts

Coconut Cherry Cobbler

2   **packages (12 ounces each) frozen dark sweet cherries, thawed and juice reserved**

1   **cup water**

1   **tablespoon lemon juice**

2   **teaspoons almond extract**

2   **cups sugar, divided**

¼   **cup cornstarch**

¾   **teaspoon salt, divided**

3   **cups all-purpose flour**

1   **cup toasted coconut***

1½ **teaspoons baking powder**

1   **cup (2 sticks) butter, softened**

4   **eggs**

*To toast coconut, spread evenly on ungreased cookie sheet. Toast in preheated 350°F oven 5 to 7 minutes, stirring occasionally, until light golden brown.

1. Preheat oven to 350°F. Spray 15x10-inch jellyroll pan with nonstick cooking spray.

2. Combine cherries with juice, water, lemon juice, and almond extract in large saucepan. Stir in ¾ cup sugar, cornstarch, and ¼ teaspoon salt; bring to a boil over medium-high heat. Cook and stir about 2 minutes or until thickened.

3. Combine flour, coconut, baking powder, and remaining ½ teaspoon salt in medium bowl; mix well. Beat butter and remaining 1¼ cups sugar in large bowl with electric mixer at medium speed until light and fluffy. Add eggs; beat until well blended. Stir in flour mixture until blended.

4. Reserve 1¼ cups dough for topping. Spread remaining dough on bottom of prepared pan using damp hands. (Dough will be thick and sticky.) Spread cherry mixture evenly over dough. Crumble remaining dough over cherries.

5. Bake 35 to 40 minutes or until crust is golden brown.

Makes 16 servings

Desserts

Creamy Coconut Cake with Almond Filling

1   package (about 15 ounces) white cake mix

1   cup sour cream

3   eggs

½   cup vegetable oil

1   teaspoon vanilla

1   teaspoon coconut extract

1   can (12½ ounces) almond filling

2   containers (16 ounces each) creamy coconut frosting

½   cup sliced almonds

1. Preheat oven to 350°F. Grease and flour two 9-inch round baking pans. Tap pans to remove excess flour.

2. Beat cake mix, sour cream, eggs, oil, vanilla, and coconut extract in large bowl with electric mixer at low speed 3 minutes or until well blended. Divide batter evenly between prepared pans.

3. Bake about 30 minutes or until toothpicks inserted into centers come out clean. Cool completely in pans on wire racks.

4. Remove cake layers from pans; cut each layer in half horizontally. Place one cake layer on serving plate; spread with half of almond filling. Top with second cake layer; spread with ½ cup coconut frosting. Top with third cake layer; spread with remaining almond filling. Top with fourth cake layer; spread remaining coconut frosting over top and side of cake. Sprinkle with almonds.

Makes 10 to 12 servings

Desserts

Tropical Angel Food Cake

- **1**   **prepared angel food cake**
- **1**   **container (8 ounces) whipped topping, thawed**
- **1**   **can (8 ounces) crushed pineapple with juice**
- **1**   **package (4-serving size) vanilla instant pudding and pie filling mix**
- **1**   **ripe banana, thinly sliced**
- **1**   **cup flaked coconut, toasted***
- **4**   **slices fresh or canned pineapple, cut in half**

*To toast coconut, spread in single layer in heavy-bottomed skillet. Cook and stir over medium heat 2 to 3 minutes or until lightly browned. Remove from skillet; cool completely.

1. Cut cake horizontally into three even layers. Combine whipped topping, crushed pineapple, and pudding mix in large bowl; mix well.

2. Arrange half of banana slices on bottom cake layer. Spread with ¾ cup whipped topping mixture. Top with middle layer of cake. Layer with remaining banana slices, ¾ cup topping mixture, and top cake later. Frost top and sides of cake with remaining topping mixture. Press coconut onto side of cake. Arrange pineapple slices on top of cake.

Tip: As a variation, add sliced strawberries and/or kiwi as a garnish or between cake layers.

Makes 8 servings

Desserts

Coconut Milk Ice Cream

    2   cans (about 14 ounces each)
        unsweetened coconut milk
    ½   cup sugar
    1   dairy-free candy bar, crushed
        into small pieces

1. Combine coconut milk and sugar in medium saucepan. Cook over medium-low heat, whisking constantly, until sugar is dissolved and mixture is smooth. Refrigerate until cold.

2. Pour into ice cream maker; process according to manufacturer's directions, adding candy pieces during last 2 minutes. Transfer to freezer container and freeze until firm.

3. To serve, let ice cream soften at room temperature, or microwave on HIGH 20 to 30 seconds.

Makes about 1 quart